Early Christian
MARTYR STORIES

Early Christian
MARTYR STORIES

An Evangelical Introduction with New Translations

BRYAN M. LITFIN

Baker Academic
a division of Baker Publishing Group
Grand Rapids, Michigan

© 2014 by Bryan M. Litfin

Published by Baker Academic
a division of Baker Publishing Group
P.O. Box 6287, Grand Rapids, MI 49516-6287
www.bakeracademic.com

Printed in the United States of America

Library of Congress Cataloging-in-Publication Data is on file at the Library of Congress, Washington, DC.

ISBN 978-0-8010-4958-3

In keeping with biblical principles of creation stewardship, Baker Publishing Group advocates the responsible use of our natural resources. As a member of the Green Press Initiative, our company uses recycled paper when possible. The text paper of this book is composed in part of post-consumer waste.

14 15 16 17 18 19 20   7 6 5 4 3 2 1

To my beloved son
William Thomas Litfin
May you always be a bold witness for Jesus Christ

Contents

Introduction

"God, I want to surrender all my plans to you today. I want to give you the complete, utter control in my life. I want to lift you high above all else."

If you are a Christian, you have probably prayed or sung words like these. Maybe you often whisper such things to God. What sentiments are being expressed here? Total abandon to the Lord's will . . . surrender of one's daily life to the all-wise God . . . earnest desire to testify to his glory. Admirable things, all of them. The person who wrote these words has set forth a worthy goal. But what makes them all the more powerful is that soon afterward, their author took three bullets in the face from a 7mm pistol because she was proclaiming Jesus in a place that didn't want him.

I remember attending chapel in November 2002 when it was announced that American missionary Bonnie Witherall had been gunned down by a Muslim extremist. I was a new professor at Moody Bible Institute, so I had never had Bonnie in class like some of my colleagues. But soon we all knew her story: how she had moved to Sidon, Lebanon, to minister among the poor; how she worked in a prenatal clinic providing health care to local Muslim women; how she and her husband, Gary, knew international tensions were high, yet could not turn back from the call of God on their lives. A few weeks after the shooting, Gary came to speak at Moody. He didn't possess the charisma of a televangelist or the rhetoric of an orator, but he didn't need to. His message of Bonnie's profound faithfulness to Jesus Christ brought a flood of students to the front of the chapel as they renewed their commitment to God.

Was Bonnie a martyr? She has been called one, and I will not argue with that designation.[1] But my point in mentioning her story at the beginning of a

---

1. Marvin J. Newell, *A Martyr's Grace: Stories of Those Who Gave All for Christ and His Cause* (Chicago: Moody, 2006), 16–23.

book like this is not to trace an unbroken line from her experience back to the ancient church. You cannot put a toga and sandals on Bonnie, or jeans and a T-shirt on Perpetua (see chap. 8), and consider them essentially the same person. Though both were young wives who relinquished their hopes of ease, security, and the joy of motherhood for the greater glory of God, their unique historical situations defy easy comparison. A very wide river—not just of time, but of spiritual outlook—separates the personal diaries that each woman left behind. Yet for all their differences, I would argue at least one thing bridges the gulf between Bonnie and Perpetua: their total devotion to the Lord Jesus, who died and rose again.

The purpose of the present book, then, must be twofold. On the one hand, it is supposed to be a work of historical scholarship. Early church history is my field of study, and it is both a privilege and a delight to offer a professor's expertise to my readers. A lot of nonsense is tossed around in the popular media about the ancient church, but here in this book you have direct access to the texts themselves. The present work collects in a single volume the most significant primary texts about ancient Christian martyrdom, newly translated in an easy-to-read style. When certain topics are unclear or could be explained further, study notes are included at the bottom of the page. I hope this enables you to investigate for yourself what the martyrs were all about.

Yet in light of this book's subject—ancient Christians bearing witness to their Lord—a second important purpose cannot be overlooked. Like most accounts of martyrdoms from the earliest days to the present, my volume intends to inspire Christian readers to greater faithfulness.[2] This is not to say every instance of ancient martyrdom can find a direct parallel in modern experience. Though Bonnie Witherall's murder or the pastor imprisoned for his faith by a foreign regime may resonate with the past, the church must not be too quick to develop a martyr complex. We can certainly expect to face opposition at times (2 Tim. 3:12), but most Western Christians do not exist in a constant state of deadly persecution. My desire is not that we point to a certain person, place, or circumstance today and say, "Look! Christian persecution! Pity us just like the ancient church!" Rather, I ask the readers of this book to reflect on what it may mean to take up their cross and follow in the Lord's footsteps.

---

2. A title that may spring to mind, even for those who have never read the book, is John Foxe's *Book of Martyrs*. The full, original title was *Actes and Monuments of These Latter and Perilous Dayes* by John Foxe. This enormously popular book has gone through many editions and abridgments since the author died in 1587. Foxe's book is about Protestant deaths in the sixteenth century. It is a controversial work; it has been accused of falsifying history for anti-Catholic polemical purposes. However, the present book has no such intent. My hope is simply that early Christian martyr stories will prompt renewed Christian devotion.

For in the end, it is not death by leaping flames or gnashing fangs that binds the modern Christian to the ancient martyr; it is an unshakeable resolve to follow hard after Jesus Christ at any cost.

The Age of Martyrdom?

As we begin to encounter the phenomenon of early Christian persecution, let us be clear about one thing: the ancient church period was not an "age of martyrdom" in the sense of continuous oppression and mistreatment. That is a myth historians have long rejected, though it has nonetheless crept into popular imagination. When a person today considers the "ancient church," the image that often springs to mind is a crowd of toga-clad Christians in a coliseum, their faces lifted to heaven as a steely-eyed lion approaches. Another common image would be a band of faithful believers scurrying into underground burial catacombs, while a Roman soldier with a red brush on his helmet searches in vain for his quarry.

We must leave such romantic notions behind. Aside from the historical inaccuracies—that all Romans wore togas, that the authorities didn't know where the Christians possessed cemeteries, that ceremonial helmet crests were worn on a daily basis—this imagery is problematic because it depicts the ancient period as an unbroken sequence of persecution. The truth of the matter is, open hostility to the faith was both localized and sporadic. Many decades passed when the church was entirely left alone, and at times it even flourished under broad popular support. So when exactly did persecution occur—and why?

Roughly speaking, the phenomenon of ancient Christian persecution may be divided into three phases. During the first phase, persecution was disorganized and welled up according to local whims. In this period it was occasionally sponsored by the Jewish authorities, as can be seen most clearly in the case of Saul. After Stephen's stoning, "there arose on that day a great persecution against the church in Jerusalem, and they were all scattered throughout the regions of Judea and Samaria, except the apostles. . . . Saul was ravaging the church, and entering house after house, he dragged off men and women and committed them to prison" (Acts 8:1, 3). However, the Jews did not possess capital authority and so could not legally execute Christians. The focus of this book is therefore on Roman persecution, which was far more prevalent than anything coming out of Jewish circles.

A noteworthy persecution from this earliest phase, one that set the pattern for future hostilities, occurred in AD 64 under Emperor Nero, who needed a scapegoat for a devastating urban fire in Rome. The historian Tacitus describes what happened:

> Nero therefore found culprits on whom he inflicted the most exotic punishments. These were people hated for their shameful offences whom the common people called Christians. The man who gave them their name, Christus, had been executed during the rule of Tiberius by the procurator Pontius Pilatus. The pernicious superstition had been temporarily suppressed, but it was starting to break out again, not just in Judea, the starting point of that curse, but in Rome, as well, where all that is abominable and shameful in the world flows together and gains popularity. And so, at first, those who confessed were apprehended, and subsequently, on the disclosures they made, a huge number were found guilty—more because of their hatred of mankind than because they were arsonists. As they died they were further subjected to insult. Covered with hides of wild beasts, they perished by being torn to pieces by dogs; or they would be fastened to crosses and, when daylight had gone, burned to provide lighting at night.[3]

Although this persecution was short lived and did not extend beyond Rome, it nonetheless signaled that the state should be hostile toward the new faith.

In the early second century, the church's experience of persecution moved into a second historical phase when Emperor Trajan issued a prohibition against Christianity. Though not a formally binding law, the letter from the emperor to his provincial governor Pliny seems to have set a legal precedent that later policy makers could follow. Pliny (often designated "the Younger" to distinguish him from his famous uncle) was governing Bithynia after AD 110 when he encountered Christianity for the first time. Accusations had been made, so Pliny presided over a trial. Those who admitted to being Christians were either executed on the spot or, in the case of citizens, sent to Rome for further adjudication. Those who denied the charge were asked to confirm their status as unbelievers by offering sacrifices to pagan idols and cursing the name of Christ. These are the actions, Pliny asserts, that no true Christian can be made to perform (and we will shortly examine their reasons for such reticence).

What about those who formerly were Christians but claimed to have abandoned their faith? Pliny asks for guidance in such cases. In response, Trajan lays down the policy that will prevail for the next 140 years. After commending Pliny for his wise actions, the emperor writes,

> These people must not be hunted out; if they are brought before you and the charge against them is proved, they must be punished, but in the case of anyone

---

3. Tacitus, *Annals* 15.44, in *The Annals: The Reigns of Tiberius, Claudius, and Nero*, trans. J. C. Yardley (Oxford: Oxford University Press, 2008), 359–60.

who denies that he is a Christian, and makes it clear that he is not by offering prayers to our gods, he is to be pardoned as a result of his repentance however suspect his past conduct may be.[4]

With this imperial decree the stage was set for local magistrates to bring the full force of Roman law against any Christian who came to public attention. Simply adhering to the name of Christianity was, in itself, a capital offense. The religion was now under state ban, even if its members weren't being sought out day after day. Whenever these scoundrels did turn up, they could be put to the "sacrifice test" and executed for refusal to comply.

We should not think, however, that persecution in this era always emanated from the corridors of power in Rome. It often tended to be a knee-jerk response at various locations across the empire. Governors were given wide latitude under the Roman legal system to resolve cases as they saw fit. Torture and capital punishment were used at their discretion, including public execution by *damnatio ad bestias*, "condemnation to the beasts" in the arena. If the emperor's majesty appeared to be threatened—or if the local populace got together and complained against the alien religion in their midst—the governors were empowered to handle the situation by whatever means suited them. Usually they were tolerant and sought to protect the rights of Christians. But sometimes an evil spirit rose up, and then the blood of the martyrs began to flow.

The third phase of early church persecution began under Emperor Decius in the year 250. What distinguishes this phase is an imperial policy to impose paganism throughout the empire. No longer would enforcement be reactionary; persecution now came from the top as part of an empire-wide program. Reacting to the political instability that characterized the mid-third century, Decius decided a renewed commitment to Roman religion would be the glue that held his society together. His edict commanded all citizens to appear before local magistrates and honor the gods by actions such as pouring libations, burning incense, and tasting sacrificial meat. Upon performing this test of loyalty, the individual would receive a *libellus*, an affidavit that proved compliance.

Though Christianity wasn't being singled out for unique persecution here, everyone knew this large religion was opposed to sacrifice and would be caught in the crosshairs. Decius himself presided over the execution of the prominent Roman bishop Fabian, possibly before the wider edict had even been issued.

4. Pliny, *Letters* 10.97, in *Pliny: Letters Books VIII–X and Panegyricus*, trans. Betty Radice, Loeb Classical Library 59 (Cambridge, MA: Harvard University Press, 1969), 291–93.

However, very few Christians held out like Fabian and became martyrs at this time. Some obtained *libelli* through bribery. Others laid low in their homes and hoped for the best, or fled to the countryside. And many just caved to the pressure and sacrificed. When the persecution passed after about a year, the problem of what to do with those who had apostatized became a major issue. The Christian community was split, especially in North Africa, between those who wanted to offer forgiveness and those who claimed the church's purity couldn't be marred by sinful idol worshipers. Eventually, after much bitter acrimony, the more lenient view won the day.

Decius's later successor Valerian renewed the persecution in 257, explicitly targeting the clergy and other Christians with high social rank. Fortunately, this effort was cut short when Valerian was captured by the Persians as a prisoner of war. The church then entered a period of respite. In fact, under Emperor Gallienus in 260, Christianity became a legal religion for the first time, gaining freedom from interference and the right to own property. The Christians of that era believed a permanent "peace" had finally arrived. But it was not to be.

In 303, Emperor Diocletian and others in his retinue initiated what has come to be called the Great Persecution (see chap. 11). In some parts of the empire it lasted only a few years, while in other provinces it raged for a decade. Many believers were tortured and executed in the most brutal fashion. Yet due to the complicated politics of that age, by the year 313 the fires of persecution had been snuffed out everywhere. The rise to power of Emperor Constantine solidified this reality and made a permanent end to Roman persecution.[5] This great moment is symbolized by his letter, issued with his brother-in-law Licinius, in which universal toleration of Christians is commanded across the realm: the so-called Edict of Milan (see chap. 12). The early church's "age of martyrdom"—which was not, as we have seen, a time of continuous persecution, but rather an era of its looming possibility—had finally come to a close. Yet the question begs to be answered: Why did it happen in the first place?

A Clash of Worldviews

Sometimes in the old Western movies, two gunfighters will square off at high noon in the middle of a dusty street. A tumbleweed usually rolls between the enemies, then one of them will be heard to mutter around his cigarette, "This

5. One historical source claims Licinius renewed persecution for a brief time when he had a falling out with Constantine, though this may be slander designed to tarnish Licinius's memory. When Constantine defeated him in 324, no other challengers remained, and the emperor could fully institute his policy of favoring the church.

town ain't big enough for the both of us." What is the gunfighter saying? He is affirming in his own colloquial way that two irreconcilable forces have come into contact, and one is going to have to give way to the other. The persecution of Christians was sort of like that. Two opposing worldviews had crashed into each other—both stubborn, both assertive, and both utterly convinced they were right. Unfortunately for the Christians, the other side held all the power for much of the ancient period.

Examining the situation from the Roman point of view, we discover persecution was a complex phenomenon. It can be interpreted from a legal, political, cultural, or socioeconomic perspective. However, the heart of the matter was *religion*. The Romans were not a "secular" people whose atheistic sensibilities were offended by the Christians' overt religiosity. Rather, the Romans prided themselves on their devotion to the gods.[6] Everyone—from the superstitious masses to the educated elites—believed the rites of state religion actually accomplished something beneficial for the public welfare. And by this I do not simply mean people thought it was good to have quaint rituals from the past to maintain traditional morality and foster patriotism, as important as those things may be. The Romans believed real spiritual powers not only observed what humans did, they also controlled earthly events and could bring about blessings or disasters. From top to bottom, the members of this society accepted the existence of potent and capricious gods.[7] Nobody should mess with powers like that. But the Christians did mess with them, and therein lies the reason for the gunfight.

Of course, since there were many gods and many temples, it would not have been immediately obvious that an individual Christian was rejecting pagan religion. Personal devotion to a specific god wasn't demanded, so Christians could quietly avoid them all and go unnoticed for a while. Earliest Christianity was a small and secretive faith. However, one particular form of religious devotion that emerged in the first century AD became a sticking point because

---

6. Historian Timothy Barnes describes the matter well when he writes, "Once it was realized that theirs was a new religion which entailed the abandonment of the established cults, the Christians could expect little sympathy or protection. The religious sentiments of the pagan world, if of a different type, were no less real and powerful than those of the Christians" ("Legislation against the Christians," *Journal of Roman Studies* 58, nos. 1–2 [1968]: 49). Likewise, my own teacher and esteemed early-church scholar Robert Wilken writes, "Given this attitude that religion is a patrimony from the past which sustains the life of the state, it was inevitable that the piety of the persecutors would conflict with the new movement that had begun in Palestine" (*The Christians as the Romans Saw Them* [New Haven: Yale University Press, 1984], 63).

7. This is not to say every single person believed in the gods. For example, a few of the philosophical schools were atheistic. Yet the culture of the Roman Empire was overwhelmingly religious, from the everyday commoners to the aristocrats who vied to occupy the prestigious priesthoods. The literary and archaeological records pour out a flood of evidence for Roman religiosity.

it was more difficult to hide: the cultural imperative to pay homage to the emperor's divinity in the imperial cult.[8]

The origins of the Roman imperial cult are diverse, with roots in Greek ruler worship and traditional Italian piety in which a clan's ancestral spirits were venerated. In any case, what emerged with Caesar Augustus and continued to expand after him was a full-blown religious system in which the innate *power* of the emperor received divine honor. Power was an amazing thing to ancient minds. Its generative source was something to revere, or even recoil from in awe. Since the emperors were the most dominant men in the world, their power must be especially fearsome and worthy of honor. Although the man himself was not, precisely speaking, worshiped in the original imperial cult, all citizens thought it useful to revere the spiritual entity called his "genius," the personification of the emperor's power that supported his actions and allowed him to bless his realm.

Devotion to the emperor's divine spirit soon became a central aspect of the broader state religion. This served as a very effective social adhesive. Festivals in honor of past and present emperors and their families rolled through an annual calendar that regulated the flow of civic life. Sacrifices and banquets were public affairs that knit the community together. Upper-class city fathers were expected to propagate the official apparatus of the imperial cult through donations and service as priests. Imperial provinces conquered by Rome began to celebrate their new Roman identity through this religious system. Emperor worship was also an important way to ensure the loyalty of soldiers in the army. In the Roman Empire, to spurn the gods, and especially the emperor's divine majesty, was to endanger the fabric of society itself.

However, Christians did exactly this, and they couldn't conceive of doing otherwise. We must keep in mind that the roots of Christianity are in Judaism. Even when the church became predominantly Gentile, it never lost certain aspects of its Jewish origins. Although wide theological diversity existed in the early church, one thing was universally agreed upon: *we are not polytheists*. The words "Hear, O Israel: The LORD our God, the LORD is one" (Deut. 6:4) were just as important to the first Christians as to the Israelites. The ancient church fathers experienced gut-level revulsion at the paganism that oozed from every pore of their society. To bow to an idol, to pray to a god, to offer even just a pinch of incense to the emperor's genius (or in Greek, his "demon") was to deny everything for which a Christian stood. It was, indeed, to become a non-Christian.

8. The term "cult" here simply means a formal system of religious observance. See the discussion of the "cult of the saints" below.

Though this might seem like extremist theology, a quick look at the early church's doctrine of salvation will help explain it. Many believers today are accustomed to think of salvation as being "saved from their sins." An ancient Christian was more likely to think of being "saved from the Devil"—which, of course, included being delivered from Satan's sinful bondage.[9] The Devil was a powerful overlord who had enslaved humans to evil deeds, but Christ the victor entered his enemy's realm, defeated him, and freed his captives from sin and death (Col. 2:15; Heb. 2:14–15; 1 John 3:8). The Christian church was a community of spiritually emancipated slaves. How, then, could the followers of the true Lord of the universe pay homage to Rome's caesar as a substitute lord? How could those whom Christ redeemed from bondage return to the chains of idolatry? How could the foul demons who posed as gods receive worship alongside the Risen One? To participate in Roman religion and its imperial cult was to spit in the face of Jesus. No Christian would do it willingly. Although many were not able to stand firm under the threat of heinous torture, those who did display such God-given fortitude were celebrated as the church's greatest witnesses—that is, as "martyrs."[10]

All this to say, it was the collision of two *religious* worldviews that ultimately led to persecution—though this had a *legal* element as well. The Roman governors considered themselves to be prosecuting Christians as criminals before the law. The magistrates were trying to follow the normal, if somewhat jumbled, legislation against crimes like treason (injury to the emperor's majesty), sedition (meeting in secret clubs, which were suspicious in principle), and disturbance of the peace (by causing periodic civil commotions). The Christians weren't being singled out for special prosecution; the laws applied to everyone alike.[11] Yet what must not be missed here is that the laws that enhanced public welfare were thoroughly intertwined with the Roman understanding of the sacred. Legal *prosecution* cannot be bracketed off from religious *persecution*. The law itself was religious. It was designed to advance a particular cult system.

9. This is clearly seen in the early Christian baptismal rite, which included a formal renunciation of Satan, an anointing with a special oil of exorcism, and rituals of transference from one domain to another.

10. The Greek word *martys* originally meant someone who gave eyewitness testimony in court or another public setting. In the New Testament, especially in Luke-Acts, the term carries the overtones of a person who confesses the gospel of Jesus Christ. Then in the mid-second century, Christians began using the word to describe those who bore witness to the Lord through their words and deeds before a watching audience in the context of persecution. At this time, *martys* came to designate a person who died for his or her faith as the ultimate proof of firm conviction (precedent for which can be found in Acts 22:20; Rev. 2:13; 11:3, 7).

11. On a few occasions Christians were targeted directly: under Nero in 64, Septimius Severus in 202, Maximinus Thrax in 235, Valerian in 257, and Diocletian in 303. However, the Christians were normally subject to general legislation against private associations like theirs.

That doesn't mean, of course, the trials of Christians were inquisitions into "heresy." Roman religion didn't have doctrines of its own, so the magistrates cared little about the church's actual theology (notice the judge's indifference in chap. 5 when Justin Martyr explains his doctrine of God and Christ). My point is simply that religion in Roman society affected every aspect of public and private life. The Christians were a political, social, and economic threat *precisely because* they did not support the ancestral customs of piety and devout social conduct. Maintenance of right relationships in both the human and divine spheres was what fostered the enduring "peace of the gods." Everyone had a vital stake in that.

The Christians' repudiation of their culture's values therefore constituted a real and present danger. The pagans often referred to them as "atheists"— people with no connection to the gods. Such individuals were like cancer cells on the face of a steadfastly religious society. Christianity was a *superstitio* in the true Roman sense of the term: not just something to mock as ignorant, but a set of beliefs so antisocial it could only lead to deadly repercussions from the heavens.[12] The outbreak of hostility at Lyons described in chapter 6 is a perfect example of how threatened the townspeople felt when a major imperial cult center was shunned or even ridiculed by a segment of the population. The persecution of the early church made absolute legal sense—not because the Christians were proven to have committed specific crimes, but because the church's intrinsic worldview aimed a sharp dagger at the throbbing religious heart of the Roman Empire.

The Fall of Rome and the Rise of Europe

Did the empire die, then? And did Christianity kill it? One of the church's more trenchant critics thought so. Edward Gibbon's *History of the Decline and Fall of the Roman Empire* (1776–88) lays the blame for Rome's demise at the foot of the cross. The robust and manly empire that had slapped around the barbarians for centuries finally acquired the bad habit of turning the other cheek. The Goths took advantage of this Christian softness by swarming into

---

12. Consider these words from the great Roman statesman Cicero. Though he wasn't speaking about Christianity, later Romans certainly applied thoughts like these to the Christian *superstitio*: "I thought that I should be rendering a great service both to myself and to my countrymen if I could tear this superstition up by the roots. But I want it distinctly understood that the destruction of superstition does not mean the destruction of religion. For I consider it the part of wisdom to preserve the institutions of our forefathers by retaining their sacred rites and ceremonies" (*On Divination* 2.72.148, in *Cicero: On Old Age, On Friendship, On Divination*, trans. W. A. Falconer, Loeb Classical Library 154 [Cambridge, MA: Harvard University Press, 1923], 537).

the territory to their south. Rome's light was snuffed out, and Europe went dark for the next millennium.

But modern historians are not so quick to make such a clean break between ancient Rome and the Middle Ages, nor to treat Christianity as the crowbar that divided the two. Augustine of Hippo, the greatest of the early church fathers, did not wake up one morning and shuck his toga, don a friar's habit, and declare himself the "first medieval man." Rather, the timeless rhythms of Mediterranean life that had reached their apex in the Roman Empire began to slide into what scholars now call "Late Antiquity"—an era of new, Christian adaptations to age-old patterns of living. The Middle Ages do not stand like a wasteland between the fertile paradise of classical antiquity and its reborn counterpart, the Renaissance. The centuries are far more intertwined than that. Green tendrils whose roots lie in Egypt, Phoenicia, Greece, and Rome stretched forth to blossom in medieval Paris, London, and Córdoba, then Florence, Genoa, and Venice, and even into our own cities today.

So if Rome did not die but only morphed, what was the catalyst of that change? What institutions channeled the culture of antiquity into medieval Europe? Perhaps several could be mentioned, but none would come close to eclipsing the importance of the Catholic Church. Separated by language and politics from the Christianity of the Greek East (today called "Eastern Orthodoxy"), the Western church, whose bishop presided at Rome, carried into Latin Christendom some of the best aspects—and some of the dregs—of the old empire. We could mention positives such as the manuscripts of antiquity, Roman law, the duty of charitable benefaction, and the principles of large-scale architecture—all of which flowed into the Middle Ages especially, though not exclusively, through Christian channels. But such topics are beyond the scope of this book. What I want to examine as I finish this introduction is a ubiquitous practice among the early Christians that became one of the hallmarks of medieval life: the attention to proper burial of the martyrs that gave rise to the veneration of saints and relics.

Holy Bones, Holy Books

Like the Jewish communities from which they emerged, the early Christians adopted inhumation (i.e., burial) rather than cremation as their preferred means of caring for the dead. Cremation signifies casting away the soul's abhorrent "shell," as well as the obliteration of individual identity. Burial, in contrast, reflects the Christian doctrine that the body is a fundamental part of the human person. When Christ became a man, he testified that physical bodies are important in the grand scheme of things. In fact, they matter so much that each person will one day be clothed anew in physical flesh. For some, this will be a resurrection unto life; for others, unto everlasting contempt—but either way, everyone will stand in a body before the Judge to face an eternal destiny. "I believe in the resurrection of the body and the life everlasting," concludes the Apostles' Creed. Christians have adhered to this truth since the very beginning, and their burial practices reflect it.

One of the primary ways we see this theology lived out is the practice of ancient congregations arranging to bury their poorest members. At first, the interment of lowly Christians was provided as charity by those who were wealthy enough to own suburban land. Later, as organizational structures progressed, the churches collectively purchased property for a cemetery out-side the city. This may seem like an insignificant matter, but consider it from an ancient perspective. Many people living in the Roman Empire could only look forward to an ignominious end to their short, difficult, often brutal lives. The majority of Rome's inhabitants were either slaves or the working poor. The cultural message conveyed to such people was that they were dispens-able. Whenever the indigent and unwanted died, their bodies were dumped in refuse pits outside the walls—stinking holes of putrid garbage, rotting animals, and human corpses. The bones of a newly deceased person would mix with everyone else's so that he or she disappeared as a distinct human being. Their lives had probably involved a lot of suffering; now, in the end, it was all meaningless. They were trash, entirely forgotten by the human race. So imagine a poor person like this who hears the message of the gospel. Not only will he or she be honorably buried among fellow believers, remembered by whoever might see the gravestone, but Jesus himself will come at the climax of history to escort the deceased to paradise! This was the great hope Chris-tianity offered. It was a message that appealed in a special way to the lonely, the downtrodden, the poor, and the afraid.

The early Christians, then, were very conscientious about their cemeteries. Usually the dead were buried in surface plots, or perhaps in stone tombs for those who could afford to buy them. But around Rome, and in a few other places where the geology was just right, the churches began to use underground burial chambers called *hypogea*, more commonly known as catacombs.[13] The

---

13. The word "catacomb" comes from an early Latin inscription that mentions a cemetery *ad catacumbas*, "in the catacombs." This appears to reflect an even earlier Greek expression *kata kymbas*, "down in the bowls." It referred to an area of volcanic-ash quarry pits outside Rome that had been turned into pagan burial areas by taking advantage of the hollowed-out excava-tions as depositories for corpses or funeral urns. In the mid-third century, one of the cemeteries (San Sebastiano) became exclusively Christian, and its catchy nickname came to stand for all

Figure 1. Sculpture of Saint Cecilia by Stefano Maderno. Church of Santa Cecilia in Trastevere. (Remi Jouan/ Wikimedia Commons)

first catacombs date to around the year AD 200. Over the next few centuries, more layers were dug even deeper until the catacombs had become multistoried mazes of narrow tunnels with tomb niches in every suitable wall. Now the poorest peasants of the empire, in death as in life, could mingle honorably with wealthier believers. The catacombs gave visible expression to the doctrine that among Christians, there was neither slave nor free, but all were one in Christ (Gal. 3:28).

However, what interests us here are not the everyday burials in the catacombs, of which there were thousands. Rather I wish to focus on the devotion attached to the final resting places of the martyrs. A classic example is the tomb of Saint Cecilia in the Callixtus (or San Callisto) catacomb at Rome. Though the story of the martyr Cecilia is the stuff of pure legend, the crowds that flocked to her tiny underground crypt certainly weren't. Yet gloomy, dank locations like this had obvious limitations, so a comfy ground-level chapel was dedicated for the use of Cecilia admirers.[14] Wherever the local topography did not allow for deep catacombs, the surface tombs of the martyrs were that much more accessible, making them wildly popular pilgrimage destinations. Soon these places were covered with spacious funeral halls that allowed visitors to file past the sacred tomb in prayerful contemplation. People vied to

the cemeteries used by the church. Today several of these underground catacomb complexes can still be toured. Not just San Sebastiano but others such as San Callisto, Domitilla, Priscilla, and Sant'Agnese are well worth a visit during any trip to Rome.

14. Today the crypt is neither dank nor dark, being properly ventilated and well lit by electric lights instead of oil lamps. Though the legends about Cecilia say that her incorruptible remains have been moved to her church in Rome's Trastevere district, a replica of Stefano Maderno's beautiful sculpture of the martyr now rests where her coffin used to sit. Cecilia's veiled face is turned to the floor, leaving the scar on her slender neck shockingly obvious to the viewer (see figure 1). Even in death, the delicate saint bears witness with her fingers to the three-and-one of the Holy Trinity. Visitors to the San Callisto catacomb will be awed by this sacred place just as they have been for centuries.

have their own graves installed in the floors, while the wealthy constructed attached mausoleums to await the resurrection in the company of a saint. The "birthdays" on which the martyrs had been reborn to eternal life were marked by annual festivals on the church calendar. Since tombs in antiquity always lay in the countryside outside the city walls, these festivals began to take on the air of a raucous picnic, or worse. Something very different was starting to happen now that the persecutions had ended. The honor accorded to the martyrs, and the loving concern for their proper burial, had evolved into what historians refer to as the "cult of the saints."

The word "cult" in this context does not mean a weird sectarian heresy. It refers to a system of religious devotion that developed around the martyrs, and later around holy men and women who metaphorically "died" to the passions of the flesh. These figures served as patrons and intermediaries who could bridge the gap between lowly humans and Almighty God. In modern American culture, where it is assumed "all men are created equal," such go-betweens seem like a needless hindrance. But ancient social systems were much more stratified. A common person could not expect to barge into the presence of the powerful. Allies were needed to make introductions and relay messages. Having friends like these was a deep comfort to those on the bottom rungs of society—and this was just as true for divine affairs as for human. Strange as it may seem, the martyrs and saints did not serve to distance ancient people from God; they brought him near. For example, the dying martyrs served as images of Christ, depicting his universal Passion through little passions of their own. When Blandina was stretched out on a pole (see chap. 6), the onlookers "saw, through their sister, the one who was crucified for them." Such *imitatio Christi*, or imitation of Christ, was one of the martyr's main ministries to the church. Through their example, other believers were encouraged to make their own hard choices along the road of costly discipleship.

Not only did martyrs picture Christ for the average person, they carried prayers to him as well. Ancient Christians delighted in the knowledge that they could share prayer requests with friends who already dwelled in the presence of God. When modern Christians struggle with some significant issue in their lives, they ask their fellow believers to intercede with the Lord. Together these friends approach the throne of grace, seeking mercy through their several petitions. But how much more glorious would it be to think that a martyr, who already resided in heaven yet remained spiritually accessible at his or her grave, might actually pray to God on one's behalf? This possibility reassured the early Christians as they faced life's uncertainties. At its best, then, the cult of the martyrs was about the twin ministries of imitation and intercession.[15] Visiting a martyr's shrine served as a profound inspiration to draw ancient believers closer to the sufferings of their Savior, and deeper into the prayer life of the body of Christ.

But this is, as I said, the cult of the martyrs at its best. An honest appraisal will conclude that it sometimes—perhaps often—took a superstitious and unspiritual turn. This is not just a modern Protestant assessment; many ancient observers, both pagan and Christian, thought so too.[16] For example, a magical view of the martyrs' relics made people expect healings and miracles as a reward for visiting the shrine. Cloths and handkerchiefs were dangled into the tombs to pick up divine power from the bones (based on Acts 19:12). Furthermore, the festivals of the martyrs sometimes turned into unruly parties. The practice of feasting at graves had long-standing precedent. The Romans often conducted funeral banquets to commemorate a departed family member. People of that time also continued the Greek practice of celebrating feasts in honor of a dead "hero" who had accomplished great deeds and become a demigod. These events included food and wine that were symbolically shared with the deceased—then consumed with gusto by the living. The early church's festivals at martyrs' shrines sometimes lapsed into such pagan practices. Ostensibly they were spiritual events, but when the whole community was gathered in the countryside for a day off work and a feast, it is not hard to imagine how good intentions might go astray. Old habits die hard, in ancient times as well as our own.

Even when an aura of holiness was retained, the exuberant devotion to the martyrs could quickly descend into something close to bone worship. Some church fathers like Augustine tried to squelch these negative tendencies.

15. Catholics today continue the practice of petitioning the saints; most Protestants (like myself) do not. I know of no firm evidence in Scripture that the dead can even hear the prayers of the living (Rev. 5:8 is unclear). However, what I do know is that ancient Christians took comfort in the fullness of the church by including within Christ's body those who already dwelled in his presence, as well as those still awaiting the beatific vision here on earth. It is this sense of communal solidarity I am trying to highlight here. The cult of the martyrs and saints did not necessarily "get in the way" of Jesus, as Protestants often imagine. On the other hand, I have no exegetical basis to think departed Christians can relay our prayers, much less affect earthly events, as saints are sometimes thought to do.

16. "You have filled the whole world with tombs and sepulchres," complains the ardently pagan emperor Julian, "and yet in your scriptures it is nowhere said that you must grovel among tombs and pay them honour. But you have gone so far in iniquity that you think you need not listen even to the words of Jesus of Nazareth on this matter. Listen then to what he says about sepulchres: 'Woe unto you, scribes and Pharisees, hypocrites! for ye are like unto whited sepulchres; outward the tomb appears beautiful, but within it is full of dead men's bones, and of all uncleanness.' If, then, Jesus said that sepulchres are full of uncleanness, how can you invoke God at them?" (*Against the Galilaeans* 1.335B–D, in *Julian: Volume III*, trans. Wilmer C. Wright, Loeb Classical Library 157 [Cambridge, MA: Harvard University Press, 1923], 415–17).

Augustine lifts up his mother, Monica, as an example of the right way to conduct such festivities: not with a picnic basket full of snacks but with a heart full of purified prayers and charitable works. When Monica learned her bishop Ambrose considered these events to be rife with drunkenness and heathen superstition, she humbly stopped attending. Instead of a party, Augustine declares, the church should celebrate Holy Communion at the shrines of those who have gloriously imitated their Lord.[17] Perhaps we can follow Augustine's lead by admiring the martyrs with warm affection while not resurrecting the excesses of medieval veneration of relics.

Of course, remembrance of the martyrs didn't have to occur only at their suburban tombs; it could also happen in civic churches as their heroic stories were retold and inspiring sermons were preached about them. From the beginning, the early church sought to capture accurate accounts of their martyrs. Sometimes these texts were shared with other congregations for documentation as well as edification. On annual feast days they were used as the basis for sermons. The intent was to strengthen one another by elevating the most eminent examples of Christian virtue. This widespread literary effort created the genre known as hagiography, or "writing about saints."

Scholars have traditionally divided hagiographical texts into three main groups (though in reality the lines between them are blurry). The "acts" of the martyrs are generally thought to be the most reliable since they often have connections to actual court transcripts. "Passions" are also fairly reliable as long as they are early texts. Yet because they include theological interpretation and crafted story lines, we cannot read them as completely neutral accounts of what happened. Some reading between the lines is always necessary. By far the largest group of hagiographical writings is the legendary material composed in the post-persecution era. Unfortunately, these texts are nearly worthless as records of real-world events. They come from the period when the cult of the martyrs was in full swing and the appetite for Christian hero tales was insatiable. Newly discovered bone fragments were supplied with marvelous backstories, turning humble graves into major pilgrimage destinations as new martyrs were created left and right. These narratives abound with evil villains, brave miracle workers, and unyielding virgins. Despite many horrible sufferings, the saints of God triumph again and again.

Although the legendary accounts are valuable because they illustrate the nature of late antique spirituality, the present volume focuses on the earliest and most historically reliable "acts" and "passions" of the martyrs. Even so, a few of the more significant legendary texts have been included as well, such

17. *Confessions* 6.2.

as the story of some pre-Christian Jewish martyrs (see chap. 1) whose noble deaths were influential on early church hagiography, and the martyrdoms of Peter and Paul (see chap. 2), whose historical kernel is of keen interest to us even though it is surrounded by pious fiction. Other early Christian letters of pastoral encouragement and works of theological reflection round out our martyrological collection.

Thus, if you read this book from cover to cover, you will have encountered the very best sources that illustrate early Christian persecution. At times you may be horrified, outraged, humbled, or inspired. Try to let your emotions flow; don't read this volume simply as a historical sourcebook. Not one of these texts was originally written without spiritual encouragement in mind. To suppress any personal reflection on them would be to ignore the authors' wishes. But if, on the other hand, you are in a receptive state of mind, I invite you to say a brief prayer, then turn the page and meet the martyrs of the ancient church.

1

The Maccabean Martyrs

Witnesses for God before Christ

In the year 167 BC the Greek king Antiochus IV initiated a policy of religious uniformity that brought great suffering to the Jewish people. A century and a half earlier, the conqueror Alexander the Great had brought the Jews under his dominion. When Alexander died, his territory was split into several Greek kingdoms that often fought with one another. In one of these kingdoms, Antiochus came to power as the fourth ruler to bear the name of his forefathers within the dynasty known as the Seleucids. The Seleucid capital was Antioch, and their great rival was Egypt—which meant the territory that occupied the boundary between these two kingdoms was ancient Israel. Therefore the holy land of the Hebrews became a battleground between the world powers of the age.

While this situation was not good for the Jews, they managed to get along for a while by accommodating Greek culture to a limited degree. The Seleucid rulers wanted their subjects to "hellenize"—that is, adopt the Greek way of life. This seemed doable, so many Jews living in Greek cities assimilated Hellenistic culture into a comfortable balance with their own ancestral religion. But King Antiochus IV took things to a whole new level. Angered that some Jews had refused to hellenize, and fearful that the Mosaic law would always undermine political unity in his kingdom, he decided to eradicate the worship of Israel's God. The final straw occurred when Antiochus profaned the altar of the Jerusalem temple, the so-called abomination of desolation mentioned in Daniel 11:31. The temple of Yahweh was now devoted to the worship of Zeus, and disgusting pagan sacrifices were being offered to a false god in the Holy of Holies.

In all the upheaval that these actions created, a revolutionary named Judas Maccabeus rallied his rebel forces against the armies of Antiochus. Eventually these "Maccabees" managed to win quasi independence from their Greek overlords. However, taking up the sword was not the only form of Jewish resistance to the evil designs of Antiochus. The ancient book of 2 Maccabees records the horrific deaths of some Jewish martyrs who gave their lives rather than submit to the commands of the king. First, a venerable scribe named Eleazar sets the martyrological pattern by refusing to violate God's law; then seven noble brothers follow in his footsteps, assisted by the courageous exhortations of their mother.

The book that recounts this story is part of the collection of texts called "apocryphal" by Protestants and "deuterocanonical" by Roman Catholics. These terms indicate Protestants do not regard the collection as belonging to the Bible while Catholics consider them a second body of scriptural works with full divine inspiration. What distinguishes the Apocrypha from the Hebrew Scriptures? The apocryphal books were written or preserved in Greek and come primarily from the period between the Old and New Testaments. Although the Jews never recognized these writings as belonging to the authoritative canon, many early church fathers did accept them as scriptural, and this trend continued through the Middle Ages. Eventually the leaders of the Protestant Reformation in the 1500s followed Jewish tradition and rejected the books' inspired status. The Catholics responded by formally accepting the books into the biblical canon, leading to the difference of opinion that still exists today among the various groups.

But aside from the question of the Apocrypha's canonical status, we can certainly find great value in these books as historical witnesses to the events of ancient times. This is especially true of 2 Maccabees, because its account of the Maccabean martyrs (2 Macc. 6–7) came to be cherished by the early Christians when they began to experience their own version of martyrdom at the hands of the Romans. Ancient church fathers such as Cyprian, Origen, Gregory of Nazianzus, John Chrysostom, and Augustine all drew great inspiration from the Maccabean martyrs. It is even likely the author of Hebrews had these martyrs in mind when he wrote Hebrews 11:35–38. Although the Maccabean martyrs were Jews who lived before the time of Christ, they came to be granted the same level of respect accorded to the Christian martyrs—for they died in the name of the same God whom Christians worshiped, just without the fuller knowledge that arrived when Jesus came into the world.

Today there is skepticism among scholars that the martyrdoms unfolded exactly as described. Of course, this doesn't mean real historical circumstances are absent from the text. The author's description of the contemporary politics is often accurate, and he claims to be summarizing a much longer source document. Yet the narrative format—such as the martyrs being allowed to deliver heroic speeches, or the seven sons each being tortured in order of age—suggests a text whose purpose was to encourage the faithful more than record pure history. The story shows signs of being shaped and embellished by its author.

Even so, the horrible dilemma faced by the story's characters is no fantasy. Jewish men and women in the age of Antiochus were tortured for refusing to abandon their ancestral religion. The account of the Maccabean martyrs sets forth an enduring pattern of bold words to the persecutors, confidence in eternal life, and uncompromising loyalty to the one true God. The ancient church fathers noticed these things and incorporated many aspects of this Jewish narrative into their own martyr stories. The Maccabean martyrs were embraced almost like Christian saints before Christ. Therefore this text makes a fitting introduction to a volume on early church persecution.

---

2 Maccabees 6–7

The Persecution of the Jews under Antiochus

A little later, Antiochus the king sent a senator from Athens to force the Jews to abandon the laws of their forefathers and no longer live by God's commandments. Furthermore, this man was to defile the temple in Jerusalem and start calling it "The Temple of Olympian Zeus," while the temple in Gerizim was to be called "The Temple of Zeus, Who Helps Strangers" (which fits what the people living there experienced).[1] The onslaught of this evil was harsh and utterly offensive.

1. Zeus was considered the supreme Greek deity, lord of the heavens and master of thunder. The biblical book of Daniel describes the desire of Antiochus IV to worship the "god of fortresses" (11:38), probably a reference to Olympian Zeus—that is, Zeus in his supremacy as he dwells atop the highest mountain in Greece, Mount Olympus. Ancient gods were often worshiped under different aspects of their character or their unique areas of patronage. Therefore, in addition to converting the Jerusalem temple to honor Zeus's supremacy, King Antiochus wanted the Samaritan temple at Gerizim to celebrate Zeus as a special helper of foreigners, strangers, and guests. The Samaritans were a religious and ethnic community whose lineage traced back to ancient Israel but became intermixed with foreign blood after settlers immigrated to Israel under Assyrian domination. Despised as "half-breeds" by the Jews of Judea, the Samaritans were often treated as unwelcome interlopers, which explains why Antiochus thought it fitting to rename their temple in honor of Zeus's hospitality. All of this was part of the king's religious policy of using Hellenistic religion to unify his realm. In the eyes of Antiochus, Judaism was an ancient cult that needed to be eradicated.

The gentiles began to fill the Holy Place with disgusting acts and revelry, lounging around with prostitutes and having sex with women even inside the sacred temple courts! To make matters worse, they brought in forbidden sacrifices, so the altar was covered with detestable offerings prohibited by the law. No one could observe the Sabbath, nor celebrate the festivals of our ancestors, nor even admit openly to being a Jew.

Every month there was a festival for the king's birthday. The Jews were compelled by harsh measures to partake of the sacrificial meat, and when there was a celebration for the god Dionysus they were forced to march in his parade wearing ivy wreaths.[2] Then, at the instigation of Ptolemy,[3] a decree was issued to the nearby Greek cities that they too should adopt the same policy toward the Jews, making them partake of the sacrifices and executing those who refrained from converting to Greek customs. So everyone understood a crisis had arrived.

For example, two women were brought in for having circumcised their children. So the authorities publicly paraded the women around the city with their babies hung around their necks and dangling at their breasts, then pushed them headfirst off the city wall. And some other folks who had secretly gathered in nearby caves to observe the Sabbath were betrayed to Philip.[4] They were all burned together, because their piety kept them from defending themselves out of respect for the day of rest.

Now, I encourage those who read this book not to be saddened by all these disasters but to consider them as chastisements designed to discipline our people instead of destroying them. For it is a sign of great kindness not to tolerate the impious for a long time but to strike them immediately with punishments. In the case of the other nations, the Sovereign Lord waits patiently to punish them until they have attained the full measure of their sins. But he has determined to deal differently with us so he won't have to execute justice upon us after our sins have reached their worst level. Thus, he never removes his mercy from us. Although he disciplines us with disasters, he does not abandon his chosen people.

2. In the apostle Paul's correspondence with the Corinthians, we discover eating meat sacrificed to idols was a problem for Christians as well. Although this is not exactly the same thing as following the kosher food laws, the early Christians made a point of having nothing to do with the pagan gods once they confessed Jesus as Lord. "What pagans sacrifice, they offer to demons and not to God," Paul writes. "I do not want you to be participants with demons" (1 Cor. 10:20). In such anti-pagan sentiments, the ancient Jews and Christians were in full agreement. Therefore, eating sacrificial meat or marching around with ivy wreaths to honor Dionysus, the Greek god of feasting and wine, was abhorrent to an observant Jew who worshiped the one true God.

3. Ptolemy is mentioned earlier in 2 Maccabees as a supporter of King Antiochus (4:45). Another way of interpreting this name is to understand it as a reference to the nearby city of Acre, Israel, which was called "Antiochia Ptolemais" at the time.

4. Philip was the governor of Jerusalem under Antiochus. He was said to be even more barbarous than the king who had appointed him (2 Macc. 5:22).

So then, let this be enough of a reminder of these things. It is now time to carry on with the story.

Eleazar the Martyr

Eleazar, a high-ranking scribe, was an aged man with a distinguished appearance. The authorities forced him to open his mouth and eat pork.[5] But he welcomed death with honor rather than life with defilement. He went of his own accord to the torture area and spat out the meat, which is what everyone should do who has the strength to refuse what is forbidden to taste, even if eating it is the only way to save one's precious life.

The authorities who were ordering Eleazar to eat unlawful meat had known him for a long time, so they took him aside privately and implored him to bring meat prepared in his own way, proper for him to consume, and only pretend to eat the sacrificial meat commanded by the king. By doing this he would be freed from the death penalty and be treated well on account of his long-standing friendship with them.

But Eleazar took a well-reasoned position worthy of a man of his years—a man of advanced old age who had earned his distinguished gray hair through excellent conduct since childhood. And since he was, moreover, committed to the holy laws established by God, he quickly made his position known by saying, "Send me on to the afterlife![6] To carry out such a charade would be unworthy of my old age. Many young folks would think ninety-year-old Eleazar had finally decided

5. To eat pork would be a violation of God's commandment in Leviticus 11:7–8: "And the pig, because it parts the hoof and is cloven-footed but does not chew the cud, is unclean to you. You shall not eat any of their flesh, and you shall not touch their carcasses; they are unclean to you." But Eleazar's concern here is not the meat in and of itself. Rather, for a Jew to partake of forbidden pork would represent an utter rejection of God's law, and therefore God himself. Like the Christian martyrs who refused to acknowledge the lordship of demons in place of Christ, so Eleazar cannot undertake an action that would tell everyone he had abandoned the God of his fathers.

6. Eleazar literally requests to be sent to *hades*, but that does not mean he thinks he will be in what we call "hell"—a place of burning fire that punishes the wicked forever. In the Second Temple period (starting around 500 BC), the Jewish view of the afterlife was evolving under the influence of new Hellenistic ideas. Since the Greek word *hades* was the normal translation of the biblical Hebrew *sheol*, we should probably see the Old Testament concept of "the grave" as the background of Eleazar's expression, though it was beginning to be colored by Greek concepts as well. In the later Old Testament writings, *sheol* was the gloomy, subterranean realm of the dead (Eccles. 9:10; Isa. 7:11). Since it is the place of death, there can be no earthly return from *sheol* (Job 7:9), yet by Eleazar's day it seems to have been viewed as a waiting area until the future resurrection of the righteous. Psalm 49:14–15 and Isaiah 26:19 hint that God will rescue his faithful from *sheol*, but the concept of resurrection is most clearly taught in Daniel 12:2. Thus an observant Jew of the second century BC like Eleazar would expect to go to *sheol* (or *hades* in Greek) until the time of his divine reward. The doctrine of bodily resurrection eventually became widespread in Judaism, though the Sadducee party denied it (Acts 23:8). Jesus rebukes them for this in Matthew 22:23–33.

to convert to foreign customs! Then, just to extend my life for a moment longer, my hypocrisy would lead them astray, and I would defile and tarnish my old age.[7] Even if I were to dodge human punishment today, I would not escape the hand of the Almighty in my subsequent life or death. Therefore, by courageously giving up my life right now, I not only show myself worthy of my years but also leave for the young a shining example of how to die a good death, with eagerness and nobility, for the sake of the holy and respectable laws."

Having said these things, Eleazar went straight to the torture area.[8] The men who just a moment before were acting friendly to him now changed to hostility, because in their minds the words he had proclaimed were utterly insane. As Eleazar was about to die from all the blows, he groaned in anguish and said, "The Lord who possesses holy knowledge clearly perceives that although I could have escaped death, I chose to endure terrible agony in my body from this beating. Yet on the inside I suffer it gladly, because I fear the Lord."

So this was how Eleazar departed this world for the next. His death left behind an example of nobility and a memorial of virtue not only for the young but indeed for the whole Jewish nation.

Seven Sons of a Jewish Mother

It also came about that seven brothers were arrested along with their mother.[9] King Antiochus was torturing them with whips and the rack to compel them to eat pork against the dictates of the law.[10] One of the brothers acted as a spokesman for the

7. The Christian martyr Polycarp (see chap. 4) likewise appeals to his old age when he says he has served Christ for eighty-six years and is not about to change his mind after so long a time. Polycarp also mentions his holy fear of God's judgment as a reason to see the martyrdom through. "Clearly you're unaware of the fire of imminent judgment and eternal punishment that awaits the ungodly," he says to his persecutor. "So what are you waiting for? Come on! Do whatever you wish." Though earthly rulers may threaten temporary punishments, Eleazar and Polycarp care more about God's divine verdict.

8. The word *tympanon* (translated "torture area") literally means a kettle drum, but by association with the act of beating it came to refer to a place for flogging, or the post to which the victim was bound. The book of 4 Maccabees tells Eleazar's story in more gruesome detail. In that account Eleazar is stripped, severely flogged, burned, and subjected to irritating fluids poured into his sinuses. The flogging takes place while Eleazar is tied to a post or other stationary object.

9. There is a substantial element of folklore in this tale. The number seven symbolizes completion, while the image of a tyrannical ruler being defeated by his wiser subjects is a stock element of folk stories. We should also note the author's thematic linkage to the preceding account of Eleazar. The old man's death provided a "shining example" for the young, and now we discover seven youths following in their mentor's footsteps.

10. As with Eleazar, the gory details of the brothers' afflictions are described in 4 Maccabees. The tortures typically involve dislocating the body's joints and vertebrae by geared machines, shredding the martyrs' flesh with metal hooks, and savagely burning them with fire or hot irons. The reader is cautioned that 4 Maccabees is a disturbing, graphic text.

rest and said, "What do you hope to ask or learn from us? For we are ready and willing to die rather than transgress the laws of our forefathers."

Infuriated by this statement, the king immediately ordered giant frying pans to be heated over fire pits. After this was done he commanded that the spokesman's tongue be cut out, his scalp be sliced away, and his limbs be amputated while his mother and brothers looked on. Then when the man was utterly helpless though still alive, the king ordered him brought to the fire and fried. Even as the fumes from the frying pan wafted everywhere, the brothers and their mother encouraged one another to die nobly, saying, "The Lord God looks down and sees us, and he truly comforts us. This is just what Moses made clear in his song when he testified against the people to their faces, saying, 'And he will comfort his servants' [Deut. 32:36]."[11]

After the first brother died like this, they brought forward the second for their mockery. As they tore away the skin of his head along with his hair, they were asking him, "Now would you rather eat pork than have your body punished limb by limb?"

But he answered them in Hebrew, "Never!" So he took his turn being tortured like the first brother. And with his dying breath he cried out to the king, "You wretch! Though you're sending us out of this life, the king of the universe will resurrect us to eternal life because we died for his laws!"

The third brother was the next victim of their ridicule. When they told him to stick out his tongue he immediately put it out and bravely offered his hands. "I received these from the God of heaven," he said with great dignity, "and because of his laws I now disregard them, and from him I expect to receive them back again." So the king himself and all his servants were utterly astonished at the young man's courageous spirit, for he regarded his tortures as trivial.

Then they abused and tormented the fourth brother in the same way after the third died. When he was close to the end he said, "It is preferable when departing the human world to trust in the hope that God will raise him up again. But as for you, O king, there will be no resurrection to life!"

Next, the fifth brother was brought forward for torture. But he looked at the king and said, "Because you have authority among men, you can do whatever

11. The full text of Deuteronomy 32:35–36 says, "'Vengeance is mine, and recompense, for the time when their foot shall slip; for the day of their calamity is at hand, and their doom comes swiftly.' For the LORD will vindicate his people and have compassion on his servants, when he sees that their power is gone and there is none remaining, bond or free." The Song of Moses was supposed to bear witness against the Israelites when they turned from the Lord, reminding them of his covenant loyalty (Deut. 31:19–22). Now the prediction of God's vengeance upon Israel's foreign enemies, and his compassion toward his loyal servants, is applied to the Maccabean martyrs as they face their Greek persecutors.

you please even though you are a mere mortal. But don't be fooled! Our people haven't been deserted by God.[12] So keep this up, O king—but be on the lookout for God's supreme power as he afflicts you and your descendants!"[13]

And after him they led forth the sixth. When he was on the verge of death he said, "Do not deceive yourself in vain. We're suffering these things because of our nation's sins against our own God, and admirable deeds have just occurred. But don't think for a minute this means you who tried to make war on God will be held blameless!"

The Mother Exhorts Her Last Son to Faithfulness

Now, the mother who saw her seven sons perish in the span of a single day was especially noteworthy and deserving of honorable memory, for she bore it with a stout heart, because her hope was in the Lord. Brimming with noble resolve, she was encouraging each of them in the Hebrew tongue. She took her female mental powers to the next level by adding manly courage. "I don't know how you appeared in my womb," she declared. "It wasn't I who graced you with the breath of life, nor did I provide the basic form to each of you. Therefore it is the Creator of the world—the shaper of the original man and initial cause of everything that exists—who by his mercy will give you back the breath of life, since you submit yourselves to mistreatment for the sake of his laws."

At these words King Antiochus thought he was being disrespected and felt suspicious of the mother's critical tone. Since the youngest brother was still alive, the king made an appeal to him not only with persuasive words but even by swearing oaths. He said he would make the youth very rich, the envy of all, a personal friend of the king entrusted with high political office—if he would just convert

---

12. A form of the same verb for "deserted" is also used in the Greek version of Isaiah 54:7–8: "'For a brief moment I *deserted* you, but with great compassion I will gather you. In overflowing anger for a moment I hid my face from you, but with everlasting love I will have compassion on you,' says the LORD, your Redeemer." The theology of the Maccabean literature suggests God is punishing the Jews for national apostasy, but thanks to the ministry of the martyrs, God will soon turn again and show his favor.

13. Later in 2 Maccabees, the disgusting death of King Antiochus is recorded. He is said to have been struck by God with a disease that filled his bowels with worms and rotted away his flesh, causing unbearable agony. No one could even carry him on a litter, because the stench of his putrefaction was overwhelming. At last, broken in spirit and suffering at every moment, the once-prideful Antiochus realizes, "It is right to be subject to God; mortals should not think that they are equal to God" (9:12 NRSV). Yet God does not accept this repentance, and Antiochus dies in torment and shame. Additionally, the king's son was captured in war and murdered (1 Macc. 7:2–4). Horrific deaths likewise befell the Roman emperors who persecuted the Christians, according to the church father Lactantius. For example, the wicked emperor Galerius endured an agonizing, stinking, worm-ridden death despite a last-minute change of heart (*On the Deaths of the Persecutors* 33–35). See chap. 11 for more on these figures.

from his ancestral religion. But since the young man refused to listen to him at all, Antiochus called the mother over and tried to get her to act as a counselor for the boy's safety. So after a great deal of urging from the king she agreed to advise her son. Leaning close to him so she could whisper, she mocked the cruel tyrant. "Feel some compassion for me, my son," she said in Hebrew. "I carried you for nine months in my womb, and nursed you three years more, and fed you, and reared you to your present age, and sustained you all this time. Now I make this one claim upon you, my child: Raise your eyes and behold heaven and earth! As you examine everything in them, know that God made all this out of nothing, and the human race came into existence the same way. Therefore do not fear this executioner, but be worthy of your brothers. Embrace death, so that by God's mercy I may receive you back along with your brothers."[14]

No sooner had she stopped speaking than the young man said, "What are you waiting for? I will not obey the king's command, for I heed the command of the law given to our ancestors through Moses. But you, O king, who have been the source of all kinds of evil against the Jews—you will not escape the hand of God![15] Our suffering is due to our own sins. Although for the sake of discipline and instruction our living Lord has been angry with us for a moment, he will soon be reconciled to his servants once more. As for you, most heinous and depraved of all men, do not puff yourself up in vain arrogance, nor prance around with false hopes when you raise your hand against the children of heaven! You haven't escaped the judgment of Almighty God, who sees all. Yes, our brothers have fallen. According to the provisions of God's covenant they have endured a brief pain now for the attainment of eternal life. But you shall receive the deserved penalty for your own arrogance according to the justice of God. Therefore I now relinquish my body and life, like my brothers before me, for the sake of our ancestral laws!

14. Notice the tension the author builds here. The woman has agreed to serve as an adviser to her only remaining son while the king awaits the outcome. She appeals to all the motherly sacrifices she has made to win the boy's compliance. But then, in a stunning reversal of expectations, the claim she makes in exchange for everything she has provided is that he give up his life. She asks for his compassion, not that he might spare her this final devastating blow, but that he would follow through with the martyrdom to the end—for what would sadden her even more than her son's death would be his apostasy. Although the tale has a legendary ring to it, we can still appreciate the author's skill in heightening the drama through irony and suspense.

15. In this speech the seventh brother alternates between God's sovereign purposes and the culpable actions of the human agents in the persecution. Like the actions of Pharaoh in the exodus, the deeds of Antiochus are wicked and blameworthy, even though God is at work for a greater good. The Jews of the Maccabean period are experiencing divine judgment, yet this does not let their Greek overlords off the hook. They will be punished for their cruel persecution of the Jewish nation, even though God has intended to use the persecution as a chastisement. The seventh brother develops both of these themes in a back-and-forth manner as he proclaims judgment against the king and at the same time explains why God has allowed his people to suffer.

I further call upon God to show mercy to his people very soon—and to make you acknowledge through afflictions and diseases that he alone is God! May the deeds of us seven brothers bring an end to the wrath of the Almighty that has justly descended on our entire nation."[16]

Feeling the sting of these taunts, the king became enraged and tortured the young man even more harshly than the others.[17] So the youth died with his integrity intact, entrusting himself entirely to the Lord. And after the seven sons died, so did the mother.

Well, then, let this be enough about sacrificial slaughters and horrific tortures.

---

16. One of the themes that sometimes appears in the intertestamental books is that certain individuals can absorb the sin of God's people or suffer on behalf of the nation. Here, the magnitude of the brothers' suffering evokes God's pity and prompts him to end the persecution against the Jews. But in 4 Maccabees, the brothers' blood is actually said to have atoning value: "The tyrant was punished, and the homeland purified—[the martyrs] having become, as it were, a ransom for the sin of our nation. And through the blood of those devout ones and their death as an atoning sacrifice, divine Providence preserved Israel that previously had been mistreated" (4 Macc. 17:21–22 NRSV). Similarly, the Suffering Servant of Isaiah 53 is depicted as wounded for the sins of others, slaughtered like a lamb, and buried in a grave on behalf of Israel. This motif anticipates the gospel teaching that Jesus suffered for the sins of the Jewish nation, and indeed the world. Caiaphas the high priest seems to be alluding to such a concept when he says in John 11:50, "It is better for you that one man should die for the people, not that the whole nation should perish."

17. According to the account in 4 Maccabees, the seventh brother was not judicially tortured but simply cast himself on the fire pits after his speech and perished.

2

Peter and Paul

Apostolic Proto-Martyrs

The biblical book of Acts records many of the heroic deeds performed by the apostles for the sake of the gospel. Evidently this was a popular subject among the early Christians, for soon Acts was followed by a slew of stories that claimed to provide even more details about the apostolic missions. Often these accounts are so highly legendary and adventurous that scholars consider them a type of ancient fiction novel. The apostles gallivant across the empire on daring escapades, defeating their heretical opponents and pagan accusers along the way. Miracles and visions abound in these tales. Sometimes there are even damsels in distress to be rescued from evil villains. The existence of this genre demonstrates how much the early Christians hungered for role models they could admire. In an age of persecution or hostility, they longed for heroes who overcame dire circumstances to win the day.

Before these apostolic adventures were collected and set down as unified narratives, they circulated widely in the churches—and also among the gnostics—as individual stories in both oral and written form.[1] Because of

---

1. "Gnosticism" was a broad religious movement that professed faith in Jesus but held doctrines that were fundamentally different from the apostolic message. Salvation centered not on Christ's death and resurrection but on the secret knowledge he could provide. Though many scholars today treat gnosticism as a type of early Christianity, it is difficult to call it that, because its entire belief system diverged from what is known to have been the original proclamation

this, scholars believe they might preserve some actual historical information. Though Christian memories and traditions from the first century were expanded by later legends, a historical core often remains. Therefore these texts cannot be considered pure fiction. Sometimes they functioned like the biblical Gospels: as biographical narratives telling a historical story from a certain theological point of view. When we find independent confirmation of their details elsewhere, these texts help us reconstruct the Christian past.

In this chapter we will encounter the two earliest descriptions of Peter's and Paul's martyrdoms. As with the Maccabean martyrs, we must remember that the stories here are only loosely based on historical events. Early traditions about the apostles have been embellished by later writers and storytellers. This situation differs from what we will encounter in upcoming chapters. The accounts of figures like Justin, Polycarp, or Perpetua are based on much more reliable sources. When it comes to the deaths of Peter and Paul, we are dealing with a possible historical core surrounded by a great deal of narrative imagination. Yet even this reveals something interesting about the early Christians. As you read the two stories below, try not to expect an account of what "really happened" to the apostles. Instead, appreciate the thrill the ancient hearers would have experienced as they encountered the daring exploits and God-empowered miracles of their original founders.

Our first text is a selection from a document called the *Acts of Peter*. This work shows every sign of being stitched together in the mid- to late second century from individual stories circulating in the ancient church. Peter's evil nemesis is Simon Magus, the same magician who appears in the biblical book of Acts (8:9–25). Simon is considered by many church fathers to be the originator of the gnostic heresy, so he functions in the *Acts of Peter* as the archvillain. Peter performs a number of miracles to refute his heretical opponent, such as making a dog and a nursing infant speak, restoring dead people and a pickled sardine to life, and making Simon crash to his death as he is flying over Rome like a bird. The modern reader can quickly discern we have departed from the historical Peter here—although perhaps not as much as we might at first think. Let us recall that the biblical Peter walked on water, healed people with his shadow, raised a woman from the dead, escaped a locked prison by angelic help, struck sinners dead with a single rebuke, and performed many additional signs and wonders (Matt. 14:29; Acts 5:1–16; 9:32–42; 12:1–19). For the early Christians, it was only natural to want to expand the mighty deeds recorded about Peter with further inspirational stories.

---

of Jesus's disciples and first followers coming out of Jerusalem. The ancient church fathers consistently viewed the gnostics as "heretics."

The martyrdom sequence in the *Acts of Peter* appears to have circulated in the early church as a self-contained unit before being edited into a larger narrative. That is the portion of the document I have excerpted and translated below. The context is Peter's conversion of certain women to Christianity, which caused them to withdraw from sexual relations with the men in their lives. We pick up the story as two unbelieving Roman politicians grow distressed at their lovers' newfound sexual reticence.

The Martyrdom of Peter (*Acts of Peter* 33–41)

Peter's Female Converts Renounce Sexuality

While Peter was staying in Rome he rejoiced with his Christian brethren and gave thanks night and day for the many people who were joining themselves daily to the holy name through the grace of the Lord. And the four concubines of Agrippa, the mayor of Rome[2]—Agrippina, Nikaria, Euphemia, and Doris—also came to Peter. After hearing the preaching of sexual purity and all the words of the Lord, they were stung to the heart. So they agreed among themselves to stay pure and abstain from intercourse with Agrippa (though he continually pestered them for sex).[3]

Now Agrippa was confused and disturbed by the women's behavior, for he lusted for them intensely. So he watched them and had men spy on them to find out where they were going, and he learned they were visiting Peter. When they returned he

2. The word translated "mayor" is literally "prefect," which has a very broad meaning but in context probably referred to the city prefect, the man who supervised all civic affairs. Though we have no record of a Roman prefect named Agrippa, there was a certain Fonteius Agrippa who ruled the province of Asia (in modern-day Turkey) around the time of Peter's death—and note that it was probably in Asia that the *Acts of Peter* came together as a text. In addition to this actual political figure, we find Peter being persecuted by Herod Agrippa I in Acts 12:1–3. The name Agrippa is even plastered across the facade of the Pantheon, which could have been seen in Rome back then just as it can be today. Therefore it seems likely the second-century editor of our martyrdom narrative has melded some vague memories of earlier politicians named Agrippa into a single character who arrests Peter in Rome.

3. Agrippa's "concubines" were high-class courtesans who serviced their master sexually but were not legally married to him. The theme of female sexual renunciation appears frequently in the various legends of the apostles, illustrating the unease Christian women often felt when they adopted a stricter sexual ethic than their promiscuous husbands. (See chap. 5 below for an example of how this issue may have led to the death of the church father Justin Martyr in Rome at the same period the *Acts of Peter* was being compiled.) Some scholars interpret early Christian sexual renunciation as a feminist rebellion in which women freed themselves from the domination of men. While Christianity did indeed dignify women in ways pagan culture did not, we should probably consider the courtesans' renunciation to be more about morality than feminist liberation. The women are pictured as abandoning pagan sexual ethics and adopting the Judeo-Christian view that sex is reserved for the marriage bed (Heb. 13:4). Yet even within marriage, sex could be viewed negatively by some early Christians, as the example of Xanthippe below demonstrates.

said to them, "That Christian has taught you not to have sex with me! I'm telling you, I'm going to annihilate you and burn him alive!" But the women resolved to suffer any of Agrippa's evil deeds rather than be used to satisfy his animalistic passions any longer, and they were strengthened in their conviction by the power of Jesus.

Likewise an incredibly beautiful woman named Xanthippe, the wife of the emperor's friend Albinus,[4] was also visiting Peter along with the rest of the ladies. She too began withdrawing from her husband. Now, since Albinus was very desirous for Xanthippe, he went crazy and couldn't comprehend why she wouldn't sleep in his bed anymore. Raging like a wild beast, he earnestly wanted to murder Peter, for he discerned Peter was the reason Xanthippe had left his bed. And many other women who delighted in the message of chastity were staying apart from their husbands, and the husbands were refraining from sex with their wives, because they all wanted to worship God in reverence and purity.[5]

Albinus and Agrippa Plot against Peter

Because of all this, a huge commotion broke out in Rome. Albinus told Agrippa what had happened to him. "Either you punish Peter, who has alienated my wife from me," Albinus said, "or I'll do it myself."

4. The character of Albinus may have been loosely based on the historical figure Lucceius Albinus, who was procurator of Judea around the time of Peter's death. James the brother of Jesus was executed by the Jewish high priest while Albinus was on his way to Jerusalem to take power. Although Albinus was infuriated by this action, his name seems to have gotten connected to the murder of an apostle in the memories of later Christian generations. Therefore he appears in our text as one of Peter's main persecutors along with Agrippa.

5. The reader may be wondering, "Why is Christianity associated with godly husbands and wives ceasing to have sex?" Biblically speaking, married sex is a potential hindrance to fervent prayer, so the apostle Paul recommends temporary abstinence during times of intense spiritual focus. Yet he counsels spouses to come back together eventually due to human weakness. Even so, Paul did express his wish that everyone could be free from the burdens of married life. The person who doesn't have to worry about a spouse can focus on service to God (1 Cor. 7:1–9, 32–35). Sex, it seems, can sometimes distract a devout believer from seeking God to the fullest. The ancient Christians did not have a theology that celebrated wild sexual passion as long as it was within the bonds of marriage. Any time a bodily urge was in charge of one's physical actions instead of self-control, the church fathers considered it problematic. Conservative sexual ethics—drawn from Jewish roots—characterized the ancient church from the beginning. Eventually this conservatism reached such an ascetic intensity that some Christians started to downplay holy matrimony. Saint Augustine had to write a book to remind everyone marriage was, in fact, a good thing. In the case of Agrippa's four courtesans, they were only trying to refrain from extramarital sex since they weren't married to him, whereas Xanthippe was married but didn't like sleeping with her pagan husband. If the Christian spouses who practiced abstinence were doing so permanently, they were approaching the type of behavior criticized by the apostle Paul in Colossians 2:18–23 and 1 Timothy 4:1–4. It was this sort of legalistic opposition to sexuality that also made the *Acts of Peter* popular among the gnostics, who abhorred, or at least disregarded, any activity conducted by the physical human body.

"I suffered the same thing!" Agrippa replied. "He alienated my concubines!"

"Well, then, what are you waiting for, Agrippa? Let's find him and execute him as a troublemaker! That way we'll get our women back, and we can take revenge for anyone else whose women he has alienated but who can't do anything about it."

But as they were plotting these things, Xanthippe learned of her husband's advice to Agrippa and sent someone to inform Peter so he could escape Rome. And all the other Christians, along with Marcellus,[6] were begging him to leave. But Peter said, "Should we abandon our cause, my brothers?"

"No," they answered, "this is so you can go on serving the Lord."

So Peter consented to the wishes of his brethren and went away alone. "But none of you can come with me," he said. "I'll escape by myself in disguise."

Now, as Peter went out the gate he saw Jesus entering Rome. At this sight he exclaimed, "Lord, where are you going?"[7]

"I am going to Rome to be crucified," Jesus said.

"Lord, are you being crucified again?"

"Yes, Peter. I am being crucified once more."

So after Peter went into his mind and saw a vision of the Lord ascending to heaven, he turned back to Rome. As he went along he rejoiced and glorified Jesus, who said, "I am being crucified"—for Peter knew this was about to happen to him.

---

6. The figure of Marcellus was introduced earlier in the narrative: a wealthy benefactor of the Christians who was drawn into heresy by Simon Magus but returned to the truth via Peter's preaching. The real historical figure appears to be Marcus Granius Marcellus, a first-century proconsul in Asia Minor. Two episodes about him recorded by the historian Tacitus show up in the *Acts of Peter* in Christianized form. According to Tacitus's account, the emperor Tiberius accused Marcellus of two crimes: embezzling funds and beheading an imperial statue in a traitorous way. Similarly, in the *Acts of Peter* the emperor first suspects Marcellus of diverting government funds to the Christians; then, while Peter is visiting Marcellus's house, a demoniac who is being exorcised knocks over a statue of Caesar and shatters it. Marcellus worries that informants will betray him to the emperor for this treasonous development, but Peter tells him to sprinkle water on the statue to restore it. The overlap between these two perspectives on Marcellus is remarkable. Once again, we find memories of actual first-century figures being adapted to the needs of this second-century martyrdom account.

7. Peter asks this same question in John 13:36, to which Jesus replies, "Where I am going you cannot follow me now, but you will follow afterward"—a prediction that Peter's death will be similar to Christ's. John 21:18–19 goes on to describe Peter's death as involving the "stretching out" of his hands, probably a reference to crucifixion. The ancient church father Clement of Rome attested around AD 96 that Peter was martyred in Rome. The historical evidence that Peter was crucified in that city is quite strong.

In the Latin versions of this text, Peter's question, "Lord, where are you going?," is *Domine, quo vadis?* The Nobel Prize–winning Polish author Henryk Sienkiewicz set his 1895 epic novel *Quo Vadis* in this historical context. It was later adapted as the 1951 film starring Robert Taylor and Deborah Kerr. Today the Church of Domine Quo Vadis stands on the Appian Way south of Rome not far from the city gate at the traditional spot where the exchange between Jesus and Peter took place.

Back in the city he approached his brethren and told them what he had seen. The Christians mourned in their souls and wept, saying, "We urge you, Peter, consider the needs of us young people!"

"If something is the Lord's will, it will happen even if we don't want it to," Peter replied. "But the Lord is able to bolster your trust in him. He will lay a firm foundation on himself and expand on it to build you up—you whom he has planted, so that by his strength you might plant others! As for me, I won't object to remaining in my body for as long as it pleases the Lord. On the other hand, if he should wish to take me away, I celebrate that with great joy."

While Peter was still speaking and all the Christians were weeping, four soldiers arrested him and led him away to Agrippa. Now Agrippa was insane with fury, so he ordered Peter to be crucified on the charge of blasphemy against the state gods. But the whole crowd of Christians came together in one accord: the wealthy and the working class, the orphans and the widows, the powerful and the weak. They all wanted to see Peter and rescue him. Crying out with a single voice that couldn't be held back, the people said, "What has Peter done wrong, Agrippa? What harm has he brought to you? Tell us Romans!" And the bystanders were saying, "We're afraid if this man is executed, his Lord will destroy all of us!"

At last when Peter arrived at the spot he quieted the crowd and said, "You men who are soldiers of Christ, who put your hope in Christ—bring to mind the signs and wonders you saw performed through me. Recall God's compassion in the many healings he accomplished on your behalf. Just wait patiently for him to come and render to each person what is due according to his works. Therefore don't be bitter now toward Agrippa, for he is only a servant doing his father's work.[8] And since the Lord showed me what is coming together, it is now unfolding in every detail. So why should I delay and not go straight to the cross?"

[A gnostic-themed speech now interrupts the brisk narrative flow. Peter's crucifixion becomes the occasion for a tedious monologue in which he offers various mystical observations, including a symbolic interpretation of the cross to which he has been nailed upside down at his own request.[9] At one point Peter even says

8. The expression here is somewhat strange. It can best be explained as an allusion to John 8:41, where Jesus uses similar language to accuse the Jewish leaders, "You are doing the works your father did." He goes on to elaborate, "You are of your father the devil, and your will is to do your father's desires. He was a murderer from the beginning, and does not stand in the truth, because there is no truth in him" (8:44). Jesus's identification of his persecutors as tools of the Devil is now applied to Agrippa's behavior as well. This fits with Peter's role of reenacting the Lord's crucifixion in his own person.

9. Peter's request to be crucified upside down is the most striking aspect of his speech in this section. "I implore you executioners to crucify me with my head down and in no other way," he says, "and I will explain the reason for this to my hearers." Then, "after they hanged

the real value of Jesus's crucifixion is not the physical event itself but the invisible secrets it conveys—a common gnostic doctrine but not the original preaching of the ancient church. After a closing benediction and "amen," the story of the confrontation with Agrippa resumes.]

At the very moment when the crowd of bystanders shouted "Amen!" in a loud chorus, Peter relinquished his spirit to the Lord. Now, when Marcellus saw the blessed Peter had breathed his last, he didn't ask anyone for permission, because he knew it wouldn't be granted, but just took Peter down from the cross with his own hands. He washed the body with milk and wine and then ground up seven pounds of aromatic resin and fifty pounds of myrrh, aloe, and other herbs to anoint the corpse. Finally, Marcellus filled a very expensive stone coffin with the finest Greek honey and buried Peter in his own personal tomb.[10]

But Peter appeared to Marcellus by night and said, "Marcellus, haven't you heard the saying of the Lord, 'Let the dead be buried by their own dead' [Matt. 8:22; Luke 9:60]?"

When Marcellus answered yes, Peter responded to him, "Everything you did for my dead body is now lost. For though you are alive, you were acting like a dead man as you cared for that dead body."[11]

---

him up in the manner he thought proper," Peter proceeds to offer cryptic remarks about the birth of the primal man and the inversion of the universe. Although his death as a martyr in Rome is attested even earlier than the *Acts of Peter* (see footnote 7 above), this is the first historical reference to the crucified apostle's head being turned downward. The stated reason for assuming this unnatural position is to convey secret wisdom about how the proper order of the cosmos came to be inverted. The more pious reason for Peter's upside-down crucifixion—that he did not consider himself worthy to be crucified like his Lord—does not appear until AD 370 in a later version of the *Acts*. Both of these explanations are fabricated, since criminals being tortured and humiliated in the Roman Empire did not have the option to make special requests about their position. However, considering that the ancients did crucify people in all sorts of grotesque ways, it is no stretch to imagine that the early Christians may have preserved an actual memory of Peter's upside-down impalement—just not for the pious reason so often attributed to him.

10. The author intends to convey that the burial preparations for Peter were costly and lavish. Milk, wine, resin (i.e., the sap of the mastic tree), myrrh, aloe, spices, and honey are all attested as having healing or preservative properties in the Greco-Roman world. The use of honey in burials was a common practice for wealthy people of various ancient civilizations. Among the more famous recipients of this preserving treatment was said to be Alexander the Great (Statius, *Silvae* 3.2.118).

11. Peter is saying he is alive in Christ and Marcellus should have recognized it. For Marcellus to go to such great lengths to care for a mere corpse indicates his lack of faith in the resurrection. The hopeful attitude of the early Christians toward death is captured by an inscription from the grave of a godly woman: "I, Petronia, wife of a deacon, of modest countenance, here lay down my bones and place them in their resting place. Cease from weeping, my husband and sweet children, and believe that it is not right to mourn one that lives in God" (Henry Bettenson and Chris Maunder, *Documents of the Christian Church*, 3rd ed. [Oxford: Oxford University Press, 1999], 94).

So when Marcellus woke up he told the brethren about the appearance of Peter. And he remained with those whom Peter had strengthened in the faith of Christ, growing ever stronger until Paul finally arrived in Rome.[12]

But later when Nero[13] discovered Peter had departed this life, he blamed the mayor Agrippa for having him executed without his knowledge. For Nero was wanting to punish Peter more severely with a much stricter penalty, since Peter had converted some of Nero's servants and caused them to rebel against their master. So Nero was furious, and for a long time he wouldn't even speak to Agrippa. Meanwhile he was seeking how he might destroy all those Christians whom Peter had discipled.

But one night, Nero saw a vision of a figure whipping him and crying, "Nero, you are not allowed to persecute or destroy the servants of Christ right now. So keep your hands off them!" Terrified by such a fearful vision, Nero stayed away from the disciples ever since the time Peter departed from this world.

And so the brethren were united with one mind, rejoicing and exulting in the Lord, and glorifying God and our Savior the Lord Jesus Christ with the Holy Spirit, to whom be glory forever and ever. Amen.

The second text in this chapter is much like the first, coming as it does from the same genre of early Christian adventure stories about apostolic heroes—except this time Paul is the protagonist instead of Peter. The *Acts of Paul* is a collection of traditional stories that circulated in the second century and were edited into a single narrative prior to AD 200. Interestingly, a large portion of the plot centers not on Paul but on his most ardent female admirer, Thecla, a young bride-to-be whose exposure to the apostle's preaching just before her

12. Since Marcellus had been swayed earlier in the narrative by the heresy of Simon Magus, the author wants us to know Marcellus has now securely returned to the true Christian faith.

13. It is widely attested in ancient church tradition that Nero was the reigning emperor at the time of the apostle's death. This would give us a date for his martyrdom in the mid- to late 60s AD. Though not without its scholarly critics, this is one of the more secure facts with respect to the life of the historical Peter. He was most likely killed by crucifixion, possibly also while being burned alive, during Nero's persecution of the local Christian community after the Great Fire of Rome in AD 64. Instead of being buried in an expensive coffin, Peter was probably interred in a poor man's grave on the Vatican Hill next to Nero's circus. A hundred years later a memorial structure was erected over the grave, the remains of which have been discovered directly beneath the altar of today's St. Peter's Basilica. The Roman Catholic Church claims to have located Peter's bones in twentieth-century excavations, though controversy surrounds the events that led to their recovery. Whatever the status of the bones, the location itself has been continuously venerated as the burial place of Peter since at least the late second century, and probably since the very beginning. The area considered to be the first-century Tomb of St. Peter may be visited by special permission from the Vatican Excavations Office (search for this term on the internet to find the official webpage, or email scavi@fsp.va).

wedding prompts her to abandon a life of marital bliss so she can follow her newfound hero on his missionary journeys. As Thecla travels with Paul she is subjected to numerous dangers, not only from her irate fiancé but also from disapproving authorities who throw her to wild beasts in the arena. Divine miracles preserve the beautiful and pious Thecla, and she eventually goes on to become a teacher at Paul's request. Thecla's example of female ministry caused the church father Tertullian to reject the *Acts of Paul* as spurious. The work is, he says, the product of a well-meaning pastor in Asia who intended to honor Paul but lost his church position for compiling such a falsified document.

Though the martyrdom narrative within the *Acts of Paul* is less adventurous than the Thecla story line, it too bears the marks of being a legendary text. Even so, certain elements hint at historical connections to the first century. The prominence of Emperor Nero helps date the martyrdom to the 60s AD, and Paul's execution by beheading is attested here for the first time. We also pick up a suggestion of where Paul might have lived during his stay in Rome. Just as with the historical Paul, so in this text we see how his bold witness inspired many conversions. Modern readers can appreciate the *Acts of Paul* not only as a record of historical details but also as a window into popular Christian spirituality in the ancient church.

The Martyrdom of the Holy Apostle Paul (*Acts of Paul* 1–7)

The Arrival of Paul in Rome

Luke had come from Gaul, and Titus from Dalmatia, and they were waiting for Paul in Rome. When Paul saw them he rejoiced. So he rented a grain warehouse outside the city and taught the word of truth there along with the brethren.[14] Soon this became well known, and "many souls were added to the Lord" [Acts 2:41]. In fact, the news spread throughout Rome, so that many were coming to Paul and

14. The book of Acts records that Paul lived and ministered in Rome for two years. Though he was in state custody awaiting trial, he was allowed to live in private lodging at his own expense and engage in preaching and ministry (Acts 28:16, 30–31). The exact location of Paul's house is not known for sure, yet a very old tradition claims the present-day church of San Paolo alla Regola stands on the site. This spot was outside the city walls that existed in the first century and was a focal point of the Christian population. It was also close to Rome's Jewish community, giving Paul ample opportunity to debate with Jewish leaders (Acts 28:17). Because the neighborhood was near the Tiber River, many leather tanners worked there, which would have allowed Paul to earn income as a tentmaker to pay for his rented space, as was his normal practice (Acts 18:3; 20:34; but his income was supplemented by a gift, Phil. 4:18). Excavations have also uncovered grain warehouses nearby, since this was a dock area where ships would unload cargoes brought upriver from Rome's seaport. Though we cannot be absolutely certain, the evidence suggests San Paolo alla Regola may stand in the general vicinity of Paul's dwelling.

believing the gospel, including a large number from the emperor's household, which gave everyone great joy.[15]

Paul Resurrects Nero's Cupbearer

Now, there was a certain fellow named Patroclus who was Caesar's cupbearer. He came one evening to the warehouse, but because of the crowd he couldn't get close to Paul, so he took a seat in a high window to hear Paul teach the word of God. And since the wicked Devil was jealous of the Christians' love, he caused Patroclus to fall from the window and die (and this news was quickly brought to Nero).[16] Paul, however, perceived through the Spirit what had happened. "Brothers," he said, "the Evil One has come up with a way to test your faith. Go outside, and you will find a boy who has fallen from a height and is about to die. Pick him up, and bring him here to me."

So they went out and carried the lad inside. And when the onlookers saw him they were very distressed. But Paul said to them, "Now, brothers, let your faith be revealed! Come, all of you—let us cry out to our Lord Jesus Christ, asking that this boy might live so we can continue without further disturbance." Then, while they were all groaning to God, the boy took breath again. So after they set him on a horse they sent him home alive, along with all the others from Caesar's household.

When Nero heard of Patroclus's death he was deeply grieved. And when he came home from the bathhouse he ordered someone else to be appointed as his cupbearer.[17] But his young servants told him the news, "Caesar, Patroclus is alive and standing by the dinner table!"

15. Paul wrote the Letter to the Philippians during his stay in Rome. In 4:22 he conveys warm greetings from the Roman Christians with the words "All the saints greet you, especially those of Caesar's household." The term "Caesar's household" included the many workers and slaves who labored in the extensive palace complex atop the Palatine Hill, the ruins of which are still visible today looming over the Roman Forum. Apparently a number of these workers converted to Christ under Paul's ministry. The Letter to the Philippians also confirms that Paul was guarded by soldiers from Rome's Praetorian Guard, among whom his teaching had become widely known (1:13), and that Paul considered his life to be endangered (1:20–26). These well-attested facts suggest that some of the traditions recorded in the *Acts of Paul* are indeed historical.

16. This story is clearly an adaptation of the account in Acts 20:7–12, when the youth Eutychus (whose name means "Lucky") fell from a window in Troas while Paul was preaching at night. On that occasion Paul raised the lad from the dead just as he does here (for Patroclus is breathing his last and is as good as dead when he is brought inside). Though the name and location have changed, this story is used for the same purpose as in the biblical Acts, to reveal the divine empowerment behind Paul's ministry. However, in the present text the story serves an additional purpose: it is the means by which Paul comes to the emperor's attention, initiating the series of events that ultimately leads to his execution.

17. Nero did in fact construct a prominent bathhouse in Rome around the time Paul was executed. The location of Nero's baths near the Pantheon is only a ten-minute walk from the traditional site of Paul's lodging (the church of San Paolo alla Regola).

So Nero grew wary when he heard Patroclus was alive, and he refused to enter the dining room. But then when he did enter, he saw Patroclus, and recoiling from him, Nero cried, "Patroclus! Are you alive?"

"I am alive, Caesar."

"Who is the one that made you alive?"

Then the youth, uplifted by the certainty that comes from faith, replied, "It was Christ Jesus, the king of the ages."

"Is he going to be the king forever and destroy all other kingdoms?" the emperor asked in dismay.

"Yes indeed! He overthrows every kingdom under heaven, and he alone will exist forever, and no kingdom shall escape him."

At this Nero slapped Patroclus across the face. "Patroclus," he barked, "are you also fighting as a soldier of that king?"

"Yes, my lord Caesar—for he has raised me from the dead."

Then several of Nero's prominent advisers—Barsabas Justus the flat-footed, Orion the Cappadocian, and Festus of Galatia—said, "And we too fight for him, the king of the ages!"[18]

So after Nero inflicted terrible tortures on these men whom he dearly loved, he threw them in prison. Then he commanded the soldiers of the "great king" be sought out. He even issued an edict that everyone found to be a Christian or a "soldier of Christ" should be executed.[19]

Paul before Nero

Among the people rounded up, Paul was brought to Nero in chains. And since all the prisoners paid attention to him, Nero could see Paul was the commander in chief.

18. A "Barsabbas also called Justus" is mentioned in Acts 1:23 as a candidate to take Judas Iscariot's place among the Twelve, but this event hardly seems likely to have prompted the editor of the *Acts of Paul* to turn the character into one of the most highly placed officials in Nero's regime. Instead, this reference may correlate to a story recorded by the second-century church father Papias in which Barsabbas Justus drank poison yet by God's grace did not die. Prominent Romans who ran afoul of the emperor were sometimes allowed to commit suicide rather than be executed, and in such cases poison was an option (e.g., the philosopher Seneca was given this opportunity by Nero). Perhaps Papias's story of divine protection from poison reminded ancient hearers of the way emperors forced suicide on their opponents, which would explain the character's insertion into the story when Nero tries to kill his friends. In the end, though, the matter must remain conjectural.

Festus of Galatia may also bear a connection to the first century. In Acts 25 we discover a high-ranking Roman official named Porcius Festus supervising Paul's court case. However, this historical Festus governed the province of Judea, not Rome. The stories that make up the *Acts of Paul* often allude to names or events from the biblical book of Acts yet differ substantially on the details.

19. Nero's fear of Christ's "soldiers" is prompted by the perceived threat to his imperial rule. Although the early Christians harbored no intentions of military rebellion, they were sometimes characterized as soldiers or fighters for Christ (1 Tim. 1:18; 2 Tim. 2:3). And as we saw in the introduction, the Christian faith actually did pose a threat to the Roman way of life.

"Man of the great king, now my prisoner," Nero said, "what made you think you could sneak into the Roman Empire and enlist soldiers in my territory?"

Paul, filled with the Holy Spirit, said in the presence of them all, "Caesar, we seek soldiers not just in your territory but in the whole world! For this is our commandment, that no one should be excluded who wishes to enlist in the service of my king. If this seems pleasing to you, join his ranks as well—for all the wealth and glittering trappings of your present life will not avail you. Only by surrendering to him and begging for his mercy will you be saved. For he is about to destroy the world by fire in a single day."

But when Caesar heard these things he ordered all the prisoners burned by fire, though Paul was to be decapitated according to Roman law.[20] Even so, Paul did not keep silent about the Word but shared the gospel with the prefect Longus[21] and the centurion Cestus. Meanwhile, Nero went throughout Rome and, prompted by the Evil One, executed many Christians without a trial. At last the Roman people gathered in front of the palace[22] and cried, "Enough, Caesar! These are our own people! You are gutting the strength of the Romans!"[23] So Nero was persuaded by this plea and held back. He ordered that no one should harm any Christian until he had thoroughly investigated the matter.

20. The depiction of Nero ordering Christians burned at the stake in the time of Paul harmonizes with what the ancient historian Tacitus recorded:

> To dispel the gossip Nero therefore found culprits on whom he inflicted the most exotic punishments. These were people hated for their shameful offences whom the common people called Christians. . . . And so, at first, those who confessed were apprehended, and subsequently, on the disclosures they made, a huge number were found guilty—more because of their hatred of mankind than because they were arsonists. As they died they were further subjected to insult. Covered with hides of wild beasts, they perished by being torn to pieces by dogs; or they would be fastened to crosses and, when daylight had gone, burned to provide lighting at night. (*Annals* 15.44, in Yardley, 359–60)

Although Tacitus attributes Nero's actions to his need for a scapegoat after the disastrous Great Fire of AD 64, it is nonetheless clear the *Acts of Paul* has recorded an ancient church memory of a mass burning of Christians at Rome. The decadence and cruelty of this event is vividly portrayed in Henryk Siemiradzki's 1876 painting *Nero's Torches*.

21. Though the term "prefect" sometimes designated the city prefect, it could also refer to various midlevel jobs in the civil service. Since Longus is paired with a centurion (a commander of about a hundred soldiers), it seems the men were influential yet not extremely high ranking. In this narrative they may symbolize the respective powers of the government and the army.

22. The modern word "palace" comes from the name of the hill where Caesar Augustus and other emperors made their homes: the Palatine Hill, overlooking the Roman Forum and the Circus Maximus. After the citywide fire in AD 64 destroyed several aristocratic villas on the Palatine's flanks, Nero used the cleared space to construct his famously opulent palace called the "Domus Aurea," or "Golden House."

23. Pity for the Christians' horrible fate is likewise recorded in Tacitus's report: "As a result, guilty though these people were and deserving exemplary punishment, pity for them began to well up because it was felt that they were being exterminated not for the public good, but to gratify one man's cruelty" (*Annals* 15.44, in Yardley, 360).

Then Paul was brought before Nero in accordance with the decree, and the emperor stayed true to his word that Paul should be executed.[24]

"Caesar," Paul answered, "with my king, my lifetime isn't just a brief span. If you have me beheaded, this is what I'm going to do: I will rise and appear to you so you can see I'm not dead but alive in my Lord Jesus Christ, who is coming to judge the world."

Longus and Cestus Seek Salvation

Longus and Cestus said to Paul, "Where did you get this king whom you believe in without changing your mind, even to the point of death?"

And sharing the gospel with them, Paul said, "You men are currently in ignorance and error. Change your mind and be saved from the fire that is coming onto the whole world! For we serve in the army of a king who is from heaven, not from earth as you seem to think. He is the living God, the one who comes as a judge because of all the lawless deeds that happen in this world. Blessed is the one who will believe in the King and live forever when he comes with fire to cleanse the earth."

"We need you to help us!" the men begged Paul. "If you do, we'll set you free!"

"I'm no deserter from Christ but a faithful soldier of the living God," Paul replied. "And even if I had known I would be killed, Longus and Cestus, I still would have enlisted. So because I live in God and care for my own well-being, I go away to the Lord, that by him I might come into the glory of his Father."

Longus and Cestus said, "But how shall we find life after you have been beheaded?"

Suddenly while they were speaking, certain men named Parthenius and Pheretas arrived from Nero to determine if Paul had been beheaded yet, but they found him still alive. Paul hailed them and said, "Believe in the living God, who raises from the dead not only me but all who believe in him!"

"We're returning to Nero now," the men replied. "But when we see you die and rise again, then we'll believe in your God."

Longus and Cestus, however, were begging Paul all the more intensely about salvation. So Paul said to them, "Come straight here to my grave at dawn, and

24. Did Paul truly appear before Nero? In Acts 27:23–24 an angel tells Paul he must testify before the emperor, though there is no biblical record of the actual event. Paul also mentions a "first defense" (2 Tim. 4:16), probably a preliminary hearing before the imperial court during his second Roman imprisonment. Though Nero wasn't as active as other emperors in hearing court cases, he did preside over some. Appealing to Caesar was a standard legal prerogative for Roman citizens like Paul. Nero knew enough about the Christians to blame them for the Great Fire, so they were not beneath his notice. He probably would have wanted to meet the movement's leaders at some point to assess them firsthand. It is not impossible that Paul could have had an audience with the emperor.

you will find two men praying, Titus and Luke. They will give you the seal in the Lord."[25]

The Death of Paul

At this Paul turned to face the east. Lifting up his hands to heaven, he prayed for a long time. After he had communed prayerfully with the fathers in Hebrew, he offered his neck without another word. And as the executioner struck off his head, milk spurted onto the soldier's tunic.[26] When the soldiers and all the bystanders saw it, they marveled and glorified God, who had given Paul such honor. Then they departed to give an account of these events to Caesar.

So when Nero heard the news he was utterly astonished and didn't know what to say. And while many philosophers and the centurion were standing around with Caesar, Paul appeared to them around the ninth hour.[27] Facing them all, he said, "Caesar, behold me here—Paul, the soldier of God! I am not dead but alive in my God. But for you, O wretched man, there will be many troubles and great punishments, because only a few days ago you unjustly spilled the blood of the righteous!" After Paul said this, he departed. Then Nero was so terribly upset by what he had heard that he ordered the release of the Christian prisoners, including Patroclus and Barsabas Justus and his friends.

Just as Paul had directed, Longus and the centurion Cestus came at dawn and approached Paul's tomb in trepidation.[28] As they drew near they saw two men

25. Paul's statement "come straight here" indicates the scene has shifted from Nero's palace to the area of execution, which would have been outside the city walls near graves and tombs. The term "seal in the Lord" could be taken in several ways. To put a seal on something was to indicate its completion, so Paul may be saying Titus and Luke will finish what he has started. Or the term could indicate ownership, meaning Longus and Cestus would become slaves of Christ. The gift of the Holy Spirit at salvation is also depicted as a seal in 2 Corinthians 1:22 and Ephesians 1:13 and 4:30, so Paul could be promising the Spirit. And in a later Christian context, the seal referred to the baptismal ritual in which a believer was marked with the cross and baptized into Christ's service instead of demons (this usage appears earlier in the *Acts of Paul*). Therefore the apostle's wording is rich in salvific associations. At the most basic level, of course, he intends to say the two seekers will receive eternal life through testimony that continues beyond his death.

26. It is hard to know exactly what this milk signifies. In the context of the narrative it probably symbolizes the holy teaching Paul offers (1 Cor. 3:2; Heb. 5:12; 1 Pet. 2:2). Yet the strangeness of this event suggests it could have been an actual eyewitness remembrance. Perhaps a spurt of Paul's body fluid later received a pious interpretation and entered the oral tradition as "milk." Such spiritual adaptation of the events surrounding a martyr's death is quite common in the literature.

27. The "ninth hour" was around three in the afternoon. This is a momentous time in Scripture: it is when Peter and John evangelized a lame beggar (Acts 3:1), when Cornelius received an angelic vision (Acts 10:3, 30), and when Christ himself uttered his final words on the cross, resulting in resurrections from nearby tombs and great fear among the soldiers (Matt. 27:46–54).

28. This text locates Paul's tomb at Rome, but where exactly was it? Like the grave of Peter, some kind of memorial structure marked Paul's grave in the late second century. This "trophy,"

praying—and there was Paul in between them! At the sight of this incredible miracle they were overwhelmed. Yet when Titus and Luke noticed Longus and Cestus approaching, they were seized with human fear and turned to run away.

Longus and Cestus followed them. "Blessed men of God, we're not chasing you for death as you might think!" they said. "No, it's for life! We want you to give us what Paul promised—he whom we just saw standing between you praying!"

So when Titus and Luke heard this, they gave them the seal in the Lord with great joy. And they exalted the God and Father of our Lord Jesus Christ, to whom be glory forever and ever. Amen.

---

as it was called, stood on the road south of Rome leading to the seaport of Ostia. When Emperor Constantine came to power in the fourth century, he (or one of his sons who succeeded him) erected a small chapel over the trophy. Within a few decades, a much larger church was constructed by Emperor Theodosius and others to replace the first one. The Basilica of Saint Paul Outside the Walls stood undisturbed on this spot from the 380s until 1823, when a worker accidentally started a fire that burned the edifice to the ground. A magnificent new basilica was then put up and can be visited today. A large arch above the tomb survived the fire. It contains mosaics from the Theodosian structure that claim the church is "sanctified by the body of Paul, teacher of the world." The 1823 fire also brought to light two ancient marble slabs inscribed with the words "To Paul, apostle and martyr." Because this spot was continuously marked as Paul's tomb from the second century to the present, the chances are good it is the actual location of the apostle's grave. In 2002 the Roman Catholic Church began excavations under the altar. Archaeologists bored through cement and confirmed the presence of a large marble sarcophagus. Then in June 2009, Pope Benedict XVI announced that carbon-14 testing on bone fragments from the sarcophagus dates them to the first or second century AD. It is likely, then, that the apostle Paul's bones lie beneath the altar of the Basilica of Saint Paul Outside the Walls in Rome.

3

Ignatius of Antioch

Final Journey to Christ

In the previous two chapters we encountered some martyrological writings with a high degree of legendary content. Though the texts emerged from real-world events, we had to dig through several layers of editorial work to discern the historical reality underneath. The human emotions of the martyrs—their fears, doubts, and misgivings—were largely obscured by their veneer of unwavering faith.

Not so with Ignatius of Antioch. Here we meet a man whose raw soul is laid bare as he marches to his death in the Roman Colosseum. Ignatius was no fearless hero from a fiction novel. The personal letter he left behind reveals a man striving to hold on to courage as he faces the kind of death none of us can truly comprehend. In this text we find no dramatic pagan conversions, no graphic descriptions of torture, no bold accusations thrown in the face of a tyrant. From the perspective of Ignatius's letter, all the tension and terror still lie ahead on the road to martyrdom. What we have here is a man contemplating his imminent and agonizing end—a man who longs to be faithful in his Christian witness yet who wonders with gut-wrenching honesty whether he has what it takes to make good on his commitment. In this chapter we will be given access to a martyr's inner mind-set as the day of his death approaches.

Chronologically, we have pressed the fast-forward button since the time of Peter and Paul. That is to say, we have rolled ahead several decades into the period just after the New Testament was written. Ignatius served as bishop of the church at Antioch during the early 100s AD. This Syrian city was not only a leading metropolis of the ancient world but also a major center of the early Christian movement. It was in Antioch that the followers of Jesus were first called "Christians" (Acts 11:26), and the community there sponsored the apostle Paul's missionary journeys. Though we do not know much about Ignatius's life, we should at least recognize he was pastoring Paul's home church (Acts 13:1–3) about fifty years after the apostle's death.

All we know of Ignatius comes from the seven letters he wrote while being carried in chains from Antioch to Rome. Somehow he had run afoul of the Antiochian authorities for his Christian faith. A squad of cruel soldiers was escorting Ignatius from his hometown to the imperial capital along much the same route that Paul traveled on his third missionary journey. When Ignatius's guards reached the city of Smyrna they stopped for a while, allowing the local bishop Polycarp (still four decades away from his own dramatic martyrdom) to encourage Ignatius as he passed through town. Several neighboring churches of Asia sent representatives to visit him as well. In gratitude for all this brotherly care, Ignatius wrote six letters of spiritual exhortation to his friend Polycarp and the churches of Ephesus, Magnesia, Tralles, Philadelphia, and Smyrna. In addition, Ignatius sent a letter ahead to his final destination. The condemned bishop had some important things he wanted the believers at Rome to know. They shouldn't try to prevent his death, he said. Ignatius longed to die for Jesus Christ—yet he wanted the Roman Christians to pray he wouldn't waver.

In the end, though, we don't know exactly what happened to Ignatius. After he wrote his seven letters he slipped off the stage of history. Later testimony suggests he met his end precisely where he believed he would—in Rome, and probably in front of a ravenous crowd in the city's amphitheater. If you ever get a chance to visit the Colosseum, be sure to locate the large bronze cross near the main entrance that commemorates the ancient martyrs. And while you're there, say a grateful prayer for the Christian witness of a man like Ignatius of Antioch.

Ignatius, *Letter to the Romans*

Salutation

FROM: Ignatius, also known as the "God-bearer."
TO: the church that has received mercy through the majesty of the Supreme Father and his only Son Jesus Christ—the church that, in accordance with the faithfulness

and love demonstrated by Jesus Christ our God, is beloved and enlightened by the will of the Creator, who chose to make everything that exists.

You, the church that presides over the whole region around Rome, are worthy of God, and of honor, blessing, praise, success, and sanctification. You stand out in your love as you bear the name of Christ and the Father. Therefore I now greet you in that name, the name of Jesus Christ, the Son of the Father. To everyone who adheres in body and soul to all his commandments, unwavering because you've been filled with God's grace, washed clean of every foreign stain—to you I offer an entirely holy and heartfelt greeting in Jesus Christ our God.

Ignatius's Request of the Roman Christians

My prayers to God have been answered, and in fact I've received even more than I asked for: I'm coming to Rome to see your actual holy faces! For I hope to greet you while in chains for Jesus Christ, if it be his will that I should be considered worthy of attaining that goal. Now, everything has started out just fine, and I can only hope to receive the grace of reaching my final end without any interference. Yet I admit, I'm worried your love might do me harm. I know it's a simple matter for you to do what you so badly want to do. But unless you purposely take a step back for my sake, it's going to be hard for me to meet my God.[1]

Now, I want you to think not like people pleasers but like God pleasers (which of course you already are). Never again will I have an opportunity like this to meet God. Nor could you ever be credited with a nobler deed—provided you just keep quiet! If you can somehow refrain from interfering with me, I'll become an eloquent and powerful testimony to God. However, if you try to show "love" for my outward body, you'll reduce me to a meaningless noise. So please grant me nothing but the chance to be poured out to God while I still have an altar available. In your brotherly love, just serve as my background chorus. Sing praise to the Father through Jesus Christ that he has deemed me, the bishop of Syria, worthy to be found in the west after being summoned from the east. What a joy it is to be like the sun slipping beneath the horizon of this world as I head toward God, knowing I will soon rise up to meet him!

Now you in Rome have never needed to be jealous of anyone. In fact, you

---

1. Ignatius seems to be aware that certain persons in the Roman church would be in a position to rescue him from death. Probably this would take the form of a bribe, or perhaps the exercise of influence from a highly placed Christian (of which there were a few in Rome, though most believers were from the lower classes). One of Ignatius's contemporaries in Rome wrote a letter that mentions how Christians often sold themselves into slavery to raise money for ransoms or to buy food for the hungry. Ignatius tells the Roman Christians not to try anything like this. He wants his death to be a powerful voice of testimony to God's glory.

have been the teacher of others.[2] Let the instructions you've issued to your follow-ers be applied in my situation as well. I ask you to pray for only one thing: that I might have inward as well as outward strength, so I won't just give lip service to martyrdom but truly desire it. I don't want to merely be called a Christian—I want to actually *be* one when everything is on the line! If I'm proven a Christian when it counts, then and only then can I be called by that name and be remembered as faithful even when I'm no longer visible in this world. The visible things of earth aren't so great! Consider Jesus Christ our God: he's all the more "visible" now that he has gone back to the Father. A divine work isn't accomplished through human techniques of persuasion. Rather, Christianity is at its very best when it's hated by the world.[3]

I'm writing to all the churches about these things. I'm telling everyone I freely intend to die for the name of God—that is, if you'll let me. I implore you: don't show me a "kindness" that is out of place! Let me instead become food for the wild animals, which are my means of attaining God. I am like a grain of God's wheat, ready to be ground by the teeth of those beasts that I might be milled into pure bread. Or to put it another way, let those beasts be coaxed near so they can become my tomb and leave no trace of my body behind. I don't want to be a burden to anyone after I've died.[4] Only when the world can no longer see my

2. Although Ignatius's language here demonstrates Rome's doctrinal authority and prestige in the early second century, the Roman church was by no means the ruler over all other Christians. Even if the city did have a single bishop at that time (which is questionable), he would not be functioning like a "pope" with recognized teaching jurisdiction over external churches. Of course, as the capital of the empire, Rome could not help but be viewed with respect by the early Christians. The prestige of the Roman church was enhanced by the fact that Peter and Paul were martyred there and buried outside the city walls. As we saw in the previous chapter, Peter's grave was in a pagan cemetery on the Vatican Hill next to the circus where he was killed, while Paul was buried near the place of his beheading on the road toward Rome's port of Ostia. Soon, little shrines were built at these locations so they wouldn't be forgotten. Then in the fourth century, grand churches were erected over these sites (known today as St. Peter's Basilica and Basilica of St. Paul Outside the Walls). Certainly this helped solidify the later Roman bishops' claims to have universal teaching authority. However, such claims weren't being made in the time of Ignatius. At that juncture the Roman church only wanted to hold on to the true apostolic faith and offer guidance to other Christian communities as needed. Ignatius seems to have been aware of, and favorable to, this role.

3. Ignatius's argument here is a little hard to follow. He is saying the most persuasive testimony comes from people who give their lives for what they believe. It might seem that a great speech of excellent rhetoric would convince the onlookers of one's sincere faith, but when it comes to divine things, the most effective witness is a ready willingness to go on to the next world. The best evidence for Christianity is provided from beyond the grave. Some of these ideas about the power of God working through weakness rather than human persuasion can be found in 1 Corinthians 1:18–2:5.

4. This statement clearly indicates Ignatius is aware the believers would try to obtain his body and give it a proper burial. As noted in the introduction, such respect for a fellow Christian's mortal remains eventually developed into the cult of the martyrs in the ancient church.

body will I be a true disciple of Jesus Christ. So petition the Lord on my behalf, asking that by the instrument of these wild animals, I might be found a worthy sacrifice for God.

I'm not, of course, issuing commands to you like Peter or Paul. They were apostles; I'm just a condemned criminal. They were free, while I'm in bondage like a slave even as we speak. Yet if I'm allowed to suffer, then I'll become the freed slave of Jesus Christ—which means I will rise up and find myself free in him! For now, though, I'm just a prisoner learning to give up all my desires.

Facing the Beasts

From Syria all the way to Rome I'm fighting wild beasts already. On land and sea, by day and night, I'm chained to ten leopards. I am referring, of course, to the squad of ten soldiers escorting me. Whenever I'm nice to them, they only treat me worse. Yet through their abuse I'm learning to become more and more of a disciple—although by no means has this resulted in my final vindication. I still need the benefit of those wild animals awaiting me in the arena. I pray they will prove prompt with me.[5] In fact, I intend to coax them so they'll devour me quickly instead of being too timid to attack as they sometimes are. And if I'm ready and willing but they aren't, I'll force them to take me! Grant me a little forbearance here—I know what is best for me. Now at last I'm beginning to be a true disciple.

Repudiation of This World and Desire for Christ

May nothing at all, whether of this world or the invisible world above, fight against me and prevent me from reaching Jesus Christ. Bring on the fire . . . the cross . . . the hordes of wild beasts! Let the cuttings and dissections begin! The wrenching of my bones, the dicing of my limbs, the grinding of my entire body, the hideous tortures of the Devil—let all this befall me; only let me attain Jesus Christ! Nothing from one end of the earth to the other matters to me anymore. The kingdoms of this age are meaningless. I would rather die for Jesus Christ than rule the entire world. He alone is the one I seek, the one who died for us. He is my desire, the one who rose again for our sake!

---

5. Modern readers will not blame Ignatius if we sense, behind his bravado, some anxiety about his suffering to come. The companions of Perpetua similarly talked with one another about what facing the beasts might be like (see chap. 8). Surely the ancient martyrs must have had many moments of trepidation like this before the day of the games. The next time you are at the zoo, take a good look at the big cats. They are fierce and deadly creatures; we humans rightly fear them. Imagine how terrifying it must have been to stand alone on the sandy arena floor as a starved lion bounded toward you. Ignatius knew full well what awaited him in the amphitheater. But he also knew what lay on the other side.

Now my birth pangs are upon me. My brothers, consent to what I'm asking. Don't hinder me from attaining true life; don't wish for my death. Why would you hand over to the world someone who longs to be with God? Why would you dangle earthly things in front of me? Let me instead attain the pure light of heaven. Once I'm there, I'll become a complete person. So give in to me! Allow me this chance to imitate the sufferings of my God. If some of you have Christ within yourselves, strive to comprehend my deep longings here, and sympathize with me! You of all people should understand what compels me.

The "ruler of this age" seeks to kidnap me and shatter my resolve to follow God. Therefore none of you in Rome should help him. Instead you should be on my side—which is God's side! You can't claim to be a follower of Jesus Christ while setting your heart on the things of the world. Don't let the Devil's trickery be in your midst!

But what if, when I arrive in Rome, I appeal to you for rescue? Even so, don't heed my pleas! Instead believe what I am writing to you now. Though I am physically alive as I write, in truth I long to die. My earthly passions have been crucified. The flame of desire for physical things is no longer present in me. Instead I am filled with living water that bubbles up from within and declares from deep in my soul, "This way to the Father!" I take no enjoyment in foods that can spoil or the fleeting pleasures of this life. The food I desire is God's bread, that is, the flesh of Christ who is descended from David, and the drink I desire is his blood, which is his eternal love.[6] I want to stop living my life according to the pattern of human beings. And I can achieve this if you'll just align your desires with mine! So desire this along with me, that you may be desirable to God.

I'm writing this short letter to tell you what I want. Don't doubt I mean what I say! But if you do, Jesus Christ will make it clear to you I am speaking in all honesty, for he is the trustworthy mouthpiece through whom the Father has spoken his truth to us. Pray for me, that I might reach my goal. I'm writing to you not with a fleshly way of thinking but according to God's divine purposes. If I suffer in the arena, it will mean you desired the right thing. But if you reject my wishes, it will only prove you hate me.

---

6. The language in this section reflects certain themes from the early Christian celebration of the Eucharist—that is, Communion, or the Lord's Supper. Ignatius longs for the kind of intimate union with Christ that the elements of the Lord's Supper foster in the believer. Chapter 6 of John's Gospel provides the background to Ignatius's thought. There Jesus declares, "Truly, truly, I say to you, unless you eat the flesh of the Son of Man and drink his blood, you have no life in you. Whoever feeds on my flesh and drinks my blood has eternal life, and I will raise him up on the last day. For my flesh is true food, and my blood is true drink. Whoever feeds on my flesh and drinks my blood abides in me, and I in him" (John 6:53–56).

Final Words of Greeting

Remember the church of Syria in your prayers. Now that I'm gone, they must rely on God alone as their shepherd. Jesus Christ is the only one who will care for them now—and so will you in your tender love. As for me, I'm embarrassed even to be named among them. I'm not worthy of those Christians. I'm the least of them, like a miscarried baby.[7] Yet if I can just reach God, then by his mercy I'll be a fully formed man.

I greet you from the bottom of my heart. All the churches that welcomed me along my route—not as a passing stranger, but in the name of Jesus Christ—send their love as well. And some churches that weren't even along my road (that is to say, my *physical* road) went before me from city to city.

I'm writing this letter from Smyrna and sending it via the Ephesians. They deserve God's richest blessings! Among the many people who are with me is Krokos, a man especially dear to me. And I believe you're already well acquainted with those who have preceded me from Syria to Rome for the sake of God's glory. Tell them I'm close to arriving. All of them deserve God's honor and yours, so it is entirely appropriate for you to refresh them in every way possible.

This letter was written on August 24. May you stand strong to the end through the endurance provided by Jesus Christ.

---

7. Ignatius is alluding to 1 Corinthians 15:8–9, where Paul remarks, "Last of all, as to one untimely born, [Christ] appeared also to me. For I am the least of the apostles, unworthy to be called an apostle." The Greek word translated "one untimely born" is the same term Ignatius uses in this passage. It refers to an ancient mother's all-too-common experience of delivering her baby before full term without any medical means to save it—in other words, a miscarriage or spontaneous abortion. In context, Paul used the term to suggest he wasn't born at the right time and place to know the earthly Jesus like the other apostles. But Ignatius follows the term's more literal meaning and compares himself to a premature infant that isn't developed enough to live on its own. According to this metaphor, Ignatius suggests that only by dying for Christ can he attain true life and reach mature adulthood.

4

Polycarp of Smyrna

A Gospel Passion

The story of Polycarp brings us to a yet another kind of text, one that again differs from those we have examined so far. As with Ignatius, so we have here a Christian letter of encouragement—but this one tells the whole story, leaving us with little doubt about how the martyrdom concluded. Furthermore, instead of having to tease out a few factual nuggets from a broad swath of fiction, the *Martyrdom of Polycarp* exhibits a high degree of historical authenticity. This is not to say the narrator has given us only the bare facts; he clearly had a theological agenda he wanted to convey, and he shaped the narrative accordingly.[1] Nevertheless he has done so around an essentially trustworthy story, making Polycarp the earliest Christian whose martyrdom we can know in detail. Yet historical accuracy is not the only reason to include this story in

---

1. Traditionally this document has been understood as an extremely reliable martyrological account (Timothy Barnes, *Early Christian Hagiography and Roman History* [Tübingen: Mohr Siebeck, 2010], 343–59). Recently this view has come under fire by a scholar who considers the text a composition from up to a hundred years later (Candida Moss, "On the Dating of Polycarp: Rethinking the Place of the Martyrdom of Polycarp in the History of Christianity," *Early Christianity* 1, no. 4 [2010]: 539–74). An excellent compromise view considers the *Martyrdom* as being written within several years or a few decades of Polycarp's death yet rooted in multiple eyewitness recollections that affected how the final story was interpreted as it was told (Paul Hartog, *Polycarp's* Epistle to the Philippians *and the* Martyrdom of Polycarp*: Introduction, Text, and Commentary* [Oxford: Oxford University Press, 2013], 186, 190).

the present book. The noble death of the blessed Polycarp is an enduring tale from the annals of church history, a text that has inspired countless generations of Christians to greater faithfulness. Polycarp of Smyrna is a church father worth getting to know.

Who was he? Some of Polycarp's biographical details are contested by scholars, but a basic outline emerges from the sources. He became the bishop of Smyrna sometime during the second century AD, which means he was entrusted with spiritual oversight of the city's Christians. Though he served alongside other elders there, by the end of his life he was the community's acknowledged leader—an aged pastor whose godliness had won him great respect throughout the churches of Asia.

Ancient Smyrna (known today as Izmir in Turkey) was a very old settlement established where a river met a sheltered bay on the Aegean Sea. Situated at such a prime location, the city thrived for several centuries. Indeed, the greatest Greek poet of all—Homer—was said to have lived there. Then, after it underwent a period of decline, Greek colonists refounded the city and launched a second era of prosperity. By Polycarp's time, Smyrna was a bustling Roman metropolis experiencing its heyday. Its monuments included many temples and bathhouses, a busy harbor, schools of rhetoric and medicine, an elegant market square, and the stadium where Polycarp was executed. A large Jewish population also flourished in beautiful seaside Smyrna. The first Smyrnaean Christians were probably Jews evangelized by missionaries from Ephesus, which lay about forty-five miles away.

Polycarp died in approximately AD 156 at the age of eighty-six. This means he was born only four decades after the time of Jesus, well within a time frame that would have allowed him to interact with the eyewitnesses of the Lord. In fact, early church tradition teaches that Polycarp was a disciple of the apostle John. Though this connection is not entirely certain, the fact remains that Polycarp spent his youth during the formational period of the first-century church. He is said by one ancient writer to have been "instructed by the apostles" and to have "conversed with many who had seen Christ." Throughout his long life he always "taught the things which he had learned from the apostles, and which the church has handed down, and which alone are true."[2] In this way Polycarp served as a link between the earliest generation of the apostles and the prominent church fathers who came later.

2. Irenaeus, *Against Heresies* 3.3.4, in *The Apostolic Fathers with Justin Martyr and Irenaeus*, ed. Alexander Roberts, James Donaldson, and A. Cleveland Coxe, *Ante-Nicene Fathers* (1885; repr., Peabody, MA: Hendrickson, 1994), 1:416. Whenever possible, quotations from the church fathers in this book are taken from the widely available *Ante-Nicene Fathers* or *Nicene and*

The legal basis for Polycarp's execution in the stadium at Smyrna is not entirely clear. The Roman officials appear reluctant to carry out the death penalty against such a devout old man. Yet in the end, the prejudice of the masses prevailed, and the governing authorities went along with popular sentiment. As the local believers watched the death of their spiritual leader in the arena, they no doubt recalled the words of Jesus to the Smyrnaean church in Revelation 2:10: "Do not fear what you are about to suffer. Behold, the devil is about to throw some of you into prison, that you may be tested, and for ten days you will have tribulation. Be faithful unto death, and I will give you the crown of life." As you are about to see, Bishop Polycarp nobly earned the eternal crown promised by the Lord.

The Martyrdom of Polycarp

Salutation and Introduction

God's church at Smyrna writes to his church at Philomelium, and to all the communities of the holy, catholic[3] church residing everywhere. May the mercy, peace, and love of God the Father and our Lord Jesus Christ abound to you.

Brothers, we're writing to give you an account of what happened to the martyrs, and especially to the blessed Polycarp, whose martyrdom brought an end to the persecution like a seal stamped on a letter.[4] Almost all the events that led up to Polycarp's death took place so the Lord could show us a martyrdom that conforms to the gospel.[5] For example, Polycarp waited until he was betrayed, just like the

---

Post-Nicene Fathers series. That way the reader can examine the citation in context at http://www.ccel.org/fathers.

3. The word "catholic" comes from the Greek expression *kath holou*, which means "pertaining to the whole"—that is, "universal." It is not, in this context, a reference to the Roman Catholic Church with the pope at its head. The early church called itself "catholic" to emphasize its communal unity across the whole known world. This term sought to distinguish those who embraced the original apostolic message of faith in Christ's death and resurrection from those who called themselves "Christians" but followed heretical doctrines. The term began to receive widespread use after the time of Polycarp.

4. Polycarp's death served to end the persecution against the Smyrnaean Christians by satisfying the bloodthirsty appetites of the crowd.

5. The parallelism between Polycarp and Christ is a major theme of this document as it has come down to us today. Here the narrator seems to view Polycarp's exile to the countryside as a Christlike move that shows his concern for his flock. Just as Jesus didn't barge into Jerusalem at the outset of his ministry to provoke the authorities, but slipped away in the crowds or deflected his accusers with a perplexing reply, so Polycarp refuses to be obstinate and stir up trouble in Smyrna. Instead he escapes out of town in deference to the wishes of his fellow believers. It is only when he is pursued and betrayed, like Christ in Gethsemane, that he is finally brought to trial. Polycarp's behavior stands in stark contrast to that of Quintus, who turned himself in to

Lord. We should become imitators of his example, "looking not only to our own interests, but also the interests of our neighbors" [Phil. 2:4]. For this is the mark of true and faithful love: to desire to save not only yourself but also all the brethren.

Therefore we count as blessed and noble every martyrdom that happened according to God's will (for we who are truly reverent must consider God as sovereign over all that occurs). Who could fail to marvel at the martyrs' nobility and steadfast endurance and total devotion to their Lord? Even when their flesh was so shredded by whips that you could see their veins and arteries and internal organs, they endured the agony with courage, while all the bystanders felt pity for them and burst into tears. Yet the martyrs themselves displayed such bravery that not one of them let out a murmur or sigh. In this they demonstrated to everyone that at the moment they were being tortured, these most noble martyrs of Christ were already away from their bodies—or rather, the Lord was right there beside them, communing with them.[6] Focusing their thoughts on the beauty of Christ, they despised their earthly torments and freed themselves from eternal punishments through one mere hour of suffering.[7] The fires of the inhuman torturers felt cool to them, because they set their eyes instead on their salvation from the eternal and unquenchable fires of hell. The martyrs gazed with the eyes of their hearts on the good things reserved for those who patiently endure—the things that "neither ear has heard, nor eye seen, nor has it entered into the heart of man" [1 Cor. 2:9]. And such marvels were personally revealed to them by the Lord, for they were no longer human but already angels.[8]

---

the authorities and compelled others to do so, then harmed the church by shrinking back from martyrdom at the last moment.

6. The theme of Christ suffering within the martyrs and enduring their pain appears frequently in this literature. For example, the story of Perpetua recounts how she is so in tune with God that she is unaware when a cow tramples her. Likewise, the pregnant slave Felicity endures pain during childbirth in prison yet is confident that on the day of her martyrdom Jesus will commune with her and alleviate her suffering. This common martyrological theme highlights the special unity between the martyrs and their crucified Lord.

7. The ancient Christians drew a tight connection between the faithfulness of the martyrs and their heavenly reward. This may sound like "works salvation," but let us recognize that in the early church, an either/or choice between "man's works" versus "God's grace" was not the way salvation was understood. (That type of thinking crystallized during the Protestant Reformation based on an interpretation of Pauline thought.) In the context of ancient martyrdom, the early Christians focused on the biblical idea that whoever "overcomes" or "endures to the end" will be saved. Many Bible verses link faithfulness under persecution and final salvation (Matt. 5:10; 10:22, 32; Mark 8:34–38; 10:29–30; 13:13; Luke 21:17–19; Rev. 6:9; 12:11). At least one church father, the great apologist Tertullian of Carthage, did make the direct (and erroneous) assertion that the martyrs' blood itself atones for their sins. However, that is not really the concept we find here in Polycarp's story. The point is that the martyrs' endurance confirms and perfects their faith in Christ, which wins them eternal life.

8. The notion that deceased believers became angels in heaven was not a widespread belief in the early church, though some writers (such as Clement of Alexandria and Origen) suggested it. In particular, Christians who demonstrated their repudiation of the things of this world, such as

Likewise those condemned to the wild beasts endured horrendous torments. They were stretched out on a bed of jagged shells or afflicted with various other forms of torture. The intent was, if possible, to force them to recant by applying continuous agony. Indeed the Devil devised many things against the martyrs. But thanks be to God, he couldn't get the victory over any of them!

Good and Bad Examples of Martyrdom

Now Germanicus, a man of the highest quality, provided strength to those who were fearful through the example of his patient endurance. Then he went on to confront the beasts in a noteworthy way. When the governor of the province tried to persuade him to recant, urging him to relent, because he was in the prime of life, Germanicus instead grabbed the animals and forcibly drew them to himself! He only wanted to be set free as quickly as possible from the crowd's immoral and lawless lifestyle. Seeing this, all the spectators were amazed at the bravery of the God-loving and God-fearing race of the Christians. They began to shout, "Get rid of the atheists! Go find Polycarp!"[9]

However, there was also a man named Quintus who had recently arrived from Phrygia. He took one look at the beasts and chickened out. Now this was a man who had voluntarily turned himself in and pressured others to do so as well. After much urging, the provincial governor convinced Quintus to swear the oath to Caesar and make a pagan sacrifice! This is exactly why, brothers, we don't praise anyone who gives himself up to the authorities. The gospel simply doesn't teach that.

The Arrest of Polycarp

But Polycarp, who is much more worthy of admiration, wasn't bothered in the least when he first heard about the persecution. He intended to remain within Smyrna's city limits, but most people advised him to slip away quietly, so he withdrew to a little farm in the suburbs, where he stayed with a few friends. Day and night he did nothing but pray for all mankind and for the whole church worldwide, as was his normal custom. Three days prior to his arrest, while he was in prayer, Polycarp fell into a trance and received a vision. He saw his pillow completely consumed by fire. Turning to his companions, he said, "I have to be burned alive."

The authorities kept pursuing Polycarp, so he moved to another farm. No sooner

---

monks who did not marry, were thought to be especially similar to angels (Mark 12:25). Here in Polycarp's story, however, the expression probably doesn't indicate the martyrs actually turned into angels, only that they have become spiritual beings who dwell with God.

9. The narrator makes the ironic point that although the Christians love and fear the one true God, the spectators can view them only as "atheists," because they refuse to worship the deities of the pagan pantheon. Amazed and repulsed at the same time, the crowd calls for the elimination of all Christians in the province of Asia, especially their leader, Polycarp.

had he departed than the searchers arrived behind him. When they didn't find him, they seized two slave boys, and one of them confessed under torture. Really it was quite impossible for Polycarp to avoid capture, since the ones who betrayed him were members of his own household. Now, the police chief—who was predestined to have the name of Herod—urgently wanted to bring him into the stadium. All this happened so Polycarp would fulfill his destiny of becoming a partaker with Christ, while the betrayers eventually received the punishment of Judas himself.[10]

So then, taking the slave boy along, the mounted police officers set out on a Friday about suppertime, armed with all their usual weaponry "as if they were pursuing a robber" [Matt. 6:55]. Late that evening they closed in on him and found him reclining in a little bedroom upstairs. Even then he still had a chance to escape somewhere else, but he decided against it, saying, "God's will be done" [Matt. 26:42]. When he heard the police arrive, he went downstairs and talked with them. The officers noticed his advanced age and quiet dignity and were astonished at all the eagerness to arrest such a respectable gentleman. Right away Polycarp ordered food and drink set before the officers, as much as they wanted. Then he asked them to grant one hour for him to pray undisturbed. When they said yes, he stood and prayed—but he was so full of God's grace that he couldn't be silent for two straight hours! All who heard him were amazed, and many regretted having to pursue such a godly old man.

At last when he finished his prayer—after remembering everyone he had ever met, whether great or small, famous or obscure, as well as the whole worldwide catholic church—it was time to depart. The officers set him on a donkey and led him into the city. Now, it was a high Sabbath day. The police chief Herod came out to meet him along with his father, Niketes. After transferring Polycarp to their carriage, they sat down beside him and tried to persuade him, saying, "What's the matter? What harm is there in saying 'Caesar is Lord' as you make a little sacrifice and do what's required? It's the only way to save your life!"

---

10. This sequence is designed to highlight certain divinely appointed parallels between Polycarp and Jesus. The judicial officer is named Herod, like Herod Antipas (Luke 23:6–12). The traitorous slaves within Polycarp's inner circle are punished for their betrayal, utterly rejected by God, and perhaps even hanged like Judas (cf. Matt. 27:5). The arrest happens on Friday (cf. John 19:14). Polycarp waits in an upper room (cf. Mark 14:15; Luke 22:12) until the officers come to him with weapons as if arresting a robber (cf. Matt. 26:55). Like Jesus in Gethsemane, Polycarp says, "God's will be done" (cf. Matt. 26:42; Luke 22:42). He offers an intercessory prayer for the whole world and the church (cf. John 17), then is seated on a donkey and comes into the city (cf., e.g., Mark 11:1–11). The day is a "high Sabbath," a term that probably refers to a Sabbath in conjunction with the annual Passover feast (cf. John 19:31). At first Polycarp remains silent before the Roman officials (cf. Isa. 53:7; Matt. 27:12–14), but when he finally gives an answer that they cannot approve, he is threatened and injured by them. Because of these parallels, some scholars consider this section to be marked by the insertion of legends from a later editor. However, nothing here is inherently impossible or even improbable. The original narrator may have noticed some details of Polycarp's story that he chose to highlight as similar to Christ's experience.

At first Polycarp gave no reply to them. But when they persisted, he finally said, "I have no intention of doing what you're advising." Once they realized they had failed to persuade him, they began to hurl curses at him, tossing him from the carriage with such haste that he ripped open his shin as he was getting out. Without turning around, as if he hadn't even suffered an injury, he marched briskly away, eager to reach his destination.

Polycarp in the Stadium

As he was led into the stadium, such a huge uproar was raging inside that no one could be heard at all. Yet when Polycarp entered, a voice rang out from heaven: "Be strong and courageous, Polycarp!"[11] No one saw any speaker, though the Christians who were there definitely heard the voice.

And then as he was brought forward, a great clamor broke out when everyone realized Polycarp had been arrested. He stood before the provincial governor, who inquired if he was indeed Polycarp. When he acknowledged it, the governor tried to persuade him to recant.

"Have some respect for the dignity of your old age," he urged, along with other things like this that they typically say. "Just swear an oath by the divine spirit of Caesar.[12] Change your mind about what you believe! Say, 'Get rid of the atheists!'"[13]

11. Polycarp is encouraged to act like Jesus's forerunner and namesake, Joshua. The message from heaven is an exact quotation of the words spoken to Israel's great general in the Greek version of the Old Testament called the Septuagint (Josh. 1:6, 7, 9, 18). The reader is supposed to recognize that Polycarp is about to fight mighty battles against God's enemies so he can enter the Promised Land.

12. Here we see a manifestation of the imperial cult, as described in the introduction. Starting at the time of Caesar Augustus, the Romans began to venerate their emperors as divinities. Very quickly this worship developed into an empire-wide religious system with its own temples, altars, priests, festivals, and images. For soldiers, this mandatory state religion meant swearing an oath of loyalty to the emperor, while the general populace participated in festivals and banquets that often included a token sacrifice (e.g., a pinch of burnt incense or a small pouring of wine). The official state cults staged even more impressive animal sacrifices. These offerings were actually made to the *genius* of the emperor—that is, to the divine spirit that indwelt the man and his family, empowering him to rule with good luck. Just about every aspect of society had its own little spiritual power, a *genius* that could be personified and named, and it was important to placate these spirits through ritual actions. How much more, then, did the emperor's divine *genius* need to be worshiped for the well-being of society! The slogan "Caesar is Lord" expressed the people's recognition of the emperor's rightful preeminence and wise beneficence to humankind. But such beliefs and practices flew in the face of the gospel. The most basic truth of Christian preaching was "Jesus is Lord" (Rom. 10:9; 1 Cor. 12:3). The tension is heightened even more when we consider that the Latin concept of the *genius* was associated with the Greek word *daimon*, which is the biblical word for "demon." The early Christians viewed the imperial cult as nothing short of worshiping demons as their "lord" in place of the Lord Jesus Christ. Some ancient believers went to an agonizing death rather than commit this blasphemy.

13. Once again, we see that Polycarp's fellow Christians are viewed as "atheists" because they worshiped an invisible deity instead of gods represented by idols. The governor wants Polycarp

With a stern expression Polycarp stared straight at the crowd of immoral pagans in the stadium and shook his fist at them. Groaning deeply as he looked up to heaven, he exclaimed, "Get rid of the atheists!"

The governor kept pressing. "Just swear the oath, and I'll let you go. Curse the name of Christ."

Polycarp answered, "For eighty-six years I have been his servant, and he has done me no wrong. How could I now blaspheme my king who saved me?"[14]

"Swear by the divine spirit of Caesar," the governor continued to urge.

"If you think I'm going to do what you're asking and swear to Caesar's demon, you're mistaken," Polycarp replied. "But since you keep pretending not to know who I am, hear me declare boldly: *I am a Christian!* Now, if you want to learn the true doctrine of Christianity, name the day, and give me a hearing."

"See if you can win over the populace," the governor suggested.

But Polycarp responded, "You indeed I might have considered worthy of a discourse; for our faith has taught us to give appropriate honor to rulers and governors, who are appointed by God—so long as we don't have to compromise our principles. But as for the mob, I don't consider them worthy of hearing a reasoned defense."

"I have wild beasts," said the governor, "and I'm going to throw you to them unless you change your mind."

"Bring them on! We Christians can't change from something better to something worse. But what is truly beautiful is to turn oneself from wickedness to righteousness."

The governor threatened again: "Since you don't think much of the beasts, I'll have you roasted by fire unless you change your mind."

"The fire you're talking about burns for a very short time and then is quickly put out," Polycarp replied. "Clearly you're unaware of the fire of imminent judgment and eternal punishment that awaits the ungodly. So what are you waiting for? Come on! Do whatever you wish."

As he said these things and much else, Polycarp overflowed with joyous courage, and his face shone with grace. It wasn't he who staggered back in despair at all the threats made against him, but rather it was the governor who was bewildered. He sent his personal herald into the midst of the stadium to proclaim three times, "Polycarp has admitted he's a Christian!" When the herald announced this, the whole mob—not just gentiles but also the Jews living in Smyrna—cried out in uncontrollable rage with a huge shout, "This is the teacher

to reject such impiety, but the martyr turns the governor's suggestion around and rejects the true atheists in the crowd.

14. In calling Jesus his "king," Polycarp draws a clear contrast between Caesar, the earthly monarch of the Roman Empire, and Jesus Christ, the one who actually rules the world.

of the Asian Christians, their spiritual father! He overthrows our gods and instructs many people not to make sacrifices or worship!" Then they screamed and demanded that Philip, who was one of the organizers of the games in Asia, turn a lion loose on Polycarp. But Philip said he wasn't allowed to do that since the beast-hunting portion of the games had already ended. Next the crowd decided to shout out in unison that Polycarp should be burned alive. Now, this happened in order to fulfill the vision he received about his pillow, when he saw it on fire while praying then turned to his faithful companions and prophesied, "I have to be burned alive."

So then, quicker than words can tell, the crowd immediately gathered logs and sticks from nearby workshops and baths. As usual the Jews were especially willing to help at this sort of thing.[15] When the pyre was ready, Polycarp took off all his clothes and removed his belt. He even tried to unlace his own sandals, which he normally didn't have to do, because all the believers were always eager to be the first to have some sort of physical contact with him.[16] For even prior to his martyrdom, Polycarp had been highly honored on account of his virtuous life.

15. While the narrator may be overstating the case here, we cannot entirely dismiss his assertion of Jewish cooperation in the wood gathering as an anti-Semitic slur with no possible basis in history. Given the frequently rancorous relationship between Christians and Jews in antiquity, it is entirely plausible to think some individuals within the sizable Jewish population in Smyrna could have supported the imperial condemnation of Judaism's primary religious competitor. This is not to say every Jewish person was an accessory to the crimes perpetrated against the martyrs, only that some of them may have welcomed the executions. Though it is unlikely any spectators—Jewish or otherwise—could have leaped from the stands and returned with wood, perhaps some event involving the collusion of a Jewish merchant near the coliseum resulted in this accusation. It is wrong, of course, to slander all Jews even if certain individuals supplied some wood.

16. The early Christians were drawn to people of great spiritual devotion because they believed these individuals, or the places and objects associated with them, could open up a door to God's presence. Men and women who lived holy lives possessed an exceptional closeness to the Lord, and this was especially true of the martyrs, who were completely identified with Christ by suffering a passion in his name. Therefore Jesus was believed to be present within the bodies of such people in a unique way. Strange as this idea may sound, it has a basis in Scripture. The notion that suffering for Jesus unites believers with him and makes his work especially present is common in the thought of the apostle Paul. For example, he writes, "I rejoice in my sufferings for your sake, and in my flesh I am filling up what is lacking in Christ's afflictions for the sake of his body, that is, the church" (Col. 1:24). Paul also considers persecuted believers to be "carrying in the body the death of Jesus, so that the life of Jesus may also be manifested in our bodies" (2 Cor. 4:10; see also 1:5; Phil. 3:9–11). Because martyrs experienced such a special connection to the suffering Savior, the early Christians believed their physical bodies—whether their shackled limbs in prison or their bones and graves afterward—deserved to be revered. No doubt there was some superstition here. Yet this ancient perspective also reminds us that the Christian faith, which centers on the incarnation, puts special value on material things as instruments to lead us toward God. Believers today could stand to discover a greater appreciation for the sacred spaces and objects that can enliven our senses to the Lord's presence.

Straightaway the wood gathered for the fire was arranged around him. Just as they were about to nail Polycarp to the stake, he said, "You can leave me as I am. The God who grants me the strength to endure the flames will also enable me to remain unflinching on the pyre. The assurance you get from the nails isn't even necessary."

So instead of nailing him they just bound his arms. He stood there with his hands tied behind him like a noble ram chosen out of a great flock to be a sacrifice, prepared as a burnt offering acceptable to God. Looking up to heaven, he said:

> O Lord God Almighty, Father of your beloved and blessed Son Jesus Christ, through whom we have learned of you! O God of the angelic powers, and all creation, and the whole family of the righteous who live in your presence! I praise you that you have considered me worthy of this day and hour, that I might receive a spot on the list of martyrs who have drunk the cup of your Christ. I know this will lead to my resurrection unto eternal life, body and soul, in the immortality granted by the Holy Spirit. May I be well received among the martyrs today, standing face-to-face with you as a rich and pleasing sacrifice. You prepared and revealed this beforehand, and now you've brought it to pass—you who are the trustworthy God, in whom there is no lie. For this reason, indeed for all things, I praise you, I bless you, I glorify you, through the eternal and heavenly High Priest, Jesus Christ your beloved Son, through whom I give glory to you, and to him and the Holy Spirit, both now and in all the ages to come. Amen![17]

The Death of Polycarp

When Polycarp had offered up his amen and finished his prayer, the men in charge of the fire put the torch to the wood. As a massive flame blazed up, those of us who were granted the eyes to see it noticed a great wonder (and we were protected from persecution so we could tell others what happened). The fire, like a ship's sail filled by wind, curved into an arch and encircled the martyr's body within a wall of flame. He stood there in its midst, not like someone whose flesh was burning, but as if he were a loaf of bread baking, or gold and silver being refined in a furnace. And we also perceived some kind of sweet-smelling odor, as if incense or another sort of precious aromatic spice were wafting in the air. At last the evildoers realized Polycarp's body couldn't be consumed by the fire. They ordered an executioner to go up and stab him with a dagger, which caused so much blood to gush out that it extinguished the fire. And the whole crowd marveled at the amazing difference between the unbelievers and the elect.

17. We must always keep in mind that the *Martyrdom of Polycarp* is an edited text. This well-constructed, almost liturgical prayer probably wasn't composed on the spot, though it no doubt reflects the kind of things Polycarp expressed as his death neared.

Indeed, the admirable martyr Polycarp truly was one of the elect! In our day he served as an apostolic and prophetic teacher, a bishop of the catholic church in Smyrna. Every word he ever spoke from his mouth was accomplished and will be fulfilled.

Polycarp's Relics

Now, the Devil is jealous, hateful, and evil—the adversary of the whole family of the righteous. He observed Polycarp's great martyrdom and his unassailable character throughout his life. Seeing that Polycarp now wore an "imperishable crown" and had won a "prize" that no one could ever snatch [1 Cor. 9:24–25], the Devil at least made sure we couldn't retrieve the corpse, though many of us dearly wanted to obtain it and commune with Polycarp's holy flesh.[18] Thus the Devil whispered to Niketes, the father of Herod and brother of Alke, that he should go talk the governor into not giving us the body. "Otherwise," Niketes said, "they might abandon the Crucified One and start worshiping this man instead." These things were said at the suggestion and urging of the Jews, who even watched us closely when we were about to take the corpse off the pyre! For they didn't understand we could never abandon or worship anyone else than Christ, who suffered for the salvation of everyone who is saved in the entire world, the innocent in place of sinners. So we worship Christ because he is the Son of God, but the martyrs we simply love as followers and imitators of the Lord—which is entirely fitting in light of their utmost devotion to their precious king and master. May we, too, become sharers and fellow disciples with the martyrs!

Therefore when the centurion saw all the fuss aroused by the Jews, he set the corpse out in front of everyone and cremated it according to pagan custom. And so at last we collected up Polycarp's bones, which are dearer to us than jewels and more esteemed than gold, and buried them in a respectable place. There, as often as possible, the Lord will allow us to assemble with great joy and delight to celebrate the "birthday" of Polycarp's martyrdom.[19] Our observance will not only

18. Early Christian reverence for the martyrs as special vessels of Jesus led to veneration of their mortal remains and burial places. The underground Christian catacombs became places of prayer, and ancient believers sought to be buried close to these departed heroes. Eventually large pilgrimage churches were erected over the tombs of the martyrs, the most famous of which is St. Peter's Basilica in Rome. See the introduction for more information on the ancient church's veneration of its martyrs.

19. As noted in the introduction, the Romans often celebrated banquets in honor of their deceased loved ones. Christians picked up certain elements of this practice, but instead of commemorating the martyr's death, they celebrated it as a "birthday" when the martyr was reborn into the presence of Jesus Christ. The commemoration of Christian martyrs at their graves was just beginning at the time of Polycarp's death (though contemporaneous markers erected at Peter's and Paul's graves at Rome attest it had already begun). The ardent devotion to relics

commemorate those who have already fought the fight as martyrs but also train and prepare those who may find themselves facing such a calling.

Conclusion

This, then, is the story of blessed Polycarp. Although he was the twelfth person to be martyred in Smyrna along with some others from Philadelphia, he alone is especially remembered by everyone and is even mentioned everywhere by the pagans. He was not only a distinguished teacher but an outstanding martyr whose death everyone wants to imitate, because it conformed to the gospel of Christ. Through his endurance he defeated the unjust governor and so received an imperishable crown. Now, rejoicing greatly with the apostles and all the righteous, Polycarp is glorifying God the Father Almighty and praising our Lord Jesus Christ—the Savior of our souls, the captain of our bodies, the shepherd of the catholic church throughout the world!

We know you asked us to report to you what happened in full detail. For now, though, we've provided a sort of summary through our brother Markion. Once you've learned the basic facts, circulate this letter among the Christians in further regions so they too can praise the Lord, who selects some for martyrdom from among his own servants.

Now to him who is able to lead all of us by his gracious gift into his heavenly kingdom through Jesus Christ his only-begotten Son—to him be glory, honor, power, and majesty forever!

Give a warm greeting to all the saints. Everyone here sends good wishes, including Euarestos the scribe who wrote this letter, and his entire household.

---

mentioned here may reflect the practice of a slightly later period, yet nothing in this account is out of step with second-century beliefs and practices.

5

Justin Martyr

Apologetics at the Ultimate Price

Justin Martyr is a church father whose name is known to many Christians today. Though some might suppose his surname was "Martyr," this was actually a title given to him in church history because he died for his refusal to blaspheme his Lord by idolatry. Yet Justin's time-honored fame stems not only from his martyrdom but also from his role as one of the earliest Christian apologists. Though a few figures before him had attempted to defend their faith to a pagan world, Justin was the first church father to cast Christian doctrine as a respectable form of Greek philosophy. After experiencing an intellectual type of conversion in which he found all schools of thought deficient compared to the principles of Christ, Justin adopted the distinct clothing of a philosopher and began serving as a freelance teacher in Ephesus and then Rome. He considered his ministry to involve instruction of Christian converts, as well as apologetic defense of the true faith to both pagans and Jews.

Bold as he was, Justin soon made enemies. Among them was a teacher named Crescens who adhered to the doctrines of Cynicism, a philosophy that competed with Christianity for converts. Justin records that Crescens "publicly bears witness against us in matters he does not understand," calling Christians "atheists and impious" in order to please the "deluded mob."[1]

1. Justin, *2 Apology* 3, in Roberts, Donaldson, and Coxe, eds., *Apostolic Fathers*, 189.

Justin publicly interrogated this man and revealed he actually knew nothing about the Christian faith. Because of this, around AD 165 Justin began to sense that Crescens, or perhaps some other intellectuals whom Justin had refuted, might be plotting his death.

An egregious act of discrimination in Rome brought Justin to the attention of the authorities. An upper-class Christian woman had grown so sick of her pagan husband's ceaseless immoralities that she could no longer stand to share his bed, so she divorced him. Furious at this rejection, the spurned husband trumped up charges against the woman's pastor, Ptolemaeus. The pastor was tossed in a prison where the accusing husband's friend was in charge. Together they arranged to have Ptolemaeus executed by the mayor of Rome—not for a specific crime or the violation of any law but simply for being a Christian. Justin Martyr was so outraged at this injustice that he published a vehement criticism of the mayor's action. Unfortunately, the mayor was a powerful ex-soldier named Urbicus who had risen to great heights from obscure origins. Now Justin's name had become known—and disliked—among the imperial elite at Rome.

And so at last we hear that Justin was dragged before the Roman authorities. The mayor who presided over the trial wasn't the one Justin had criticized. He was Junius Rusticus, a noted philosopher and close confidant of Emperor Marcus Aurelius. As quickly becomes obvious in the text translated below, Rusticus held no sympathy for Christianity. Justin hardly stood a chance against such hostility.

The story of Justin's martyrdom is recorded in a different literary genre than the well-developed passion stories of figures like Polycarp or Perpetua. In Justin's case, what has survived is not an account of the events leading up to the martyrdom but simply the "acts" of the trial and execution. This "acts" genre is often based on court transcripts and is therefore quite reliable. Three versions of *The Acts of Justin and His Companions* have come down to us: a short one, a longer and more pious one, and a late version embellished with legends. The first one, though briefest, is the most accurate account of what actually happened, so it is the one translated here.

The Martyrdom of Saints Justin, Chariton, Charito, Euelpistos, Hierax, Paion, Liberian, and Their Comrades

The Interview with Justin

In the days of illegal decrees of idolatry, the saints listed above were arrested and brought before the mayor of Rome, whose name was Rusticus. After they were brought into court, Mayor Rusticus said to Justin, "What sort of life do you lead?"

"A blameless and innocent one toward all people," Justin replied.

"What sort of teachings do you live by?"

"I've tried to become familiar with all doctrines," Justin said, "but I've committed myself to the true doctrines of the Christians, though I realize that might not please those who hold to falsehood."[2]

"Yet these doctrines do please you?"

"Yes, because I follow them according to the correct belief system."

"And what is your belief system?"

"We reverently profess faith in the Christian God, whom we believe to be the sole architect of the entire created world from the very beginning, and we believe in Jesus Christ, the Son of God, whom the prophets predicted was about to come down to the human race as a messenger of salvation and a teacher of excellent doctrines.[3] I consider what I'm telling you to count very little in comparison to Christ's divinity. Yet I do acknowledge a certain prophetic power—namely, the prophecies announced about the one I just declared to be the Son of God. For you should know that in times past, the prophets predicted he would appear among us."

"Where do you meet?" Mayor Rusticus demanded.

"Wherever each of us wants to or can. Do you actually imagine we could all gather in the same place?"

"Tell me where *you* meet. In what specific place do *you* assemble?"

"I have been living in an apartment above the bathhouse of Martin for my entire stay in Rome, which is my second period of residence here. I have no knowledge

2. Justin tells us in one of his works that when he was a young man seeking divine wisdom, he tested various philosophical schools of antiquity but found each one lacking. The Stoics, Aristotelians, Pythagoreans, and Platonists all came up short. At last Justin met a wise old man walking by the sea. The man showed Justin that human philosophies are empty and contradictory; only the wisdom of God and his Christ could satisfy humanity's inner longings. "Straightaway a flame was kindled in my soul," Justin recalls, "and a love of the prophets and those men who are friends of Christ possessed me" (*Dialogue with Trypho* 8, in Roberts, Donaldson, and Coxe, eds., *Apostolic Fathers*, 198). At that moment Justin committed himself to the truth that Christianity is the only "safe and profitable" philosophy. It is a conviction he maintained all the way to his death.

3. Note Justin's apologetic method here. A Roman bureaucrat wouldn't understand Jewish ideas about a messiah, yet he might respect a wise teacher whose eternal truths could improve human morality. Therefore Justin presents Jesus in a manner that would be understood by his pagan opponent. In doing so, he is part of a long tradition of intellectual Christians from the Greek-speaking East who presented Jesus as the "Logos," or Word of God (John 1:1–18)—that is, as a teacher of the soul. Ancient philosophy sought to discover how to reach the highest divine world. In answer to this fundamental question, the early Christians claimed Jesus was the supreme messenger of the Heavenly Father. Rusticus, however, remains unimpressed by what Justin has to offer, despite the added confirmation of predictive prophecy.

of any other meeting place but this one. Anyone who wished could come to me, and I would share the doctrines of truth with him."[4]

"So then," the mayor said, "you are indeed a Christian?"

"Yes, I'm a Christian," Justin declared.

Rusticus Examines the Other Christians

Mayor Rusticus spoke to Chariton. "Are you a Christian too?" he asked.

"I am," Chariton said, "by the decree of God."

Turning to Charito, the mayor asked, "What do you have to say, Charito?"

"I am a Christian according to God's gift," she replied.

"And what are you, Euelpistos?"

Euelpistos said, "I too am a Christian, sharing in the same hope as these others."

The mayor asked Hierax, "Are you a Christian too?"

"Indeed I am, for I worship the same God."

"Did Justin convert all of you to Christianity?"

"No, I have been a Christian for a long time," Hierax said.

A man named Paion stood up and spoke. "I too am a Christian," he declared.

Mayor Rusticus asked him, "Who instructed you?"

"I received it from my parents."

"I also received my Christian faith from my parents," Euelpistos added, "though I listened willingly to Justin's teachings."

"And where are your parents?"

"In Cappadocia."

4. The earliest Christians typically met in private houses, because they believed God did not have to dwell in temples like the pagan deities. According to what Justin describes elsewhere, the believers gathered on Sunday for Scripture readings, spiritual exhortation from the church's leader, corporate prayers, the celebration of Communion, and the collection of charitable offerings. Baptism also took place in a setting like this. In the smaller towns and midsized cities of the empire, this would have been the normal church practice. Rome's large size, however, created a scenario in which various Christian groups remained isolated from one another. The Roman Christians were not spread equally across the urban area but were clustered near the docks that lined the Tiber River or along the roads that entered the city—fringe places with an impoverished immigrant population. This lack of strong centralization in Rome created the situation Justin describes to Mayor Rusticus, in which a learned Christian philosopher could rent a room and gain a following in his neighborhood yet be isolated from other cells of believers. In the late second century (just after the time of Justin's death) several successive bishops of Rome became more active in establishing a central authority structure. They purchased residential properties—sometimes renovating them extensively—to serve as meeting spaces, and they also secured land outside the city for Christian burials. These early churches of Rome were functional buildings to gather a congregation for worship and store charity for distribution to the poor. They were not, like Roman temples, inherently sacred places where a god's presence was invoked to take up permanent residence. The universal God of the Christians dwells wherever his followers are found.

The mayor turned to Hierax. "What about you—where are your parents?"

"They're dead. I was dragged here a long time ago from Phrygia."[5]

Rusticus asked Liberian, "You aren't a Christian too, are you?"

"Yes, I'm a very committed Christian," he replied.

Justin Defends His Hope

Turning back to Justin, the mayor said, "Are you convinced that if I have you whipped and beheaded you'll go up to heaven?"

"If I endure these things, then yes, I have hope because of my endurance," Justin replied. "I know God's blessing will remain upon everyone who lives a devout life, lasting even through the final judgment by fire."

"So you suppose you'll ascend to heaven?"

"I don't just suppose it. I'm absolutely certain of it."

The Martyrs Take Their Stand

"If you don't obey me," Mayor Rusticus said, "you will be punished."

But Justin replied, "If we are punished, we have the sure promise of salvation."

Mayor Rusticus then proclaimed, "Let those who refused to sacrifice to the gods be whipped and led away for execution in accordance with the laws."

So the holy martyrs, glorifying God, went out to the appointed place. There they fulfilled their martyrdom through confession of our Savior. To him be glory and power, along with the Father and the Holy Spirit, now and forevermore. Amen.

---

5. The Christians apprehended with Justin were part of the school that met at his house. Hierax, who was forcibly "dragged" from his homeland, appears to have been a slave brought to Rome against his will. We cannot be sure the others were slaves, but at least they were probably poor, for they have Eastern names that indicate they were immigrants without high social standing. Many of the names listed in Romans 16 in the New Testament reflect these same social demographics, which serves to illustrate an important fact about early Christianity: the new faith held special appeal to social outcasts. Why? It is hard to say for sure, but one reason must be that Christianity dignified the lowly as valuable to God and promised them a better afterlife. In a society that tossed aside the poor like garbage, the message of a loving Creator who offered eternal life was often irresistible to those who possessed no earthly privileges.

6

The Martyrs of Lyons and Vienne

A Crown of Many Flowers

In the year 177 a persecution broke out against the Christians in what are today the French cities of Lyons and Vienne (known back then as Lugdunum and Vienna in Roman Gaul). The cities are close to each other, with Vienne being only a few miles downstream along the Rhône River from Lyons. Of the two cities, Lyons was the more important. As the capital of the three main regions of Gaul it hosted an annual congress of the sixty Gallic (i.e., Celtic) tribes. It is certainly no coincidence that the terrible Christian persecution occurred during the festivities of the congress in August, the month of Caesar Augustus, when patriotic fervor was at its height and the populace was reaffirming its loyalty to Rome and its worship of the emperor.

Christianity was a relative newcomer in this part of Gaul. All evidence points to a foundational relationship with the churches in the province of Asia (modern-day Turkey). This evangelistic connection wouldn't have been made by land, for the entire Alpine range stood in the way. Instead the connection was established via Massalia (Marseilles), a port city on the busy sea-trading route with Asia. Greek-speaking immigrants from the East had found their way to the interior of Gaul through Massalia and up the Rhône River as merchants, businessmen, and slaves. Among them were Christians, so by this means faith in Jesus made the leap from the lands Paul and John had evangelized to a brand-new region: a land of pagan Celtic tribes that had finally bowed the knee to the Roman Empire. In this context Christianity was viewed—not only by the indigenous Celts but also by the aristocratic Roman bureaucrats who now ran the province—as an alien and suspicious religion from far away. The believers were suspected of practicing magic and committing secret moral atrocities, such as orgies and cannibalism. Though these suspicions may have had some basis among the local gnostic sects,[1] the Christians utterly rejected such behavior. Unfortunately, the pagans couldn't tell the difference between the two groups.

As you will see in the text below, the vicious persecution killed Christians from the upper ranks of society all the way down to slaves. Lyons's first bishop, the elderly Pothinus, died in prison from the harsh conditions. Others died in the Amphitheater of the Three Gauls, which was part of the temple complex that hosted the annual Gallic congress. The remains of this structure can still be seen today in the Croix-Rousse neighborhood of Lyons at the confluence of the Rhône and Saône Rivers.

After the persecution finally subsided, the church father Irenaeus became the city's next bishop. He was probably the one who arranged for a letter describing the martyrs' faithfulness during these terrible days to be sent to the sister churches in Asia. Like all historical documents of the ancient world, this is a work of interpretation, not a record of bare facts. The events of 177 have been "theologized" for the benefit of the church. Even so, the details of the letter lodge it squarely in late second-century Christianity. This text survived for over a century until the ancient historian Eusebius obtained a copy and incorporated it into his book *Church History*. Because of this, we can still read the letter today in its original form. Here it is.

The Martyrs of Lyons and Vienne
(Eusebius, *Church History* 5.1.1–63)

Salutation

The servants of Christ living at Vienne and Lyons in Gaul write to our brothers in Asia and Phrygia, who have the same faith and hope of deliverance as we: peace, grace, and glory be yours from God the Father and our Lord Jesus Christ.

[Eusebius tells us there are some other prefatory remarks, then the text continues.]

---

1. Irenaeus of Lyons accuses the local gnostics of orgies, while other sources denounce the sects for eating aborted fetuses and consuming bodily fluids. Since many gnostics disparaged the social pattern of marrying and begetting children, and since they sometimes had mystical theologies of eating and drinking, the Christian accusations of sexual or cannibalistic rituals are not so utterly ridiculous as to be impossible. This sort of thing certainly did happen at times in the ancient

The Beginning of the Intense Persecution

We can't even begin to put into words, much less describe in detail, the magnitude of the persecution here: how the pagans raged so terribly against the saints, and how the blessed martyrs endured so patiently. No letter could possibly contain what must be said about the persecution.

Our adversary the Devil, giving us a foretaste of his final appearance, which is surely very close, fell upon us with all his might. He used every trick available to prepare and train his followers to attack God's servants. Eventually we weren't just banned from homes, baths, and the market square; we were ordered not to appear publicly in any way whatsoever.

However, God's grace joined the fight and protected the weak! He set up an array of sturdy pillars—the martyrs who by their endurance could draw all the fierce wrath of the Evil One onto themselves. These heroes ran into battle, enduring every sort of scorn and punishment. Indeed, they considered their massive abuse to be a mere trifle as they sped toward Christ, proving that "our present sufferings aren't worth comparing to the glory that will be revealed in us" [Rom. 8:18].

To begin with, they nobly endured all the abuse the whole mob collectively piled on: screaming at them, punching them, dragging them through the streets, plundering their homes, stoning them, locking them up, and everything else a savage horde loves to inflict on a despised enemy. Next they were led into the public square and interrogated in front of the populace by the military commander and the city officials. When they admitted to being Christians they were tossed in jail until the governor arrived.

The Advocacy of Vettius Epagathus

A while later, after the believers had been hauled before the governor and he had attacked them with all the typical savagery directed at us, a Christian brother named Vettius Epagathus stepped from the crowd, a man abounding in love for God and his neighbor. Though he was still young, his life had already reached such a degree of sanctification that the same testimony could be said about him as was said about the old man Zechariah: that he had truly walked "blameless in all the commands and precepts of the Lord" [Luke 1:6]. Epagathus never hesitated to serve his neighbor in any way he could and was extremely devoted to God with a fervent spirit.

---

world. On the other hand, making charges like this was an easy way to discredit one's enemy. Even if no babies were being eaten, some gnostic sects probably did have looser sexual rules than the orthodox Christians, though others were highly ascetic. Regardless of who actually did what, it is easy to imagine how a climate of runaway rumors could lead to a persecution like the one that broke out at Lyons in 177.

So, a man like this couldn't stand to see such an irrational judgment imposed on us. Outraged at what was happening, he demanded a private hearing to speak in defense of the brethren and prove we are neither atheistic nor impious. Since he was a man of high station, the bystanders around the judgment seat could only shout their objections. The governor refused to entertain the reasonable request Epagathus had made and simply asked if he was a Christian too. In a ringing voice he confessed himself a believer and was admitted to the ranks of the martyrs.

Though Epagathus was nicknamed "the advocate of the Christians," he in fact had the Advocate within him [John 14:16], the Holy Spirit who also filled Zechariah. Epagathus demonstrated the fullness of his love by choosing to lay down his life to defend his brethren. Surely he was (and now is!) a genuine disciple of Christ, "following the Lamb wherever he goes" [Rev. 14:4].

Faithful and Weak Martyrs

Now the rest who were in prison fell into two groups. Some were clearly prepared to become the first martyrs of Gaul, for they made the ultimate confession with all eagerness. Others, however, didn't appear ready. They were untrained and feeble, incapable of bearing the tension of a great conflict. About ten of them succumbed to the strain like a baby that dies in childbirth, which caused us immeasurable grief and distress. And this certainly undermined the eagerness of those who hadn't yet been arrested—those who, despite the martyrs' terrible sufferings, were coming to help them instead of deserting them.

At that point, then, we were all desperately worried about the uncertain outcome of this moment of confession. It's not that we were afraid of the tortures being applied. Rather we were looking ahead to the final end, very concerned that someone might fall away. Even so, our most honored leaders kept being arrested day after day in order to fill up the ranks of the martyrs. In this way the authorities collected from the two churches of Lyons and Vienne all the most devoted Christians, the ones on whom everything here was especially dependent.

Now, some of those arrested were our unbelieving household servants, since the governor had publicly ordered a full investigation of all Christians. These servants became Satan's trap for us. Terrified by the tortures they saw the believers suffering and pressured by the soldiers, they falsely accused us of eating children like Thyestes or committing incest like Oedipus,[2] and other sorts of crimes that

---

2. Thyestes and Oedipus are Greek mythological figures who are noted, respectively, for cannibalism and incest. Thyestes was secretly served his own cooked sons at a banquet, while Oedipus unknowingly married his mother. This same terminology is used by the church father Athenagoras of Athens in his apologetic defense of the Christians written around the same

are inappropriate for us even to name or consider. Indeed, it is difficult to imagine such things ever happened among the human race at all! Yet once these sordid rumors began to circulate among the people, they all raged against us like wild animals. Even those who at first were more moderate because they were our friends now grew incredibly furious and bared their teeth at us. Thus the saying of our Lord was fulfilled: "The time is coming when whoever kills you will think he is doing a service to God" [John 16:2].

The Torments of Some Specific Martyrs

Then at last the holy martyrs suffered tortures beyond all description as Satan tried to wring a word of blasphemy from them too. The full wrath of the mob and the governor and the soldiers came crashing down with overwhelming force on Sanctus, a deacon of Vienne; on Maturus, a newly baptized Christian who nonetheless proved to be a noble contender; on Attalus from Pergamum, who had always been a "pillar and buttress" for the believers there [1 Tim. 3:15]; and on Blandina, in whom Jesus Christ proved that what people consider worthless, ugly, and contemptible, God considers worthy of great glory. For Blandina's love of God was demonstrated by her steadfast strength, not by any boasting in her outer appearance.[3]

Blandina

Figure 6.1. Saint Blandina. Nineteenth-century stained glass window, Chapel of Saint Blandina, Église St. Martin d'Ainay, Lyons, France. (Gianni Dagli Orti/Art Resource, NY)

Now, we were all very concerned, and Blandina's earthly mistress (who was herself one of the contenders among the martyrs) was especially worried that her servant wouldn't be able to make a bold confession because of her frail body. But Blandina was filled with such strength that the

---

time as the martyrs of Lyons (*A Plea Regarding the Christians* 3). Evidently it was a common accusation in the late second century.

3. Blandina is sometimes depicted in pious Christian art as a beautiful "damsel in distress." However, the eyewitnesses who told her story went out of their way to note she was unlovely in appearance—a woman whose inner beauty far outshined her external form.

torturers, who worked in shifts from dawn to dusk tormenting Blandina with every possible method, were exhausted and finally gave up. They admitted they were beaten, that there was nothing left to do to her that hadn't been done already. In fact they marveled she was still alive with her entire body ripped open and broken in every place. The men acknowledged that even one form of torture should have released her soul, not to mention such terrible ones like the many they applied. But instead this blessed woman, like a well-trained athlete, kept growing stronger throughout her confession. Blandina was refreshed and experienced rest and relief from her agony by exclaiming, "I am a Christian! We don't do anything wrong!"

Sanctus

Sanctus was another martyr who encountered all the cruelties men could dish out, yet he endured them nobly with immeasurable, indeed superhuman, strength. Though the wicked men hoped that by intense and unrelenting tortures they could make him say something unworthy, he withstood them with such firmness that he refused even to divulge his name, race, hometown, or status as slave or free. To all their questions he answered in Latin, "I am a Christian!" He kept repeating this over and over instead of giving his name, birthplace, nationality, or anything else. The pagans heard no other word from him but this confession.

Because of this, the governor and the torturers became obsessed with breaking him. At last when they had nothing left to do to him, they attached red-hot metal plates to his most delicate body parts. And although his tender parts were indeed scorched, Sanctus remained unbent and unbroken, firm in his confession—for he was sprinkled and refreshed by the heavenly fountain of living water that flows from Christ's side [John 4:10; 7:38; 19:34].

Even so, his poor body bore witness to all that had happened to him. It was traumatized from head to toe—a continuous raw wound and bruise, shriveled everywhere by fire. Sanctus's frame was so mangled that he had lost any visible resemblance to a human being. Yet Christ, who suffered in Sanctus's body, achieved great glory. Obliterating the Enemy's power, he gave living proof to all the other believers that when we have God's love, we have nothing to fear, and when we have Christ's glory, nothing is painful.

A few days later the evil men tortured the martyr again. Since they knew his body was so swollen and inflamed that even a light touch of the hand would cause him unbearable agony, they thought if they reapplied the same torture instruments to Sanctus they'd get the best of him.[4] Or, if he happened to die under torture, that

---

4. Anyone who has ever had a bad burn, a broken bone, or a surgical operation knows how sensitive a wound can be a few days after the trauma. Poor Sanctus, who had terrible wounds all over his body, was left without any painkillers in the dungeon for several days until the inhuman

too would strike fear in the hearts of the remaining Christians. Yet nothing of this sort took place. Instead, contrary to what anyone would ever expect, the renewed tortures restored Sanctus's mangled body and made it straight again! He actually recovered his former appearance and the use of his limbs! Thus, we might say the second round of torture served not as a punishment for Sanctus but—by the grace of Christ—as a cure.

Biblis

Now, there was a certain woman named Biblis among those who had denied the Lord. Though the Devil supposed he had already devoured her [1 Pet. 5:8], he wanted to see her condemned even further for slander against the Christians. So, thinking she was a fragile coward, he put her under torture again to force her to attribute atrocities to us. But once she had been stretched out on the rack, Biblis came to her senses and awoke, so to speak, from a deep coma. The temporary punishment of the torture caused her to consider the eternal chastisement of hell,[5] so she directly refuted the slanders directed against us. "How could the Christians be guilty of eating human children," she asked, "when they aren't even permitted to consume the blood of irrational animals?" [Acts 15:29]. From then on Biblis confessed herself a Christian and was given a place among the martyrs.

Other Terrible Sufferings

Through Christ, then, the tyrant's tools of torture were rendered useless by the endurance of the blessed martyrs. So now the Devil considered other devices he might use, such as confinement in the darkest and most oppressive parts of the prison; spreading the legs in the stocks as widely as possible; and all the other horrors the Devil's enraged, demon-possessed servants typically inflict on prisoners.[6]

---

torturers attacked his broken body again. Such pain is unfathomable. It is no wonder the letter writer made a point of showing how Christ gave strength to the martyr in his time of need.

5. To judge from the evidence of the second through fourth centuries, the ancient Christians did not believe in what is commonly called "eternal security" or "once saved, always saved." Although I personally accept this doctrine, it is nonetheless clear that the earliest church fathers believed true salvation could be lost. Apostasy brings eternal condemnation, and a Christian who denies the Lord will be judged. In this belief the fathers were only trying to take literally the words of Jesus in Matthew 10:33, "Whoever denies me before men, I also will deny before my Father who is in heaven," or Mark 8:38, "Whoever is ashamed of me and of my words in this adulterous and sinful generation, of him will the Son of Man also be ashamed when he comes in the glory of his Father with the holy angels." The first Christian writer to lay out a formal doctrine of assured perseverance in salvation, grounded in God's eternal decree of predestination, was Augustine of Hippo in his treatise *On the Gift of Perseverance*, written around AD 428.

6. Prisons in Roman times provided absolutely no comforts. The conditions were more like Nazi or North Korean concentration camps than the humane prisons we know today. Typically a Roman jail had, in addition to its more-tolerable rooms, a dreaded high-security inner

In fact, the majority of the Christians were strangled in the prison—whomever the Lord ordained to die like that to display his glory. Yet some, tortured so cruelly it seemed impossible for them to survive even with extensive medical care, still managed to stay alive in the prison. Though they were deprived of any human attention, the Lord provided the refreshment they needed, empowering them physically and spiritually so they could urge on the other believers with words of encouragement. However, some of the young people were arrested only recently, and their bodies had never been mistreated before. They couldn't bear the weight of imprisonment, so they died in jail.

Pothinus

The blessed Pothinus, more than ninety years old and physically very frail, was the man entrusted with the bishop's ministry at Lyons. Though scarcely able to breathe due to his bodily weakness, he had such an intense desire for martyrdom that his strength was renewed by his spiritual eagerness. Thus, he too was dragged before the judgment seat—this old man whose body was worn out by age and disease, yet whose life had been carefully preserved so Christ might triumph in it.

Now when the soldiers brought him before the governor, Pothinus gave a good witness despite the civic leaders and the whole mob shouting all kinds of abuse at him as if he were Christ himself.

"Who is the Christian God?" the governor inquired.

"If you seek in a worthy manner, you will find out," Pothinus replied.

At this the crowd began to drag him around, raining down blows mercilessly from every direction. The bystanders punched and kicked him with no regard for his old age, while those who stood farther away hurled at him whatever they could grab. Everyone thought it would be a great religious travesty if they held anything back in their vicious attack on Pothinus. They imagined that by beating

---

dungeon (cf. Acts 16:24). This underground area possessed no ventilation, light, or sanitary facilities. In many cases it was just a pit into which people were tossed through a trapdoor in the ceiling. The darkness at night was absolute. Human waste piled up and was not removed. Rats and fleas were everywhere. Disease was rampant. The stifling heat was unbearable in summer, and water was scarce, resulting in desperate dehydration. At times the air became so polluted in the overcrowded conditions that prisoners (the elderly in particular) simply could not obtain enough oxygen and slowly suffocated. Detainees were confined in such places for weeks, months, or even years at a time while they awaited trial. Often they were chained in uncomfortable positions and left to languish. Rations were entirely inadequate, resulting in near starvation, which is why Christians visiting their fellow believers in prison and attending to their needs was such a vital ministry. Indeed, to fail in this responsibility was to disobey the direct command of Jesus and be guilty enough to go to hell (Matt. 25:35–46). Because prison life was so hard in Roman times, a special term developed for those who had been incarcerated or tortured without being executed as a martyr: "confessors," those who maintained their confession of faith amid incredible adversity.

him up they would avenge their gods' honor. At last Pothinus was thrown in prison, scarcely breathing. And two days later, he breathed his last.

The Deniers Are Ashamed

At that time God gave us a great gift. Jesus's immeasurable mercy was shown in a way that rarely occurs among the Christian brotherhood yet certainly isn't beyond his ability to achieve. It came about that those who denied their faith during the initial arrests still found themselves imprisoned with everyone else, and since they shared in all the same hardships of incarceration, their denials at the outset didn't really gain them anything. So whereas those who confessed their Christian identity were jailed on the sole charge of being Christians and no other charges were brought against them, the deniers were held as murderers and common criminals, which meant that they—unlike the confessors—ended up getting a double punishment. For the confessors' burden was lightened by their joy in martyrdom, their hope in God's promises, their love for Christ, and the presence of the Father's Spirit. In contrast, the deniers were greatly tormented by their conscience, which produced such a sad demeanor in them that they were clearly distinguishable from the others as they went about. The confessors strode forward joyously, with glory and great favor mingled on their faces. Even the chains encircling them were a lovely ornament—like a royal bride adorned in a gold-fringed robe of many colors [Ps. 45:13–14]. Together they exuded such a "sweet aroma of Christ" [2 Cor. 2:15] that some people thought they had actually anointed themselves with literal perfume.

But the deniers couldn't even lift their heads. They were dejected . . . ugly . . . full of disgrace. Moreover, they were ridiculed by the pagans as despicable cowards. By taking on the label of "murderer," they had forfeited the family name that is truly honorable, glorious, and life-giving. When the other imprisoned Christians saw this, their resolve was strengthened. And further, any newcomers to the prison confessed their faith without hesitation and paid no attention to the Devil's tempting arguments.

[At this point Eusebius skips ahead in his excerpt of the letter. More will be said in a moment about what happened to the deniers.]

Triumph in the Amphitheater

From then on the martyrs' deaths began to take every possible form. They offered to the Father one multicolored crown woven out of many different flowers. Certainly it is fitting that such distinguished champions, after they endured this diverse contest and won a great victory, should be awarded the splendid crown of immortality.

So the day came when Maturus, Sanctus, Blandina, and Attalus were led in to face the wild beasts—and also to serve as a public display of the pagans' universal inhumanity. Now, this day of animal-fighting games was specially arranged for the Christians. In the amphitheater Maturus and Sanctus once again faced every kind of punishment—as if they hadn't already suffered the whole range of tortures before! Or maybe it would be better to say, it was as if they'd already tossed their opponent out of the ring in numerous previous matches, and now they were vying for the victor's crown itself. Once again they endured a gauntlet of whips[7] as is customary there, and mauling by wild beasts, and everything else the crazed horde demanded with shouts that rained down from all corners of the arena. And to top it off the martyrs were put on the iron chair, where their frying bodies gave the crowd its fill of savory smoke. But the onlookers didn't stop there. They kept on raging, driven insane by their desire to overcome the martyrs' endurance. Yet they never heard a single thing from Sanctus except what he'd been saying from the beginning: the cry of his confession, "I am a Christian!" At last, after the martyrs survived the great contest for a very long time and were made a spectacle before the world all day long (including the afternoon, instead of the assortment of gladiator fights),[8] they were sacrificed to God.

As for Blandina, she was hung on a pole so wild animals could be turned loose to eat her as food.[9] The sight of Blandina hanging there in the posture of a crucified person, and the intense way she was praying, caused utmost devotion to well up in the other martyrs suffering the ordeal. Gazing at Blandina in the midst of their own agony, their outward eyes saw, through their sister, the one who was crucified

7. The Roman spectacle of hunting games included certain people called *bestiarii* who were trained to fight wild animals and had weapons such as whips, while other *bestiarii* were simply condemned criminals thrown naked and defenseless to the beasts. Sometimes these unfortunates had to run a course across the arena floor while the hunters lined up and cracked whips across their shoulders. Tertullian refers to this sort of punishment in his letter *To the Martyrs* (see chap. 9 below).

8. Normally the cruel hunting games took place in the morning and were concluded by midday. During the lunch break some spectators would go find food, while others ate a sack lunch and stayed to watch the executioners finish off the half-dead victims who had been mauled by wild beasts (as depicted, for example, in the martyrdom of Perpetua and her companions). After lunch, the main show would begin, when more-evenly matched gladiators fought each other. In the case of Lyons, however, a special full-day animal show had been arranged for the Christians. These believers were publicly tortured and exposed to fierce animals all day long for the citizens' entertainment. No gladiator combat was arranged for the afternoon; the spectacle of prolonged torture simply continued. In this we are reminded the Roman Empire was extremely brutal—not nearly as noble as it is often made out to be in popular depictions. Life was cheap in that culture, and collective violence was relished. Christianity, of course, introduced a very different attitude toward the sanctity of human life.

9. Today a post stands in the Amphitheater of the Three Gauls in Lyons to commemorate this event (see fig. 6.2 on p. 81).

Figure 6.2. Wooden post in honor of Saint Blandina. Amphitheater of the Three Gauls, Lyons, France. (Otourly/Wikimedia Commons)

for them. Christ was seeking to convince[10] the believers that everyone who suffers for his glory has eternal fellowship with the living God.

But since the animals refused to attack Blandina that day, she was taken down from the pole and cast back into prison to await another ordeal, so that by triumphing in those upcoming matches she might put into effect the judgment already decreed against the crooked serpent. In this way she could spur on her brothers— even she, who was petite and weak and despised. For Blandina had clothed herself in Jesus Christ, her mighty and invincible champion. Having knocked out her opponent after many rounds, she won an imperishable crown in her hour of trial.

The crowd also demanded vehemently that Attalus be brought forward, since he was famous around town. He entered the fray as a ready contestant, because his conscience was clear before the Lord. For Attalus had been superbly trained in the disciplines of the Christian army and had always been a model of truth to us. He was marched all around the amphitheater behind a man with a sign that said in Latin, "Here is Attalus the Christian." This really got the crowd worked up to a frenzy against him. However, when the governor discovered Attalus was a Roman citizen, he ordered him brought back to the prison where some of the

10. It has been argued by certain scholars that Blandina, not Christ, is the proper subject of the verb "to convince" in this passage. However, the meaning seems to be that the invisible Christ is conveying a message *through* Blandina's visible posture and actions, so he is the one doing the convincing. Most translators have understood the sentence the way I translate it here.

others were as well; for the governor had written to the emperor about the citizens and was awaiting his decision.

The Deniers Are Reborn

This waiting period, though, wasn't a wasted and unproductive time for the martyrs who were returned to jail. Through the example of their endurance, Christ's immeasurable mercy was revealed: the dead were restored to life by the living! The martyrs ministered grace to those who had failed to bear witness, and so the virgin mother rejoiced greatly at recovering alive her stillborn babies.[11] For through the martyrs, most of the deniers were reconceived and reimpregnated in the womb and restored to new life, learning at last how to confess. Alive now and fortified, they came before the judgment seat so the governor could question them again. And God, who does not desire the death of the sinner but shows favor to the repentant,[12] made this moment sweet.

The emperor had sent back his decree that the Christians should be tortured to death, but if someone denied his faith he could be set free. So at the beginning of the festival in Lyons, which was very crowded because representatives from all the tribes attended it,[13] the governor summoned the blessed martyrs to assemble before

11. The motherhood analogy depicts the deniers as spiritual offspring who are spontaneously aborted before full term—but then, miraculously, they are reimplanted in the womb and come to life again as healthy children. Note that the term "virgin mother" here is a reference not to Mary but to the Christian church, of which Mary is a symbol. The word "virgin" should be taken to mean "chaste, pure," as in Ephesians 5:26–27. The idea of the church as a symbolic mother figure can be seen in the writings of Irenaeus, the bishop of Lyons, when he wrote that the Holy Spirit is found only in the true church and whoever does not partake of the Spirit is not "nourished into life from the mother's breasts" (*Against Heresies* 3.24.1, in Roberts, Donaldson, and Coxe, eds., *Apostolic Fathers*, 458). More famously, the third-century African bishop Cyprian said, "He can no longer have God for his Father who has not the Church for his mother" (*On the Unity of the Church* 6, in *Hippolytus, Cyprian, Caius, Novatian, Appendix*, ed. Alexander Roberts, James Donaldson, and A. Cleveland Coxe, *Ante-Nicene Fathers* [1885; repr., Peabody, MA: Hendrickson, 1994], 5:423). In other words, salvation can be found not among separatists and heretics but only within the true body of Christ. The Protestant Reformer John Calvin used similar imagery when he wrote that the church is the mother "into whose bosom God is pleased to gather his sons, not only that they may be nourished by her help and ministry as long as they are infants and children, but also that they may be guided by her motherly care until they mature and at last reach the goal of faith." Like Cyprian, Calvin longed that "those to whom [God] is Father the Church may also be Mother" (*Institutes* 4.1.1, in *Calvin: Institutes of the Christian Religion*, ed. John T. McNeill, Library of Christian Classics 21 [Philadelphia: Westminster, 1960], 1012; cf. 1016). All of these ideas stem from the biblical assertion in Galatians 4:26 that "the Jerusalem above" (which symbolizes the church) is "free, and she is our mother."

12. The author seems to have in mind texts like Ezekiel 18:23, 32; 33:11; 1 Timothy 2:4; and 2 Peter 3:9.

13. As noted in the introductory comments to this chapter, the amphitheater where the martyrdoms took place was part of a religious and governmental complex at Lyons called the Sanctuary of the Three Gauls. The sanctuary served as the focal point of political unity for the Gallic tribes

the judgment seat so he could make a big display of them and flaunt them before the crowds (for that was why he was examining them again). And everyone who appeared to have Roman citizenship, he beheaded; the rest he threw to the beasts.

But Christ was greatly glorified when those who had denied him at first suddenly began confessing him again, to the pagans' utter surprise. For the deniers were examined individually as if they were actually going to be released—but then they confessed Christ and were added to the ranks of the martyrs. However, some of the deniers remained outside the church: those who never possessed any trace of faith at all, who had never even touched the "wedding garment" [Matt. 22:11–13], who gave no thought to the fear of God. Instead they tarnished the reputation of the Way by their behavior. These men are the "sons of destruction" [John 17:12].[14]

Alexander Joins Attalus

All the others, though, were included in the church. Among those being questioned was a man named Alexander, a doctor from Phrygia. He had been employed for many years in Gaul, so he was known to almost everyone for his love of God and his bold preaching—in fact, he had a share of the same spiritual gifting as the apostles [Acts 4:29–31]. As Alexander was standing before the judgment seat, he was using gestures to encourage his fellow Christians to maintain their confession. Thus it was clear to the bystanders that he was, so to speak, a spiritual mother giving birth. Now the pagans were extremely annoyed that the deniers had started

---

that had been conquered by Rome and incorporated into the empire. Every year a festival was held in August to worship the emperor for whom that month is named—Caesar Augustus. An important congress was held in conjunction with the festival, attended by representatives of the sixty tribes. As a time of renewed devotion to the imperial cult, it was a natural opportunity to heap abuse on a competing and seemingly foreign religion, like Christianity.

14. Both of these scriptural passages describe people who appear to be inside Jesus's group and have his favor yet end up being rejected by him. Similarly, those who did not continue to confess their Christian faith during the persecution at Lyons were viewed as apostate unbelievers. Such criticism seems unnecessarily harsh to us today. Perhaps these folks did believe in the Lord but were too weak to face the tortures their brothers and sisters did. In the centuries ahead, the ancient church would be severely divided over what to do with persecuted Christians who had given in under pressure—known as "traitors" or "the lapsed." Two parties emerged: those who wished to grant mercy and restoration, and those who believed the deniers had so defiled the purity of Christ's bride that they could never again function as leaders. This division led to the formation of a breakaway sect of moral rigorists called the Donatists, who would not accept any leaders who had lapsed. But the more merciful viewpoint, led by figures such as Cyprian of Carthage and Augustine of Hippo, eventually won the day. They said the church must be a hospital for broken sinners, not just a haven for perfect saints. Nevertheless, the letter from Lyons and Vienne is actually quite strict: whoever does not maintain his confession to the end is viewed as eternally condemned. Such beliefs were based on passages like Matthew 10:22, "You will be hated by all for my name's sake. But the one who endures to the end will be saved." It was difficult for the church in the era of martyrdom to understand how someone who had cursed the name of the Lord Jesus Christ could be a true Christian.

confessing again, so they shouted that Alexander was to blame. The governor made him come forward and demanded to know who he was. When Alexander replied, "A Christian," the enraged governor condemned him to the beasts.

The next day Alexander entered the ring along with Attalus (for the governor was exposing Attalus to the beasts once more to please the mob). In the amphitheater the two men were made to endure the full range of the instruments invented for torture. They suffered through the most terrible struggle imaginable until at last they were sacrificed to God. Alexander didn't groan or make any sound at all but only fellowshipped with God in his heart; while Attalus, when he was fastened to the iron chair and was being scorched from head to toe—even as the stench of his burning flesh was rising from his body—shouted to the crowd in Latin, "Look at what you're doing! *This* is eating human flesh! We Christians aren't cannibals! And we don't practice any other evils either!" When he was asked what God's name is, he replied, "God doesn't have a name like people do."[15]

Blandina and Ponticus

At last, on the final day of the gladiator games, Blandina was brought in again, along with a boy of about fifteen named Ponticus. Every day they had been forced to watch the others being tortured in the arena while the pagans pressed them to swear to the idols. Because the martyrs remained steadfast and rejected these attempts, the crowd grew enraged at them like savage animals. They felt no pity for the boy's age nor any respect for the woman's gender. The evildoers cast Blandina and Ponticus to all the hideous torments, subjecting them to one form of torture after another all day long. They kept trying to force the martyrs to swear to the idols, demanding it over and over, but it was no use! Ponticus was so inspired by his sister's exhortations that even the pagans could see she was urging him on and upholding him. After he nobly endured all the tortures, he gave up his spirit.

The blessed Blandina was the last martyr of all. Like an aristocratic mother exhorting her children to faithfulness, she sent them ahead of her triumphantly to the King. Then, retracing the footsteps of her children's many trials, she hurried on to join them. Blandina rejoiced and took delight in her death, considering herself not to be thrown to wild beasts but invited to a wedding banquet. After enduring the whips, the fierce animals, and the frying pan, she was finally wrapped in an encumbering net and set before a bull. The creature knocked her around for so long that she lost awareness of her surroundings, thanks to her

---

15. It is not exactly clear how this statement fits into the flow of the narrative. Apparently Attalus thought his accusers were reducing the status of the one true God by attributing a common name to him. In this letter Attalus is portrayed as a "pillar of truth"—a man with sound theology who engages in what we would call "apologetics" toward his pagan adversaries.

heavenly hope, her firm grasp on what she believed, and her spiritual intimacy with Christ.[16] At last Blandina was sacrificed, and the pagans were forced to admit that in their experience no woman had ever suffered so many tortures as fearsome as these.

Desecration of the Martyrs' Corpses

Yet even all this wasn't enough to satisfy the pagans' rabid cruelty toward the saints. For those wild and barbarous tribes—stirred up by the Wild Beast himself—were incapable of controlling their urges. Their senseless violence took a new form in the things they did to the bodies. The people weren't even ashamed of their defeat by the martyrs, because they lacked the basic human intelligence to realize what had happened. Instead, their natural instincts were inflamed like brute beasts. Both the governor and the people exhibited the same unfair hatred toward us, so that in this way the Scripture might be fulfilled, "Let the wicked continue to do evil, and the righteous continue to do good" [Rev. 22:11].

The Christians who had been strangled in prison were thrown to the dogs. Guards carefully watched the bodies day and night to keep us from providing any sort of burial. Next they pitched out whatever human remains the beasts or the fire had left behind—some of it torn to bits, some charred to a crisp—along with the severed heads of those who were decapitated and their torsos. All this the pagans likewise left unburied, guarding it with a detachment of soldiers for many days. Some of the passers-by snorted and gnashed their teeth at the remains like they wanted to take even further revenge on the bodies. Others mocked them with derisive laughter, exalting their gods as the source of the martyrs' punishment. Even those who were kinder and seemed to have a measure of pity still criticized us intensely, saying, "Where is their God? These people chose faithfulness to their religion over their own lives—but what good did it do them?"

So these were the various ways the pagans responded. As for us, we experienced great sorrow that we couldn't bury the bodies in the ground. Nothing could change this: the cover of darkness didn't help, bribes didn't persuade the guards, our pleading didn't shame them into action. The pagans kept a close watch at every turn, thinking they'd get a big advantage by preventing the burials.

[Eusebius skips a few lines and then resumes.]

Therefore the martyrs' bodies were desecrated in every possible way to set a public example. After being left out in the elements for six days, they were set

---

16. Here is an obvious example of the author's theologizing of the events observed in the arena. Blandina was knocked unconscious by the rampaging bull, but this is given a more pious interpretation. So too, Perpetua is said to be caught up in the Spirit after she is trampled by a wild cow (see chap. 8 below). While we cannot dispute the spiritual rapture these women may have experienced, we must also recognize the physiological effects caused by trauma to their bodies.

ablaze and burned down to ashes. Then the evildoers swept the ashes into the Rhône River that flows nearby, so that not a single piece of the martyrs' bodies would remain on earth. This the pagans did as if they'd be able to defeat God and thwart the bodily resurrection of the martyrs.

"Let's prevent the Christians from having any hope of resurrection," the pagans said in their own words. "These people who introduce this strange new cult among us place all their hope in resurrection. They despise every torture and are ready to face death with joy. Now let's see if they will rise again! Let's see if their God can help them and deliver them from our hands!"[17]

---

17. In the ancient church, the hope of bodily resurrection at the second coming of Christ was a central doctrine. The early Christian view of salvation did not focus attention where we tend to today, on Christ's payment for sin at the cross. Though that idea certainly was not missing, the church fathers put special emphasis on the triumphant victory of Jesus over death and the power of Satan by his resurrection and ascension to the Father's right hand. This perspective, already seen clearly in Acts 2:24–36 and 1 Corinthians 15, became part of the essential preaching and creedal proclamation of the church. We should remember that most early Christians were simple, illiterate people. Many were slaves who were ill-treated during their earthly lives. They did not understand complex theology. What they knew was this: when they died, or when they lost a Christian loved one, the hope of bodily resurrection awaited the deceased person through their victorious Lord. Inscriptions from the cemeteries of the early Christians make this abundantly clear. The dead are frequently said to be "in peace," and the confident assertion "may you live" appears often as well. "To my good and sweetest husband Castorinus," said a Christian wife to her sixty-one-year-old husband on his gravestone, "you are well-deserving. Live in God!" "To dear Cyriacus, our sweetest son," cries another epitaph across the centuries, "may you live in the Holy Spirit" (see J. Spencer Northcote and W. R. Brownlow, *Roma Sotterranea: Or, An Account of the Roman Catacombs*, Part Second: Christian Art [London: Longmans, Green, and Co., 1879], 80–81 [translation modified]). An echo of this ancient confidence is found in the last line of the Apostles' Creed: "I believe in . . . the resurrection of the body and the life everlasting. Amen." Consider the glorious hope you share with Castorinus and Cyriacus—as well as Blandina, Sanctus, and the martyrs of Lyons and Vienne—the next time you recite the historic creed.

7

The Scillitan Martyrs

Africa Takes Its Stand

On July 17, 180, the governor of a province in North Africa, P. Vigellius Saturninus, became the first Roman persecutor to draw Christian blood on a continent that would soon become famous for its martyrs. Twelve commoners from Scilli, a village near Carthage,[1] were hauled into the governor's personal office and interrogated before him. He comes across to us as reasonable, offering the Christians a merciful opportunity to bypass a death sentence. Yet the lone alternative he presented was entirely on his own terms: worship and pray to the gods for the welfare of the emperor. To the seven men and five women on trial that day, this would have meant a fundamental rejection of Christianity, whose first commandment proclaims, "You shall have no other gods before me. . . . You shall not bow down to them or serve them, for I the LORD your God am a jealous God" (Exod. 20:3, 5). Governor Saturninus was urging the Christians to do the one thing they could never do.

The *Acts of the Scillitan Martyrs* has come down to us in the terse genre of "acts" that we have already encountered in chapter 5 with Justin and his companions. Though it is based on a court transcript, there are hints of a theological perspective as well. For example, the explicit mention of Paul, a

1. See the introduction to chap. 8 for more about this prominent ancient city.

quotation from 1 Timothy, and an emphasis on spiritual unity indicate these African Christians were especially devoted to Pauline thought. Another interesting aspect of the text is that it is written in Latin and thus stands as the first surviving example of a Christian document in that tongue. The African writers of the ancient church, such as Tertullian, Cyprian, and above all Augustine, would soon take the Latin language to new heights in the service of Christian faith and doctrine.

Though the individual Scillitan martyrs remain obscure to us, and other than their leader Speratus we can say virtually nothing about them, they nonetheless speak volumes about an emerging trend within African Christianity. Their utter rejection of not only pagan worship but the very world in which they lived would become a distinctive of the North African church, which was prone to fanaticism and dogmatism. Martyrs were elevated as Christian superstars in whose grace-filled footsteps many imitators sought to follow—some with wisdom and dignity, like Perpetua, others with an extremism that could only be considered suicidal. And when the era of martyrdoms finally passed, the African church found itself terribly divided between those who wanted to forgive and those who could only condemn the believers who didn't have the stamina to hold fast under persecution.

As you engage with the text below, consider the way these early Christians wrestled with the age-old dilemma of how to be in the world but not of it. Though at times it can be difficult to know where to draw the line, the Scillitan martyrs instinctively sensed they could have no part in worshiping demons alongside the Lord Jesus Christ.

The Acts of the Scillitan Martyrs

The Arraignment of the Accused

On July 17 in the year that Praesens was consul for the second time, along with Claudian,[2] the following persons were brought into the governor's office at Carthage: Speratus, Nartzalus, Cittinus, Donata, Secunda, and Vestia. The governor Saturninus said, "You can earn the pardon of our lord the emperor if you return to a proper way of thinking."

2. "Consuls" were a pair of powerful elected officials in the old Roman Republic, though under the empire they were appointed by the emperors to a more symbolic office. The Romans used the consulship, which rotated annually, as a means of recording years. The year during which Praesens and Claudian were the two consuls was the year we refer to as AD 180. The emperor at that time was Commodus.

Interrogation of Speratus

Speratus said, "We have never done wrong. We have never carried out an evil deed. We have never uttered a curse. Instead, whenever we were abused, we gave thanks, for we honor our own Emperor."

"We too are religious," Governor Saturninus replied, "and our religion is simple: we swear by the divine spirit of our lord the emperor and offer prayers for his well-being—which is what you should do as well."[3]

"If you will just offer me the chance to speak undisturbed, I will tell you the mystery of simple faith."

"I'm not going to give you the opportunity to start slandering our sacred rites! Instead, swear by the divine spirit of our lord the emperor."

"I do not recognize the empire of this world," Speratus said. "Rather I serve the God whom no one has seen nor can see with physical eyes [1 Tim. 6:16]. Yet I have committed no theft, and if I buy something I pay the tax on it—for I recognize my Lord, who is 'Emperor' over kings and the entire human race" [Rom. 13:6–7].

Interrogation of the Other Martyrs

To the rest of the prisoners Governor Saturninus said, "All of you, abandon this persuasion!"

"An evil persuasion," Speratus remarked, "is to commit murder or bear false witness."[4]

"Have no part in this man's insanity!" said the governor.

"We have no one to fear but the Lord our God, who is in heaven," Cittinus replied.

"Give honor to Caesar as Caesar but fear to God," Donata added [cf. Mark 12:17].

Vestia testified: "I am a Christian."

Secunda also said, "What I am, that I wish to remain."

"Do you intend to continue as a Christian?" Governor Saturninus asked Speratus.

"I am a Christian," Speratus declared. And everyone voiced their agreement with him.

"So you wish no time for deliberation about your decision?" asked the governor.

"In a cause so just as this, no deliberation is needed."

"What do you have in your satchel?"

---

3. The same demand was made of Bishop Polycarp, and just like the Christians of Scilli, he utterly refused to pay homage to the emperor's *genius*, which was viewed as a demonic spirit (see chap. 4 above).

4. Speratus makes an objection here that a few years later Tertullian will emphasize as well in his *Apology*. The Romans were punishing the Christians solely for their beliefs—that is, for following the name of Christ itself—not for any specific misdeed. This was a departure from normal legal procedures by which a person would have to be convicted of an actual crime such as murder, theft, or sedition before receiving punishment. The legal policy by which the "name of Christ" was illegal had been established by Emperor Trajan (see the introduction).

"Books and letters of Paul, a righteous man," Speratus replied.[5]

"You are granted a thirty-day reprieve," the governor said. "Think it over."

But Speratus said once more, "I am a Christian!" and the others said it too.

Pronouncement of Sentence

Governor Saturninus read out his decision from a tablet: "Whereas Speratus, Nartzalus, Cittinus, Donata, Vestia, Secunda, and the others confess themselves to be living according to the Christian religion, and since they obstinately persisted even when offered the chance of returning to Roman ways, it is proper that they are to be punished with the sword."

"We give thanks to God!" Speratus cried.

"Today we are martyrs in heaven! Thanks be to God!" Nartzalus added.[6]

Governor Saturninus also had the following proclaimed by a herald: "I have commanded that Speratus, Nartzalus, Cittinus, Veturius, Felix, Aquilinus, Laetantius, Januaria, Generosa, Vestia, Donata, and Secunda are to be led forth to execution."[7]

"Thanks be to God!" they all exclaimed. And straightaway they were beheaded for the name of Christ. Amen.

---

5. Evidently Speratus was carrying a *capsa*, either a cylindrical case that could contain scrolls or a leather satchel for small volumes with bound pages. In early Christian times, the older writing format of the scroll was quickly being replaced by the adoption of the codex, that is, the book. But the ancient church in Speratus's day did not collect all of its inspired writings into a single codex like modern Bibles. That development did not begin to happen until the fourth century, and even then it would have been rare. For example, the famous conversion scene from Augustine's *Confessions* depicts him picking up not a complete Bible but a book of Paul's letters to find the voice of God (8.12.29). Virtually all ancient Christians encountered the canon of Scripture as a collection of scrolls or codices that would be kept in a cabinet. Some groupings of biblical materials quickly appeared together in a single volume, such as the four Gospels or the Pauline Epistles. Other books remained a matter of debate for many years as the early church determined what belonged in its cabinet. When Speratus was asked about his satchel, he may well have possessed the letters of Paul and the book of Acts. He also may have been carrying certain writings that recounted heroic stories about the apostle Paul, which came to be compiled in a work known as the *Acts of Paul and Thecla*. The church father Tertullian attests that this text had become known in Africa at the time. In addition, the martyrdom account from chap. 2 would be another likely candidate for Speratus's library.

6. In martyrological literature, the expression "Thanks be to God!" (*Deo gratias*) serves as the usual exclamation of the martyr upon receiving a sentence of death. The statement comes from 1 Corinthians 15:57, where Paul uses it to express the joy of conquering death through the hope of resurrection. The phrase eventually became a common Christian name in Africa. For example, Saint Deogratias was a bishop of Carthage in the 400s AD.

7. The six additional names in this list probably refer to Christians who were tried and convicted in this same persecution but whose personal interrogation by Saturninus was not, for whatever reason, included in the earlier part of the document. Names ending in -*us* are male and -*a* are female. The names also indicate these believers were of the lower classes, possibly including slaves, and probably of indigenous Punic descent rather than the Romanized cultural elite. Speratus appears to be the only literate person among them. As such, he may have been the Christians' catechist, or teacher, like Saturus in the Perpetua account.

8

Perpetua and Felicity

Heroines of Faith

It would be hard to find a more noble and heroic woman in all of church history than Vibia Perpetua of Carthage, who was arrested for her faith and thrown to the wild beasts in AD 203. If you have never met her, it's time you did. You will be impressed.

A personal encounter with Perpetua is possible for us today because she, unlike most women in the ancient church, has left a written record of her thoughts. Since she was an aristocrat, Perpetua had the ability to read and write. And since she was a woman of profound devotion to Jesus Christ, her prison diary was cherished enough by subsequent generations to be copied by countless hands until it reached the modern age. The entire Latin text, as preserved in nine medieval manuscripts, is translated below.

Perpetua was about twenty-two—the age of a college senior—when she was executed in the amphitheater of Carthage in Roman North Africa (modern-day Tunisia). The city was as old as Rome, having been founded by sea explorers from faraway Phoenicia around the same time that shepherds were beginning to colonize Rome's seven hills. As the Romans rose to power, they quickly came to view Carthage as one of their main rivals. Eventually the Romans defeated Carthage in the Punic Wars and razed it to the ground. The city lay abandoned for decades until Caesar Augustus decided to renew its former glory. By Perpetua's day, Carthage was once again a thriving metropolis with a thousand-year history, a city whose size and splendor were second only to Rome in the western half of the empire. Exports of grain and olive oil had made the province rich. Life was sweet for the Roman aristocracy of North Africa. We won't properly understand Perpetua until we realize how much she gave up when she relinquished her life in front of thirty thousand spectators.

The full extent of Perpetua's biography is lost to us, but we do know she came from a noble family, was married, and was nursing an infant son when she met her end through martyrdom. Although her devotion to the Lord Jesus is obvious, the exact nature of her faith has puzzled historians. The church in Perpetua's context was marked by a movement called the New Prophecy. Scholars today call it Montanism after its founder Montanus, who began spreading his ideas in Asia Minor during the mid-second century. The primary distinctives of Montanism were divine prophecies received in a trance, a stricter lifestyle than most Christians observed, and the belief that the end times were at hand. Somehow this radical movement crossed the sea and came to the shores of Africa, where it appealed to the famous church father Tertullian for its earnest spirituality and austere morality. Although its beginnings under Montanus were somewhat cultish, the New Prophecy in Africa operated as a theologically orthodox and Spirit-led faction within the broader church. It claimed the material things of the world were passing away, God was speaking anew to his people, and no price—not even death—was too high to pay for the glory of Jesus's name. These are the ideals for which the smart and virtuous daughter of a pagan aristocrat found herself imprisoned in 203.

We should remember, of course, that Perpetua didn't go to her death alone. As was often the case with the ancient church martyrs, Perpetua journeyed down the road of persecution with a band of faithful companions. The scribes of antiquity saw fit to mention in the martyrdom account's title not only the noblewoman Perpetua but also the pregnant slave Felicity. Obviously these women were especially revered for the depth of their faith. Several male martyrs, including an educated man named Saturus, were among the group of jailed Christians as well. The prison diaries of Perpetua and Saturus form the nucleus of the text as we have it today.

The Christian community of Carthage so cherished these martyrs that their heroic deeds had to be captured in writing. Perpetua's and Saturus's firsthand recollections were set into an editorial framework that introduced the account and recorded the final outcome in the coliseum. Quite possibly, this skillful editor was Tertullian. With the kind of rhetorical eloquence and dramatic flair Tertullian so often displayed, the editor wove the martyrs' stories into a coherent narrative that was part history, part theology, and part apologetic.

Yet at heart, the editor's goal for the text was the same as Perpetua's: to glorify God before a watching world through the testimony of ultimate witness. The early Christians understood that faithfulness unto death has the power to edify the church long after ancient times have passed.

The Passion of Saints Perpetua and Felicity

The Editor's Introduction

Illustrations of true faith from earlier times[1] achieve two things: they testify to God's grace and work toward human edification. Such illustrations are set down in writing so that God might be honored and his people comforted by reading and recalling the very facts themselves. If this is so, shouldn't we also set forth new documents equally suitable for these purposes? Surely our current examples will one day become ancient as well! In the coming ages they will be very useful, though now they might enjoy less authority, because we tend to respect older things. But let those who would limit the power of the one Holy Spirit to certain times and seasons take notice! Sometimes accounts that come later must be considered superior to earlier things because they are closer to the end times, and thus closer to the abundant grace promised for the last period of the world. For "'in the last days,' says the Lord, 'I will pour out my Spirit upon all flesh, and their sons and daughters will prophesy. On my servants and handmaidens I will pour out my Spirit, and the young men will see visions, and the old men will dream dreams'" [Acts 2:17–18; cf. Joel 2:28].

We who recognize and respect not only these new prophecies but new visions too as being equally promised to us—we likewise consider all the other powers of the Holy Spirit as a provision for the church.[2] This same Spirit was sent to administer all his gifts to everyone, according to the way the Lord distributed them to each person. That is why it's absolutely essential to set forth exemplary stories and celebrate them by reading them for God's glory. We have to make sure no one with weak or hopeless faith should suppose that divine grace—the grace that honored us with martyrdoms and revelations alike—was present only

1. The editor is probably thinking of accounts such as Stephen's execution in Acts 7 or the martyr stories of Peter and Paul. He is saying that just like apostolic times, so in his own day (150 years later) the Holy Spirit is empowering the church for steadfastness under persecution.

2. Here we see evidence of the editor's Montanism. Followers of the New Prophecy like Tertullian believed they were living in the end times, so they expected to receive the outpouring of spiritual gifts promised for that age. In the third century AD, such beliefs were the hallmark of the Montanists. Yet, as we noted in the introduction above, the Carthaginian church at this time was very open to Spirit-led prophecy and miraculous gifts, so we should not make a hard-and-fast distinction between Montanists and other Christians.

in former times. The truth is, God always brings about what he has promised! And when he does, it serves as a testimony to unbelievers as well as an encouragement to Christians.

And so, my dear brothers and little children, "what we have heard and touched with our hands, we declare also to you" [1 John 1:1–3]. We proclaim it so you who actually witnessed these events may recall the glory of the Lord, and you who are now hearing about it for the first time may "have fellowship with" the holy martyrs—and through them, with our Lord Jesus Christ. To him belong bright splendor and high honor forever and ever. Amen.

Some young unbaptized believers[3] were arrested: the slave Revocatus, his fellow slave Felicity, Saturninus, and Secundulus. With them was Vibia Perpetua, a woman nobly born, educated in the liberal arts, and respectably married. She had a father and a mother and two brothers (one of whom was also an unbaptized believer like her), as well as an infant son, who was still nursing. Perpetua was about twenty-two years old.

From this point on, the whole description of her martyrdom is narrated in first person. It was written by her own hand and reflects her own point of view.

Perpetua under House Arrest

While we were still under house arrest, my father earnestly tried to dissuade me with words and kept seeking to break my resolution out of his great love for me.

"Father," I said, "let me give you an example. Do you see this vessel lying here, this little pitcher or whatever?"

"Yes, I see it," he replied.

"Could you call it by another name than what it really is?"

"No."

"It's the same with me. I can't be called anything other than what I am: a Christian."

3. A "Christian" in the ancient church was a person who had formally accepted all the responsibilities of the faith through water baptism. This rite, carried out before the gathered community, was the unmistakable sign of entrance into the church. It was an oath of allegiance and citizenship, akin to the oath a soldier swore when he left civilian life and entered the service of a new commander. People who were still exploring the Christian faith but hadn't yet crossed the definitive line of baptism were known as "catechumens." The root meaning of this word indicated they were undergoing preparatory instruction, like military recruits learning about the army but not yet sworn in and enlisted. The process of catechesis in Perpetua's day might take several years. Because she and her friends were known to be followers of Jesus but hadn't taken the step of baptism, they were put under house arrest for observation. Clearly, at this final stage of Perpetua's catechesis, she considers herself a fully committed Christian. Yet it is only after she and her companions are baptized that the authorities take them away to jail. Even today in countries where Christians are persecuted, it is the definitive act of water baptism that often elicits retaliation from families or the government.

That word "Christian" so infuriated my father that he lunged at me like he was going to tear out my eyes. But he just shook me and went away defeated, taking with him his arguments from the Devil.

Over the next few days my father was gone, and I thanked the Lord for that. I was actually comforted by his absence. During that time I was baptized. The Holy Spirit spoke to me and emphasized that I should not desire anything after this water except the endurance of my flesh.

Perpetua Is Jailed

It was only a short time later that we were thrown into the dungeon.[4] I was terrified, because I had never experienced such gloomy darkness before. What an awful day that was! The heat was stifling due to the overcrowded conditions, and the soldiers kept harassing me so I would pay them a bribe. But worst of all, I was tortured by worry for my baby the whole time I was there!

Then Tertius and Pomponius, those blessed deacons who ministered to us, offered a bribe so we would be sent to a better part of the jail to refresh ourselves for a few hours. We all left the dungeon and could tend to our needs. I nursed my baby, who was weak with hunger. Since I was so anxious about him I spoke to my mother and strengthened my brother, and I committed my son into their care. But then I started to waste away, because I could see they were consumed with worry for me. Oppressive fears like these tortured me for many days. At last I arranged for my baby to stay with me in the jail. Once my distress and concern for my child had eased up, I recovered my health right away. All of a sudden the prison became like a palace to me. I wanted to be there more than anywhere else!

The Vision of the Ladder to Heaven

Then my brother said to me, "Honorable sister, you are now greatly privileged.[5] You can ask for a vision to show you whether there is to be a martyrdom or a release."

4. Some scholars believe the Roman emperor Septimius Severus instigated this persecution. He was personally devoted to the Egyptian deity Serapis. To promote this god's worship, around AD 202 he issued an edict forbidding conversion to Christianity and Judaism. When Perpetua and her companions accepted Christian baptism, they placed themselves in formal violation of the imperial decree and were moved from house arrest to the prison. We should recognize, however, that in this particular instance the actions of the local governor were of greater relevance than a decree from distant Rome.

5. Perpetua's brother was a catechumen like her; yet apparently he wasn't baptized with her, so he wasn't taken to jail. In Roman times people were allowed to visit their friends and relatives behind bars, and here we see Perpetua's family doing so. (Alternatively, the reference might be to a brother in the Lord, not her physical sibling.) When the speaker calls Perpetua "greatly privileged," he is reflecting the early Christian belief that those imprisoned for their faith were uniquely chosen by God to receive a special measure of his Holy Spirit. This doctrine was based on the Gospel saying, "And when they bring you to trial and deliver you over, do not be anxious

I confidently promised him I would tell him, for I was certain I could speak with the Lord, whose immense blessings I had come to know well. "Tomorrow," I declared, "I will announce the answer to you." So I requested a vision, and this was what God revealed to me.

I saw a bronze ladder of astonishing height reaching all the way into heaven. It was so narrow that only one person could ascend it at a time. To the sides of this ladder all kinds of iron weapons were attached. There were swords and spears and hooks and curved daggers and darts. If people tried to climb without paying attention or looking upward, they would be gouged or snag their flesh on the blades.

At the foot of the ladder crouched a dragon of enormous size. It was ensnaring those who tried to climb, or frightening them so they wouldn't dare ascend. Saturus was the first to go up.[6] (He who had so often strengthened us Christians wasn't present when we were first arrested, but he subsequently gave himself up to the authorities.) Arriving at the top of the ladder, Saturus turned around and said to me, "I'm waiting for you, Perpetua. Just make sure the dragon doesn't bite you."

"He will not hurt me," I replied, "in the name of Jesus Christ."

From underneath the ladder, the dragon slowly stuck out its head like it was afraid of me. I trampled on its head and used it as my first step as I ascended the ladder. I discovered an expansive garden, in the middle of which sat a white-haired old man in shepherd's garments. He was a tall man and was milking sheep. All around him were many thousands of people in white robes. Raising his head and looking straight at me, the shepherd said, "You are welcome here, my child."

The man called me over and gave me a mouthful or so of the curd he was making from the milk. I took it into my cupped hands and ate it. Everyone standing around said, "Amen!" At the sound of their voices I woke up, still tasting a sweetness I cannot describe. Immediately I recounted this to my brother, and we realized there would be a martyrdom. From then on we no longer placed any hope in this world.

Perpetua Resists Her Father

A few days later a rumor circulated that we would be granted a hearing. Then my father arrived from the city, consumed with worry. He came to see me in order to

---

beforehand what you are to say, but say whatever is given you in that hour, for it is not you who speak, but the Holy Spirit" (Mark 13:11; cf. Matt. 10:19–20; Luke 12:11–12).

6. Who is this Saturus? Though he wasn't arrested at first, Perpetua tells us he professed his faith voluntarily and was thrown in jail with the others. Because of his close relationship with Perpetua, it has been suggested he was her husband—a figure who is otherwise absent from the story, which is somewhat hard to explain. However, the husband hypothesis hasn't gained much acceptance among scholars. The terminology used to describe Saturus more likely indicates he was the Christians' respected teacher. This father figure, who had held the converts' hands as they took their first baby steps into Christianity, now desired to walk alongside his fully grown children on their road to martyrdom.

shake my resolve. "Have pity on my gray hairs, daughter," he said. "Have pity on your father—if I am worthy to be called your father! With my own hands I tended you like a blossoming flower. I favored you over both your brothers. So don't cast me aside now to be scorned by men! Think of your brothers . . . your mother . . . your aunt . . . your son! He won't be able to live without you. Don't be so stubborn, or you're going to destroy us all! We'll never be able to speak freely again if anything happens to you."

My father said these things like any loving father would. He kissed my hands and threw himself at my feet. With tears in his eyes he didn't just call me his little girl but addressed me as a lady. I felt so sorry for my father's misfortune, because out of all my relatives he was the only one who wouldn't rejoice at my martyrdom.

I attempted to comfort him. "Everything that happens at my trial will be God's will," I said. "Rest assured that we are upheld not by our own strength in that moment but by God's." And so he left me, grief-stricken.

The day finally came when, while we were eating lunch, we were suddenly hustled to a hearing. We were taken to the main public square. Immediately the news ran through the whole neighborhood nearby, and a huge crowd gathered. We climbed up on the prisoners' platform. Everyone with me confessed their faith when asked. Then it was my turn. At that moment my father appeared there with my baby boy. He dragged me away from the steps and urged, "Perform the sacrifice! Have pity on your baby!"

The governor Hilarian, who had recently obtained jurisdiction over capital crimes when the previous governor Minucius Timinianus died, said to me, "Spare your gray-haired father! Spare your infant son! Just make a sacrifice for the emperors' well-being."

I replied, "I won't!"

"Are you a Christian?" Hilarian asked.

"I am a Christian," I declared.

My father kept trying to dissuade me, so at last Hilarian ordered him to be thrown down and beaten with a rod. My father's suffering hurt me as if I myself had been beaten! It broke my heart to see him endure such misery in his old age.

And so Hilarian sentenced us all to face the wild beasts. Rejoicing, we went down into the dungeon. Then, because my son had gotten used to staying with me in the prison and being nursed, I immediately sent Pomponius the deacon to ask my father for the baby. But my father refused to hand him over! However, God made sure the baby no longer desired to nurse and I didn't suffer any inflammation, so I wouldn't be burdened by anxiety for my son and pain in my breasts.[7]

7. As mothers who have nursed are aware, the sudden cessation of breastfeeding often leads to an infection of the milk ducts called mastitis. Perpetua's praise that God spared her this pain is one of the touching little details that make this story such a uniquely feminine account.

The Vision of Perpetua's Brother Dinocrates

A few days later when we were all praying, my voice suddenly broke out in the middle of the prayer, and I uttered the name "Dinocrates." I was amazed by this, because his name hadn't ever popped into my mind before. It pained me to remember what had happened to my brother. Right away I knew I was in a privileged position and ought to intercede for him. I began to pray fervently and groan deeply before the Lord. That very night I had a vision.

I saw Dinocrates come out of a shadowy place where many others were with him.[8] He was very hot and thirsty. His appearance was filthy and pale, and he still had the lesion on his face that he had when he died. (Dinocrates was my physical brother who died horribly at age seven from a facial lesion that caused absolute disgust in everyone.) So as I made my prayer for him I saw there was a great gulf between us and we couldn't cross over to each other. Where Dinocrates stood, there was a basin full of water, but its rim was higher than the height of a child. Dinocrates kept trying to stretch up and drink from it. I was so sad that even though this basin held water, its rim was too high for Dinocrates to get a drink. Then I woke up and knew my brother was in distress. Yet I believed by faith I could alleviate his suffering. I prayed for him every day until we were transferred to the military prison (for we were supposed to confront wild beasts at the military games in honor of Caesar Geta's birthday).[9] So I

8. The early Christians were not entirely clear about what happened to human beings between their physical death and bodily resurrection at the second coming. The souls of the dead were sometimes thought to go to a subterranean place called Hades to await the return of Christ. Because the righteous dead stayed in a better compartment of Hades called "Abraham's bosom" (Luke 16:22–23), they experienced a more tranquil wait than did the wicked, who could see, smell, and feel the lake of fire that awaited them. Although other church fathers believed the souls of all Christians went directly to paradise (Luke 23:43), many believed only a martyr could bypass Hades and go straight to the altar of God (Rev. 6:9). The fact that dead Christians had to wait in Hades (albeit in a better compartment) meant they were probably enduring a rather dank and gloomy existence under the earth. According to Tertullian, this waiting period in Hades might include some divine discipline to prepare the Christian for final judgment. Such ideas reflect a particularly apocalyptic and Jewish view of Hades, a view that Perpetua's vision likewise displays. Her dead brother Dinocrates is stuck in a dark and unhappy place until the prayers of the faithful release him. The notion that one's fate is not entirely sealed at death but can still tip in one direction or the other is stated even more clearly in the writings of Saint Augustine. Though the ancient church did not teach a full-blown doctrine of "purgatory," these hints about a believer's undetermined fate at death, or the value of prayer for the dead, would eventually lead in that direction. Purgatory became a formal doctrine of the Roman Catholic Church by a papal decree in 1254 and a council in 1274.

9. The Romans sponsored gladiator games in conjunction with festival days as a means of winning the favor of the masses. The mornings were devoted to animal shows, while gladiators fought in the afternoon. Though sometimes these games were funded at imperial expense, on other occasions local bureaucrats paid for them to gain public approval. In the case of Perpetua and her companions, it appears the governor Hilarian wanted to butter up Emperor Severus by putting on a show in honor of his youngest son, the fourteen-year-old Geta. (The term "caesar"

prayed for Dinocrates day and night with groans and tears, asking that God would grant my request.

And one day while we were in chains, I received another vision. I saw the same place as before, but now Dinocrates was clean and well dressed and refreshed. The tumor on his face was healed and scarred over. The rim of the basin I saw before had been lowered to the level of a child's waist, and my brother was drinking as much as he wanted. On the basin's rim there was a golden bowl. Dinocrates approached and began to drink from it, yet the bowl never went empty. When he had drunk enough water, Dinocrates began to play happily in the way children do. Then I awoke, knowing my brother had been delivered from his punishment.

A Prison Visit from Perpetua's Father

A few days after this, the junior officer in charge of the prison, named Pudens, began to honor us because he recognized the spiritual power at work in us. He began to let many people visit us so we could mutually encourage one another.

Now, as the day of the games approached, my father came to see me, overwhelmed with grief. He started tearing the whiskers from his beard and threw them on the ground.[10] He fell down on his face and cursed the years of his life, uttering the kind of words that would move heaven and earth. All this made me mourn for his unhappy old age.

The Vision of the Egyptian Gladiator

The day before we were to confront the beasts, I saw another vision. Pomponius the deacon came to the prison gate and knocked loudly. I went out and opened the gate

---

at this time meant Geta would one day reign as emperor—which he did for about a year, until his brother had him killed.) Once Hilarian had decided to sponsor the games, he needed bodies to throw to the beasts, so he determined to enforce Severus's decree against conversion to Christianity. The evidence suggests Hilarian was a religious conservative who viewed the Christians as an affront to the traditional pagan gods. Probably he expected to catch only some slaves and rabble in his deadly net, not a distinguished young noblewoman with a regal bearing. To prosecute such a refined lady was unseemly. This explains why Hilarian so vehemently urged Perpetua to recant, and why several other officials got flustered when she faced them down. They were used to executing the worst sort of criminals, not a high-class woman with the fire of God in her eyes.

10. The actions of Perpetua's father here are stunning. Roman men were never supposed to express grief through emotional outbursts or pulling their hair. Such dramatic gestures belonged solely to the realm of grieving women. Furthermore, Roman fathers had complete authority over their daughters—traditionally even the power of life and death. So for Perpetua's father to flail about at her feet while she remains placid is to overturn the normal social roles in their culture. Do not miss the poignancy of this moment. Perpetua's father clearly loved his little girl. Her death in the arena would be a family catastrophe, which explains why he was reduced to a blabbering fool in her presence. In light of this, it is all the more remarkable how Perpetua steadfastly resisted her father's pleas and remained true to her convictions. To belong to the Christian faith was to take on an allegiance that superseded even the ties of family (Luke 14:26).

to him. He was wearing a loose white robe and elaborate sandals. "Come, Perpetua," he said. "We're expecting you." So he offered me his hand and led me by a winding path through rough country. With difficulty we finally arrived at the amphitheater, gasping for breath. Pomponius led me into the middle of the arena and said, "Do not be afraid. I am with you, struggling alongside you." Then he went out.

I looked around at the enormous crowd of astonished onlookers. Surprisingly, no animals were set loose on me, even though I was condemned to face them. But then a fierce-looking Egyptian gladiator came out to confront me, along with his assistants. He made ready to fight me. However, some splendid young men approached me to serve as my own assistants and comrades-in-arms. I was disrobed and became male. My supporters began to rub me down with oil like gladiators do before a match. Across the way I saw the fearsome Egyptian rolling in the sand.

Just then a man of extraordinary size came forth—a man even taller than the highest point of the amphitheater.[11] He wore an unbelted purple toga with two stripes running across his chest, and his intricate sandals were wrought with silver and gold. He carried the rod of a gladiator referee, along with a green branch hung with golden apples. The referee called for silence and announced, "If this Egyptian wins, he will slay her with his sword. But if she conquers him, she will receive this branch." Then he stepped back.

The gladiator and I drew close. We began to pound each other with our fists. He lunged to grab my feet, but I kept smashing him in the face with my heel. Suddenly I was lifted high, as if I could walk on air, and I started punching him from that stance. Then I noticed he had paused, so I interlocked the fingers of my two hands and squeezed his head. He toppled face forward onto the ground, and I crushed his head underfoot.

The crowd began to cheer, and my comrades started singing psalms. I approached the referee and accepted the victory branch. He kissed me and said, "Peace be with you, daughter." Just as I was heading in triumph toward the Gate of Life, I awoke.[12]

11. The giant man represents an authority figure associated with gladiatorial combat. He seems to be wearing the kind of garment called a *toga picta*, a purple toga with gold embellishments. This garment was normally worn by triumphant generals but was also associated with the civic official whose job was to put on spectacular shows and games. At the same time, the man is described as a *lanista*, the owner of a gladiatorial school who sometimes acted as a referee during matches. In this capacity he carried a wooden rod as a symbol of his authority, with which he could separate the combatants. Clearly this figure is in charge of the bout between Perpetua and the Egyptian. He declares the terms of combat and rewards the victor.

12. The ancient amphitheater at Carthage had two points of access to the arena floor: the Porta Sanavivaria, or Gate of Life, for those who were victorious in combat or were spared after defeat, and the Porta Libitinensis, the Gate of Death through which the slain were dragged away (named for Libitina, the Roman goddess of funerals). Even though Perpetua knows that as a martyr she will be slain in the physical world, her vision reminds her she is not defeated but "alive" spiritually. For this reason she must exit through the gate that leads to eternal life.

This vision told me it wasn't wild beasts I'd be facing in the arena but the Devil himself. Yet I knew I would win the victory!

Here ends the account of how I conducted myself up to the day before the games. Concerning what happened at the games themselves, let someone else write about that if he sees fit.

Saturus's Account of His Heavenly Vision

Now the blessed Saturus also had a vision and made it known by writing it out himself. He said:

We suffered and had already put off the flesh. Four angels began to carry us toward the east, though without touching us with their hands. We were transported along, not on our backs looking upward, but as though we were climbing up a gradual slope. As soon as we were freed from this present world we saw an infinite expanse of light. Perpetua was at my side, and I said to her, "This is what the Lord promised us! Now we have gained the reward he promised."

While those four angels were carrying us along, a great space opened up before us, like a garden with rose bushes and all kinds of flowers. The trees were as tall as cypresses, and their leaves were continually floating down. In that garden we found four angels even more glorious than the first ones. As soon as they spotted us, they honored us and said to the other angels with admiration in their voices, "Look! They've arrived! Here they are!"

Now, when the first angels who were carrying us heard this, they grew frightened and set us down. Then we walked across the park by a broad path, where we found Jocundus and Saturninus and Artaxius, who were burned alive in the same persecution, and also Quintus, who became a martyr himself when he died in prison. We were asking them where they had been, when the four new angels said to us, "Wait, first come in here, and greet the Lord."

Then we approached a place whose walls seemed to be constructed of light. Four more angels stood at the building's gate, clothing everyone who entered in white robes. So we went in and heard a choir of voices endlessly singing, "Holy, holy, holy!" Sitting nearby we saw someone who looked like an old man with snow-white hair, yet with a youthful face. We couldn't see his feet. On his right and left stood four elders, and behind them were several other old men.

With great awe we drew near and remained motionless before the seated man's throne. The four angels lifted us up, and we kissed him, and he reached out and caressed our faces with his hand. Then the elders cried, "All rise!" So we stood up and exchanged the kiss of peace. The elders commanded us, "Go now, and have fun."

"Perpetua, you have what you always wanted!" I exclaimed.

"Thanks be to God," she replied. "Although I was happy while in the body, I'm even happier now."

Then we left the building. But outside the gate we saw Bishop Optatus on the right and the presbyter and teacher Aspasius on the left.[13] They were standing far apart from each other, looking sorrowful. They threw themselves at our feet and urged, "Reconcile us! For you've gone away and left us in a state of division."

But we cried, "What? Aren't you our bishop and our presbyter? How can *you* cast yourselves at *our* feet?" So our hearts were deeply troubled, and we embraced our friends. We took them over to the garden in the shade of a rose tree, where Perpetua began to converse with them in Greek. But as we were talking, the angels commanded them, "Leave the martyrs alone, and let them enjoy their rest! Whatever divisions have arisen between you two, it's time to put them aside." The angels brought our friends to a crisis point and said to Optatus, "Discipline your congregation! They come to you like a bunch of hooligans fighting for their teams at the chariot races!"

Then it seemed the angels wanted to close the gates. Suddenly we noticed a whole host of fellow Christians there, many of them martyrs. All of us were strengthened by an odor too wondrous to describe. The scent of it completely satisfied us. At last I woke up in great joy.

The Editor Describes the Other Martyrs

These, then, were the remarkable visions experienced by the supremely blessed martyrs Saturus and Perpetua. They wrote the accounts themselves. As for Secundulus, God called him to leave this world earlier than the others while he was still in prison. This was a special grace so he could be spared from facing the beasts. Instead his body was slain with a sword—though his soul certainly wasn't!

What about Felicity? She too received a special grace from the Lord, and it happened like this. She was pregnant when she was first arrested, and now she was in her eighth month. As the day of the show drew near she became deeply distressed. She feared her swollen belly would delay her martyrdom, because it is against the law to publicly punish pregnant women. Felicity didn't want to shed her holy and innocent blood later among a bunch of common criminals. The

13. We know nothing else about these two figures, nor do we know the basis of their dispute—though we might imagine the divisive issues surrounding the New Prophecy might have been at work here. The martyrs clearly defer to the authority of the bishop and presbyter. At the same time, we glimpse the spiritual power that the ancient church invested in the martyrs. They are especially Spirit-filled individuals, which means they have the ability to reconcile their fellow believers and even pronounce forgiveness of sins (John 20:22–23). See Tertullian's treatise *To the Martyrs* in chap. 9 for more on this theme.

burden weighed heavily on her fellow martyrs as well. They worried they'd have to leave behind such a fine companion to travel all alone on the road to hope. And so, two days before the games began, they joined together and poured out their prayer to the Lord in a single united groan.

Immediately after the prayer Felicity's birth pangs came on strong. Now, because preterm deliveries are naturally difficult, she was suffering great pain as she struggled to give birth. One of the prison workers saw it and said, "Ha! So you're suffering now? What are you going to do when they toss you to the beasts? Little did you think of them when you refused to sacrifice!"

Felicity answered, "Right now I must endure what I'm suffering. But on that day there will be someone inside me to bear the pain on my behalf, since I'll be suffering for him."

So Felicity gave birth to a little girl, and a Christian sister raised the baby as her own daughter.

Therefore, since the Holy Spirit permitted the events of this contest to be written down (and by permitting it, he willed it) I must carry out the command of that truly righteous woman Perpetua—indeed, not just her command, but the sacred trust of her final request.[14] Admittedly I am unworthy to write an addition to such a glorious story. Yet even so, I will add one more example of Perpetua's courage and inner beauty.

The Events Leading Up to the Games

The military commander had imposed an unusually harsh imprisonment, because he was concerned about the warnings of certain fools who suggested the martyrs might be spirited out of prison by some kind of magic spell.[15] In response, Perpetua got in the commander's face and said, "Why won't you let us refresh ourselves sometimes? Aren't we the most prominent of the criminals? Aren't we important even to Caesar, on whose birthday we're going to face the animals? Wouldn't it be more to your credit if you displayed us on that day not looking so scrawny?"

At this, the commander grew horrified, and his face flushed red. He ordered the prisoners to be treated with more lenience, so Perpetua's fellow Christians

14. The editor is referring to Perpetua's remark at the end of her diary after the vision of the Egyptian gladiator, where she charges someone else to finish the narrative she has begun. Scholars believe certain clues in the diary indicate Perpetua intended it as much more than a personal journal. She clearly hoped to edify the Christian community through her story. Yet she probably didn't imagine that believers would still be reading her words more than eighteen hundred years later!

15. Superstitious belief in magic spells was widespread in the Greco-Roman world. Many people outside the Christian faith would have viewed Jesus as a magical wonder-worker. Rumors based on the stories of prison escapes in Acts 12 and 16 might have influenced popular opinion.

and others had the right to enter and provide food and comfort. In fact, the head jailer himself was now a believer.

The day before the gladiator games, the martyrs ate the final meal, called a "free banquet."[16] As much as possible, they tried to turn the supper into a Christian love feast. With their usual unwavering confidence they bandied words with the mob of spectators—warning them of God's judgment, bearing witness to their joy in suffering, and ridiculing the morbid curiosity of the people who had gathered to watch the meal.

"Will tomorrow not be enough for you?" Saturus asked. "Why are you so eager to gawk at those you hate? Today you're friendly; tomorrow you'll be our deadly enemies! Just make sure you pay close attention to our faces so you can recognize us when the time comes." Thus, all the spectators were leaving the prison astonished, and many of them became believers.

The Martyrs in the Amphitheater at Carthage

At last the day of their victory dawned. The martyrs proceeded cheerfully from the prison to the amphitheater as though they were marching to heaven. Their appearance was honorable, and if they happened to tremble it was not from fear but from joy. Perpetua went along at a calm pace with a radiant countenance. She was a true wife of Christ, beloved of God. The intense expression in her eyes made all the onlookers avert their gaze. Felicity was there too, rejoicing to have given birth safely so she could face the beasts. She was going from one kind of blood to another, from the midwife to the gladiator. Her postpartum washing would be a second baptism![17]

---

16. The reference here is to the Roman practice of the *cena libera*, a banquet the night before the games that included gladiators as well as the prisoners condemned to the beasts. Because the meal was visible to the public, the curious would come and examine the participants. Gladiators were superstars in the ancient world, so many people wanted to see them up close and maybe place bets on the matches the next day. As for the condemned criminals, a kind of lurid voyeurism drove people to stare at them the night before they died. Some Bible commentators consider this the background behind the expression quoted in 1 Corinthians 15:32, "What do I gain if, humanly speaking, I fought with beasts at Ephesus? If the dead are not raised, 'Let us eat and drink, for tomorrow we die.'" The apostle says facing death from wild beasts is meaningless without the hope of resurrection, so the condemned might as well gorge themselves. But because Perpetua and her companions had an eternal hope, they turned the meal into an *agape*, that is, the love feast shared between Christian brothers and sisters.

17. This is just the sort of wordplay so often found in Tertullian, which is one of the reasons we can consider him the possible editor of this text. Yet there is an important theological point here that should not be missed. Martyrdom was described in the ancient church as a "baptism of blood." Just as the purpose of water baptism was total identification with Christ, so dying for his name created a special association between the martyr and his or her Lord. The themes of martyrdom and baptism are brought together in Mark 10:38–39 when Jesus predicts the sons of Zebedee will undergo the same suffering as he. The crucifixion

The martyrs were brought to the amphitheater gate, where they were forced to wear pagan garments—the men dressed like priests of Saturn, and the women like priestesses of Ceres. But the noble Perpetua adamantly refused right to the end. She complained to the commander, "We came to this day of our own free will, precisely so our freedom wouldn't be violated. We offered our lives on the understanding that you wouldn't try to pull something like this. We had an agreement with you!"

Injustice acknowledged justice: the commander acquiesced. He decreed the martyrs should be led into the arena wearing the simple garments they had on before. Perpetua began to sing a psalm, already treading on the Egyptian's head.[18] Meanwhile Revocatus, Saturninus, and Saturus were threatening the watching crowd with judgment. Then, when they came within sight of Hilarian, they used motions and gestures to tell him, "What you do to us, God will do to you!" This infuriated the mob. The people demanded they be harassed by whips as they passed a line of animal fighters.[19] And the martyrs gave thanks indeed that they had obtained a share in the Lord's sufferings.[20]

---

is called a "baptism" (cf. Luke 12:50) and a "cup" of shed blood (cf. Mark 14:36; 1 Cor. 11:25) that these two brothers must experience like the Savior himself. Sure enough, James the son of Zebedee was put to death by the sword (Acts 12:2), and tradition describes John as being persecuted as well, though the Bible does not specifically describe his death, and in all likelihood he was not martyred. Because of the thematic connections between baptism and bloodshed, the church fathers could consider the martyr's death another kind of Christian "washing." The martyr is purified by his or her union with Jesus Christ. This allusion resurfaces in our text when a leopard's bite drenches Saturus in blood. The shouted cry of "A healthy washing!" was a typical greeting for a bather emerging from a bathhouse, but the editor turns the crowd's macabre pun into a veiled reference to baptism (see "Saturus Is Mauled by a Leopard" below).

18. We do not know what psalm Perpetua was singing, but perhaps it was Psalm 91:11–13: "For he will command his angels concerning you to guard you in all your ways. On their hands they will bear you up, lest you strike your foot against a stone. You will tread on the lion and the adder; the young lion and the serpent you will trample underfoot." Jesus also connects treading on serpents with defeat of the Devil (Luke 10:17–20; cf. Gen. 3:15). It is a prominent theme in this martyrdom story.

19. As was the case with the martyrs of Lyons and Vienne (see footnote 8 in chap. 6), so we see here that the Romans staged animal games in the morning, during which trained animal fighters hunted ferocious and exotic beasts. Often these men were equipped with whips or spears. But to increase the bloodshed, condemned convicts were also forced into the arena, helpless and unarmed, to be mauled by the animals. If they survived, they would be finished off by the executioner during the lunch break, as happened to Perpetua and her friends. Then in the afternoon, the main event would occur when skilled gladiators fought one another. Wealthy Romans loved to depict scenes from the games on mosaics in their homes (see fig. 8.1 on p. 106).

20. In being whipped, the believers participated in what their Savior had experienced. The early Christians believed suffering for Jesus's name was a special sort of fellowship with him—a common theme in the New Testament. Look up and reflect on these Bible verses: 2 Corinthians 1:5; 4:10; Philippians 3:10; Colossians 1:24; and 1 Peter 4:13.

Figure 8.1. Gladiator games with animals. Zliten Mosaic, Archaeological Museum of Tripoli, Libya. (© Gilles Mermet/Art Resource, NY)

Now, he who said, "Ask, and you shall receive" [John 16:24] answered the martyrs' prayers by granting them the specific deaths they requested. For whenever they discussed what they hoped for in martyrdom, Saturninus always insisted he wanted to be exposed to all the beasts so he would be assured of receiving more heavenly crowns. And that's exactly what happened: at the beginning of the show he and Revocatus had to contend with a leopard, while later they were put on a stage to be mauled by a bear. Saturus, on the other hand, hated the thought of a bear above all else. He was confident he'd be dispatched right away by one bite of a leopard. However, he was matched with a wild boar—but the hunter who tied him to the beast was gored by the boar instead! He died after the contest was over, while Saturus was only dragged around a little bit. Then, when he was bound to the platform to await the bear, it refused to come out of its pen. So for a second time Saturus was taken back into the holding cell unhurt.

Perpetua and Felicity Are Trampled by a Cow

For the young women, however, the Devil had arranged a very fierce cow.[21] This wasn't the normal custom, but it was done to mimic the women's sex. So they

21. The milk-giving cow was a universal symbol of maternal nurture. Perpetua and Felicity, who had released their claims on their children, are matched with a wild cow to heap scorn on them for rejecting the traditional maternal role. Such an action would have been repugnant and incomprehensible to Roman sensibilities. The women are likened to cows who have gone wild

were stripped naked and draped in nets, then brought out into the arena. But the spectators were horrified when they saw one was a delicate young woman, and the other had just come from childbirth with her breasts still lactating. So the authorities put loose tunics on the women.

The cow tossed Perpetua first, and she landed on her hip. Sitting up, she immediately straightened her tunic where it was ripped along the side to cover her thighs—for Perpetua cared more about modesty than pain. Then she sought her hairpin and straightened her disheveled hair. She believed it was improper for a martyr to die with her hair unbound, which would make it look like she was mourning in her moment of triumph.

She got to her feet. Seeing Felicity's crumpled form lying on the ground, Perpetua went over and offered a hand, helping Felicity to stand. The two of them stood there, side by side. With the brutality of the crowd satisfied, the two martyrs were brought back into the Gate of Life.

While they waited, an unbaptized believer named Rusticus stayed close to Perpetua and supported her. Then she awoke from what seemed like a sort of sleep, though actually she had been enraptured in the Spirit.[22] She began to look around. To everyone's amazement she asked, "When are we going to be thrown to that cow or whatever it is?" When she heard it had already happened, she couldn't believe it until she noticed the gashes on her body and the rips in her clothing.

Then Perpetua called for her brother and spoke with him and Rusticus. "Stand firm in the faith," she urged, "and all of you must love one another! Don't let our martyrdom be a stumbling block to you!"

Saturus Is Mauled by a Leopard

Meanwhile Saturus was in a different gate, evangelizing the junior officer named Pudens. "It has all come down to this, exactly as I foresaw and predicted," he said. "Until this moment I haven't been touched by any of the beasts. So believe

---

and turned ferocious. But as we have seen, the women did not reject motherhood *per se*—they simply found it superseded by an even more compelling loyalty. "Whoever loves son or daughter more than me is not worthy of me," Jesus said (Matt. 10:37).

22. Without doubting Perpetua's Spirit-filled strength at this moment, we may nonetheless imagine she is physiologically in a state of shock from the abuse and is having difficulty understanding her surroundings. Her actions—covering herself, groping for her hairpin, reaching out for Felicity, gazing at the crowd in a stupor—are not inherently impossible, nor even improbable as this traumatized woman sought to recover her dignity or regain her bearings. Yet the actions probably weren't performed with the kind of mental clarity and intentionality the author wants us to perceive. In an ancient context, this wouldn't have been considered a misrepresentation of the facts. The audience of this text understood its "theologized" nature and did not expect a journalistic account of the events.

me now with all your heart. Watch and see, I'm going back in there to be finished off by one bite of a leopard."

And immediately, at the climax of the animal show, a leopard rushed upon Saturus. After just one bite he was so drenched in blood that as he returned to the gate, the people's shout bore witness to his second baptism. "A healthy washing! A healthy washing!" they cried—and clearly he who had been washed like this was "healthy" indeed. Then he said to the soldier Pudens, "Farewell! Remember me and my faith. Don't let these things dismay you. Be strengthened instead!" As Saturus was speaking, he asked Pudens for his finger ring, which he dipped in his wound and handed back as an inheritance. In this way Saturus left behind a symbol and reminder of his bloody martyrdom.

The Martyrs Give Their Lives for Christ

A little later Saturus was tossed unconscious with the other martyrs in the room where the throats of the dying are normally slit.[23] But the mob demanded the martyrs be brought into the open. So when the sword pierced their bodies, the spectators joined the murder with their eyes and became accomplices to the crime.

The martyrs willingly stood up and went over to the place the people wanted. But first they kissed one another, and in so doing they consummated their martyrdom with the kiss of peace. Each of them remained completely still and took the sword silently, especially Saturus. Just as he was the first to ascend the ladder in the dream, so he was the first to give up his spirit. Once again, he was waiting for Perpetua!

She, however, had to experience some pain. Perpetua shrieked as the sword was thrust between her bones. Then she herself guided the young and inexperienced

---

23. This room in ancient coliseums was called the *spoliarium*, a place where dead gladiators were stripped of their armor and dying criminals were finished off by the executioner. The *spoliarium* of the Carthage amphitheater has been identified by one scholar as being located near the Gate of Death on the western side of the structure (David L. Bomgardner, "The Carthage Amphitheater: A Reappraisal," *American Journal of Archaeology* 93, no. 1 [January 1989]: 89, 100). Although a cemetery was situated outside this part of the building, Perpetua and her companions were not buried there. The martyrs' remains eventually came to rest in the great church of ancient Carthage called the Basilica of the Ancestors, built on the ancestral burial grounds of Perpetua's wealthy family. That church is now destroyed, and the bones of the saints have been lost. However, a museum in Tunisia contains a stone plaque that reads, "Here are the martyrs Saturus, Saturninus, Revocatus, Secundulus, Felicitas (and) Perpetua, who suffered on the 7th of March." Near the place where the plaque was found in 1906, in the church's apse, archaeologists uncovered the grave of a child whose body was wrapped in a gold-embroidered cloth. They also found two coffins for adults, in one of which the deceased was wrapped in a similar rich cloth. It is surely tempting to imagine these are the aristocratic relics of Perpetua and her younger brother Dinocrates, though perhaps this is stretching the evidence. Even so, wherever those bones may lie today, I will not be surprised if they begin to stir when the final trumpet sounds.

gladiator's wavering hand to her throat. Perhaps we might say that such a great woman, who was feared by the demon within the executioner, couldn't be killed unless she herself allowed it.

Benediction

Hail, you supremely brave and blessed martyrs! Truly you have been called and chosen for the glory of our Lord Jesus Christ! Anyone who magnifies and honors and worships him ought to read these exemplary stories for the edification of the church. These new accounts of miraculous power are no less important than the stories of old. They remind us that one and the same Holy Spirit is always at work, even now, along with God the Father Almighty and his Son Jesus Christ our Lord, to whom be glory and infinite power forever and ever. Amen!

Tertullian

"The Blood of Christians Is Seed"

Tertullian of Carthage is one of the most energetic and colorful figures of the ancient church. We have already met him briefly as the possible editor of Perpetua's passion account. But he was much more than an editor. Trained in courtroom argumentation and the art of rhetoric, Tertullian directed the persuasive ability of an orator against pagans and heretics alike. His brilliant mind, sharp wit, and uncompromising style make him one of the foremost defenders of the Christian faith the church has ever known.

Yet as is so often the case, Tertullian's strengths could be drawbacks as well. His passion for holiness slipped too easily into legalism. His unwillingness to give an inch of ground to the heretics crept into his relations with his fellow Christians. His belief that the Holy Spirit was speaking anew to prophets in the church gave him a sense of spiritual elitism. These tendencies galvanized in Tertullian's life once he became more heavily invested in Montanism, or the New Prophecy (see introduction to chap. 8). Eventually he and his band of followers alienated themselves from the broader Christian community at Carthage.

Despite Tertullian's shortcomings, his contributions to the Christian faith are incalculable. A generation after him in Carthage, the famous martyr-bishop Cyprian would ask his secretary to bring him Tertullian's works with the instruction, "Give me the master." In fact, as the first known church father to write in Latin instead of Greek, Tertullian set the theological trajectory for much of Western Christianity. For example, he was the first theologian to use the word "Trinity" (*trinitas*) to describe God as both three and one. Tertullian argued the Christian God is not a single being who reveals three different facets of himself at various times, as some heretics were saying at the time. That would mean Jesus was nothing but God the Father viewed from a different angle. No, Tertullian insisted, Jesus has to be understood as a distinct *persona* who can relate to his Father as another *persona*. And yet they must both share the same divine *substantia*, for both are fully God. This sort of theological reasoning—three distinct persons, one divine substance—was pioneered by Tertullian in light of the biblical evidence. Eventually the early church expressed it in the Nicene Creed as the doctrine of the Trinity, which is still held by all orthodox Christians today.

Tertullian's active period of writing spans the years AD 196–212. As noted earlier, the Roman emperor Septimius Severus instituted a policy in 202 that forbade conversion to Christianity, which was what got Perpetua and her friends arrested after they were baptized. Probably it was this event that prompted Tertullian's treatise *To the Martyrs*. Though scholars debate this point, good evidence suggests that what we have here is a theologian's letter of encouragement to Perpetua's band of imprisoned believers. As you read this document, note the extensive overlap with her story: the invocation of the Holy Spirit, the trampling of the Devil underfoot, the gladiatorial language (including the presence of a divine trainer and referee for a wrestling match), and the problem of dissensions besetting the church. In addition, Tertullian's direct address to female martyrs at one point in the text is a strong indication that a literate noblewoman like Perpetua was among the jailed Christians. In light of such parallels, it is quite possible we are reading Tertullian's actual letter to Perpetua and her companions. Though at times the author's language veers into exaggeration or awkward analogies, it nonetheless provides a beautiful picture of how highly the ancient church esteemed its faithful martyrs.

To the Martyrs

Salutation

I greet you, blessed martyrs-to-be! In addition to the bodily food supplied to you in prison by our lady and mother the church from her own breasts, and by individual Christians from their private resources, please accept a little something from me that will nurture your spirit as well.[1] For it isn't good that the body should be well fed while the spirit goes hungry. On the contrary, since your bodily weakness is being cared for, it is only fitting that I not neglect what is stronger. Not that I'm qualified to give you any words of encouragement! However, even the most highly skilled gladiators are sometimes spurred on, not just by their trainers and managers, but by those idiots who shout unnecessary advice from up in the stands—yet quite often these suggestions yelled by the mob turn out to be useful.

So, blessed ones, my main advice to you is "Do not grieve the Holy Spirit" [Eph. 4:30], who escorted you into prison. For if he hadn't accompanied you inside, you wouldn't be there today. Therefore, bring forth the kind of works that will cause the Spirit to remain there with you and lead you from your jail cell to the Lord.

Martyrs in Prison Should Demonstrate Harmony

The prison is undoubtedly the Devil's house. His gang of household slaves lives there. But you have arrived in the prison so you can crush him underfoot in his own home. Of course, you have already stepped on him when you met him in spiritual warfare outside those walls. So don't let him say, "Aha! Now that they're in my domain, I'll tempt them with petty quarrels, or their own weaknesses, or arguments between them!" Let the Devil flee from your sight [James 4:7]. Like a snake driven out by charms or smoke, let him hide away, coiled up and sluggish, in the deepest recesses of his den. Don't let him prosper in his own kingdom by setting you against one another. Instead let him find you well protected and armed with harmony—for peace among yourselves makes war against him. But certain people who don't have this peace in the church have become accustomed to seek it from the martyrs in prison.[2] Therefore you martyrs must be sure to have such

1. Concerning the church as a "mother," see footnote 11 in chap. 6. The language here depicts the loving maternal care that the church provided to jailed Christians. Prison inmates in Roman times were dependent on friends and family for nourishment, a responsibility the early church took seriously. In Perpetua's case we saw how individual Christians, like her mother and brother, as well as the deacons Tertius and Pomponius, cared for her and the other believers in jail (see chap. 8). One of the main purposes of monetary collections in the ancient church was to provide for the needs of Christians who had been imprisoned for their faith or sent to hard labor in the mines. Here Tertullian says he knows the martyrs are being well cared for physically. He hopes to offer them the additional "food" of spiritual encouragement.

2. Most commentators interpret this as a reference to persecuted Christians who denied their faith asking the martyrs to grant them "peace" (forgiveness) so they can be restored to church fellowship. It is true that ancient believers sought forgiveness from imprisoned martyrs for grievous sins such as apostasy or adultery. Tertullian mentions this practice elsewhere, and it is attested by other writers as well. The early Christians believed the Bible taught that martyrs have a special portion of the Holy Spirit (Matt. 10:19–20; Mark 13:11), which allowed them to grant forgiveness in God's name (John 20:22–23). However, I am not sure this is what Tertullian is referring to here. The context is divisions within the church, not apostasy. Possibly these divisions were over how to handle "lapsed" Christians who denied Jesus, but the problem could

peace in your midst, cherishing it and guarding it, so that if you get the chance, you can offer it to others.

The True Value of Prisons

No doubt some other spiritual burdens, equally heavy, went with you to the prison gate. And perhaps certain members of your family could accompany you that far. But from then on you've been isolated from the outside world. Shouldn't you, therefore, be all the more isolated from its secular ways? Don't let this segregation from the world bother you. When we stop and think what a greater prison house our world truly is, we realize you actually left the prison rather than entered one! The world has more darkness than a dungeon, for it blinds our hearts instead of our eyes. The world burdens us with heavier chains, the kind that constrict our very souls. The world exhales something much worse than a prison's noxious vapors: the lusts of men. And the world contains the most criminals of all—the whole human race! For every single person awaits final judgment, not from a human governor, but from God himself.

And so, blessed ones, consider yourselves (if you can) to have been transferred from a prison to a sanctuary.[3] Yes, it's dark in jail—but you are the light. You may be in chains, yet you're free before God. Though the place exudes a foul stench, you are a sweet odor there.[4] In prison you may await the judge, but the reality is, you will pass sentence on those very judges [1 Cor. 6:2]! Let all the prisoners who long for worldly pleasures be sad and gloomy. In contrast, the Christian—even one who is outside of jail—has renounced secular ways. All the more has the locked-up Christian rejected the very prison itself! It doesn't matter where you're located in the world, for it isn't your true home. And if you have to part with some of life's joys, remember the saying "In business you have to lose a little something to make greater profits."

Now, I'm not going to say anything yet about the reward to which God invites the martyrs. For the moment, let's just compare prison life to worldly life and try to determine whether your soul gains more than your body has to give up. The

---

just as easily be a doctrinal controversy that had driven a wedge between fellow believers. Tertullian's reference is remarkably similar to the scene in Saturus's vision in which Perpetua seeks to reconcile Bishop Optatus and the presbyter Aspasius. The house churches in Carthage had separated into factions like fans rooting for their own teams at the chariot races. Here Tertullian uses the spiritual authority of the martyrs to address the problem of factionalism head-on, just like he did in Perpetua's story (if he was the unnamed editor of that account). Apparently Tertullian prized harmony within the church, even though he wasn't always able to live it out.

3. As Perpetua herself puts it, "The prison became like a palace to me. I wanted to be there more than anywhere else!"

4. Similarly, the martyrs of Lyons and Vienne were said to possess such a sweet odor of Christ that those around them thought they had been anointed with literal perfume.

truth of the matter is, the body doesn't actually lack what it needs in prison, thanks to the care of the church and the charity of the brethren. The soul simply gains some extras that are always helpful to faith. For example, you don't have to look at weird gods or encounter their idols. You don't have to participate in pagan holidays, even just by intermingling in the crowd. You aren't afflicted by the disgusting smells of sacrifices or the raucous noise of the gladiator shows. The atrocities, mad passions, and sexual immorality of the pagan revelers cannot constantly hammer you in prison. Your eyes don't keep falling on houses of prostitution right out in the open. You're free from stumbling blocks, temptations, and seductive mental images. And in fact, you're now free even from persecution.

The prison offers to the Christian what the desert used to provide to the prophets. The Lord himself often went to a remote place so he could pray without interruption and withdraw from public life. In fact, it was in a secluded place that he revealed his glory to his disciples [at the transfiguration]. So let's drop the name "prison" and start calling it a spiritual retreat. Though your body is shut inside a building and your flesh is restrained, the whole world is open to your spirit. Come! Wander freely in your spirit, and take a walk. But instead of walking down shady paths or lengthy colonnades, steer your feet onto the road that leads to God. Whenever you walk that spiritual path, you won't be in jail. Your leg doesn't feel the chain when your soul is in heaven. For the soul encompasses the whole self, taking you wherever you wish. And let us recall: "Where you heart is, there will your treasure be also" [Matt. 6:21]. So let our hearts go where we want to find our treasure.

The Christian's Call to Endure Hardship

Now, I admit, blessed ones, the prison is unpleasant even to Christians. But we were called into the army of the living God at the very moment we responded with the words of the baptismal oath.[5] No soldier goes to war equipped with all

5. Tertullian's word for "baptismal oath" is *sacramentum*. Contrary to what some people today might believe, the term "sacrament" does not refer to magical rites that bring about salvation. The original meaning of a sacrament involved an oath: that of a soldier entering the army, and, by implication, anyone accepting a sacred new loyalty. The Latin word *sacramentum* was also connected with the biblical Greek word *mysterion*, or "mystery." The apostle Paul, for example, speaks frequently about the "mystery of Christ." In what way is Christ mysterious? The ancient Christians understood it to mean that intimate knowledge of the Lord is available not to just anyone but only to those who have committed themselves to him in a personal profession of faith. This was done in private, not out in front of the unbelieving crowds. A parallel to this could be found in the pagan "mystery religions," whose adherents made secret pledges to their chosen gods. What the mystery religions and Christianity had in common was a binding oath as part of the initiation ceremony. For the Christians, this involved not arcane cultic rituals but the simple act of water baptism in the presence of fellow believers. In this holy moment, the terms of a specific "contract"—the baptismal creed, or rule of faith—were stated aloud and accepted by the convert. It was an oath of loyalty to a new God, even if that meant persecution,

sorts of luxuries. He marches to the battle line not from his bedroom but from a bare and cramped tent where all sorts of hardships and annoyances and discomforts are endured. Even in peacetime, soldiers are taught by hard work and inconveniences to bear the rigors of war. They have to march around fully armed, practice their drills in an open field, dig trenches, or bunch together to form the "tortoise."[6] Everything is covered in sweat! The soldiers' bodies and spirits can't be afraid to go from pleasant shade to hot sunshine, and then straight to icy cold. They can't fear the transition from comfortable tunics to body armor, from peace and quiet to the battle cry, from relaxation to the chaos of war.

Therefore you too, blessed ones, should consider whatever hardships you now face as strength training for your bodies and souls. You are about to "fight the good fight" [1 Tim. 6:12]. The living God himself presides as the overseer of this contest, and the Holy Spirit is your trainer.[7] The prizes you can win are the flower wreath of eternity, the victory medal of angelic existence,[8] citizenship in heaven, and glory forever and ever. And so your coach Jesus Christ has oiled you down with the Spirit and led you to the wrestler's exercise ground.[9] He intends to rid you of a lazy lifestyle before the actual day of the contest, leading you through a much tougher regimen so your inner strength can be hardened.

This is of course what happens to all athletes. They're set apart for a life of strict discipline so they can spend their time building their endurance. All luxuries, rich foods, and delicious drinks are kept away from them. Athletes are driven hard . . . forced to endure trials . . . pushed to the limits of their strength. The more they labor in their exertions, the more they long for the day of victory. According to the apostle Paul, the athlete competes to win only a perishable crown [1 Cor. 9:25]. But we who will obtain an eternal crown view the prison as our exercise ground. We must be well accustomed to all hardships when we're led to the competition

and at the same time it was a repudiation of all former allegiances to pagan deities. Tertullian refers to the profound commitment Perpetua and her friends made when they were baptized as a stimulus for them to endure present affliction in jail.

6. The "tortoise" (*testudo*) was a military maneuver for approaching walls in a siege, or whenever light missiles were expected from above. The soldiers clustered together with their shields interlocked above and around them, creating the appearance of a giant tortoise encased in its shell.

7. In this section Tertullian artfully illustrates his point through a series of technical terms from Greek athletics. He compares an athlete's physical discipline in training to the martyrs' spiritual preparation for the day of their contest.

8. See footnote 8 in chap. 4 for more about deceased Christians existing like angels in heaven.

9. Perpetua asserts in her vision of the Egyptian gladiator that "some splendid young men approached me to serve as my own assistants and comrades-in-arms. I was disrobed and became male. My supporters began to rub me down with oil like gladiators do before a match." Could Perpetua's vision have been stimulated, in part, by her meditation on the imagery in Tertullian's letter?

before the seat of the Judge. For strength is built up through austerity, but soft living definitely tears it down.

Weak Flesh Can Be Aided by a Strong Spirit

We know from one of the Lord's sayings that "the spirit is willing but the flesh is weak" [Mark 14:38]. Now, when the Lord admits our flesh is weak, let's not kid ourselves and use it as an excuse. He intentionally started out by saying "the spirit is willing" so he could indicate which part of us should be obedient to the other. In other words, he wanted to show how the weaker flesh is submissive to the spirit, which is stronger. Thus the flesh can draw strength from the spirit. Let the spirit converse with the flesh about the salvation they share in common. Instead of focusing on the hardships of prison, begin to think about the actual confrontation at the games. Perhaps the flesh will fear the painful sword, the elevated cross, the enraged beasts, and the worst punishment of all, burning alive—not to mention the many excruciating skills of the torturer. But then let the spirit remind itself and the body about the other side of the argument: that while these things are extremely painful, many people have embraced them with a calm demeanor. In fact, some people have even sought out suffering voluntarily for the sake of fame and glory. And I don't mean only men. Women have done this too. May you likewise, O blessed women, respond in a manner worthy of your gender!

Famous Examples of Bodily Denial among Unbelievers

It would take a long time for me to list every single figure who stayed true to their convictions and chose to end their lives violently.[10] Among women, Lucretia comes

10. Tertullian now embarks on a litany of famous (and sometimes legendary?) people who suffered or died for their beliefs. The Roman noblewoman Lucretia killed herself after being shamed by rape, an act that caused the original monarchy of Rome to be replaced by the republic. Mucius Scaevola (the "Left Handed") was captured by hostile forces yet proved his courage to the enemy king when he held his right hand in a fire without flinching. Ancient accounts say the philosopher Heraclitus tried to cure his edema through heat by lying in the sun while smeared with a poultice of dung; Empedocles leaped into a volcano to prove his immortality; and the Cynic philosopher Peregrinus Proteus gave himself a funeral speech and then cast himself on a burning pyre during the Olympic Games of AD 165. Similarly, in Virgil's *Aeneid* the first queen of Carthage, Dido, commits suicide on a funeral pyre after she loses her lover Aeneas, an act imitated by Carthage's final queen, who hurled herself into the flaming wreck of her city after her husband Hasdrubal cowered before the conquering Romans. The death of Marcus Atilius Regulus was especially famous in Roman history. After being captured by the hated Carthaginians, he was sent back to Rome to arrange for peace and the exchange of prisoners. Regulus didn't view peace as Rome's best interest, so he honored the terms of his release by putting himself back into enemy custody. The Carthaginians executed him in a spiked box or cask. Likewise, Queen Cleopatra of Egypt, after the death of her lover Mark Antony, famously chose suicide by snakebite rather than face humiliation and defeat from Octavian (soon to be known as Caesar Augustus) as he rose to imperial power. And finally, a certain Athenian courtesan named

quickly to mind. After being raped she stabbed herself with a knife in front of her whole family so she would win praise for her commitment to sexual integrity. Mucius burned his own right hand over a sacrificial fire so he would always be remembered for this deed. And have the philosophers achieved less? Heraclitus roasted himself while smeared with an ointment of cow dung; likewise, Empedocles hurled himself into a fiery chasm on Mount Etna; and just recently, Peregrinus threw himself onto a funeral pyre. Why, even women have boldly embraced the flames—like Dido, for example, so she wouldn't be forced to marry any man after the departure of the one she loved the most. Or what about the wife of Hasdrubal? When Carthage was set ablaze she cast herself and her children into the flames that consumed her city rather than see her husband begging for mercy at Scipio's feet.

The general Regulus, after being captured in battle, refused to be the only Roman hostage exchanged for multiple Carthaginian prisoners of war. He preferred instead to be returned to the enemy, who stuffed him into a sort of chest and hammered in spikes from the outside. Each time a nail came through from another angle, he experienced yet another crucifixion.

Or consider a woman who intentionally sought out fearsome animals—even asps, those snakes that are far scarier than a bull or bear. I mean Queen Cleopatra, who allowed asps to bite her so she wouldn't fall into enemy hands.

Now, you might reply, "Yes, but the fear of death isn't as strong as the fear of pain." Well then, did the Athenian courtesan give in to the torturer? She was a conspirator in a plot against a tyrant. Even when he brought her under intense agony for her involvement, she refused to betray her co-conspirators. In the end she bit off her tongue and spat it in the tyrant's face so he could see that his tortures couldn't break her, no matter how long he kept them up.

And it's no secret that even now among the Spartans, their most important ceremony is the *diamastigosis*, that is, a severe whipping.[11] In this sacred rite all the aristocratic Spartan teenagers are scourged with whips beside an altar while their parents and relatives gather nearby and shout encouragement for the boys to stand firm. For the Spartans consider it a much greater mark of distinction and glory when a person submits to the lashes with intentional willpower, not just his outward body.

Leaena who possessed secret information about an assassination plot was reputed to have bitten off her tongue and spit it out rather than betray the man she loved. If we are honest, we must admit Tertullian belabors his point here. He probably didn't encourage the jailed martyrs too much with these unprofitable remarks. The passage does, however, say a lot about the ancient world's respect for heroic endurance and noble death, of which Christian martyrdom can be considered a certain type.

11. The ancient Spartans were famous for their endurance contest in which young males were ritually flogged to prove their manly fortitude. Around the time of Tertullian, so many tourists were coming to watch the bloody spectacle at the temple of Artemis Orthia in Sparta that eventually an amphitheater was constructed to hold them all.

Look how much earthly glory is heaped on those with steadfast bodies and minds! People will scorn the sword, the fire, the cross, the beasts, or the rack—all for the reward of human praise. Therefore I have to tell you, your present sufferings are insignificant compared to the heavenly glory and divine reward you're about to receive [Rom. 8:18]. If people so highly value a cheap glass bead, how much more valuable is an actual pearl? Who wouldn't gladly spend for a true pearl what others pay for an imitation?

The Vanity of Human Glory

But let me stop talking about the motive of human glory now. The prideful ambition so common among men these days—in fact, a kind of mental insanity—has revealed the utter corruption in all these contests of savagery and torture. Think about how many leisured aristocrats have become gladiators out of longing for combat glory.[12] Surely it is vanity that makes them go down and face the wild beasts—and then they fancy themselves all the more handsome because of their bites and scars! Others have made a deal with fire by hiring themselves to cross a certain space while clad in a burning shirt. Still other men with very tough shoulders have walked a prescribed course among the bullwhips of the beast hunters in the arena.[13]

Blessed martyrs, know that the Lord has allowed these events to happen in the world for good reason. Why? Certainly they can spur us on right now. Yet they will also condemn us on judgment day, if we hesitate to suffer for saving truth the very things that unbelievers long to suffer out of their damnable pride.

12. Though gladiators were slaves, it is widely attested in the historical sources that sometimes aristocrats and free men would lower themselves into slavery as gladiators because they longed for the glory that would accrue to them through skill at arms. In ancient Rome the best fighters were adored the way superstar athletes are today. Well-to-do women were known to call these men to their beds. Even the emperors weren't above the allure of gladiatorial fame. The cruel and insane emperor Commodus, who died shortly before Tertullian wrote this treatise, was famous for killing many exotic animals in the arena and even murdering opponents in staged gladiatorial contests (as is fictionally depicted by Joaquin Phoenix in the movie *Gladiator*). Tertullian argues that if men will compete for such earthly glory, how much more should the martyrs strive for heavenly praise?

13. Obviously, some people in antiquity were willing to endure outrageous pain for the sake of monetary gain. Tertullian is thinking of two specific instances that have recently come to his attention. In his apologetic work *To the Nations* he mentions a man who won a prize by walking a certain distance with his clothes on fire, and another who traversed a set course while the animal hunters cracked whips on his shoulders. That work of Tertullian's also mentions several of the same figures from pagan history he has just cited here (Regulus, Cleopatra, Dido, Leaena, etc.). These illustrious pagans served as a reply to critics who claimed the martyrs were fanatical in their willingness to suffer and die. Tertullian wanted to show that heroic endurance is something his society respected and considered noble. Therefore the martyrs should be honored for their faithfulness to God.

Endurance of Everyday Suffering

So then, enough with all these examples of endurance motivated by human ambition. Let us turn our attention to our normal everyday experience. Perhaps we
can learn from the things that often happen to people unwillingly, in case we ever
require the courage to face something similar.

Think, for example, how many people have been burned to death in house fires.
Or consider how many people have been devoured by animals in the woods—
and sometimes even in the heart of the city when a beast escapes its cage! Many
others have fallen to the robber's knife, or been crucified by their enemies after
being tortured and afflicted with every kind of abuse.

Furthermore, some people are willing to suffer things for the sake of a man that
they wouldn't suffer for God. Our present times bear witness to this.[14] Look how
many high-ranking noblemen are meeting with deaths that are quite surprising
in light of their birth, their dignity, their bodily condition, or their old age. They
suffered all this because of one man—being killed either by him if they opposed
him or by his enemies if they were on his side.[15]

Tertullian's letter *To the Martyrs* bears a close relationship to another of
his works, the great *Apology*, in which he makes a comprehensive defense of
the Christian faith. Many scholars believe both works were written in 197,
but I take the view that only the *Apology* dates to that year. The content of

14. Most commentators suggest Tertullian is referring to the purge of aristocrats that happened in AD 197 when the triumphant emperor Septimius Severus massacred the followers of
his rival, Clodius Albinus. Tertullian probably did have this event in mind, but his phrase "our
present times" does not necessarily indicate he wrote the treatise in 197. The expression is impre-
cise enough that the treatise could have been written a few years later at the time of Perpetua's
imprisonment in 202/3. Tertullian may have borrowed material from his earlier *Apology* (where
he does mention Albinus) for use in *To the Martyrs*, which would explain the presence of this
statement about the emperor's purge of noblemen. This would be a case of an author lifting
some arguments from a previous writing and inserting them (somewhat awkwardly) into a later
work. Some modern scholars, however, see the *Apology* as being written just after *To the Martyrs*,
which would invert the textual borrowing that was occurring between the two works. It is hard
to be dogmatic here, but I do think a good case can be made that Tertullian wrote this letter to
Perpetua and her companions in jail, even if he reworked some material from his earlier writings.
15. The manuscript of Tertullian's treatise ends here in a most disappointing way. The reader
will probably sense a lack of closure. At the very least we would expect to find a final address
to the imprisoned martyrs. It may be that some part of this treatise was lost in the historical
process of its preservation. On the other hand, contemporary scholars have discerned a rhetorical structure to this entire work that would have satisfied the ancient mind. Be that as it
may, the modern reader is left with the distinct impression that *To the Martyrs* does not end
where it should. We must appreciate this text as an insight into early Christian perspectives on
martyrdom, even if the treatise doesn't conclude with a stirring exhortation as we might wish.

To the Martyrs fits so precisely with what Perpetua and her companions were facing in 202 that the letter appears to have been addressed directly to them. Of course, it may be that Tertullian has reworked an earlier letter to other Christian prisoners, which would explain some of the overlap with the *Apology*.

As you read the concluding chapter of the *Apology* below, compare its tone and content to what you have just read in Tertullian's letter of spiritual encouragement. Here the addressees are not fellow believers in jail but the magistrates of Carthage who are perpetrating abuse upon the faithful. The judges are urged to give the same honor to the martyrs' self-sacrifice that they do to pagan examples of endurance. The valor of the Christians should inspire admiration and conversion, not disdain. It is in this context that we find the famous slogan so often quoted incorrectly as "the blood of the martyrs is the seed of the church." What Tertullian actually said was *semen est sanguis Christianorum,* "The blood of Christians is seed." In other words, death causes new life to spring up. As the onlookers see the bravery and steadfastness of the martyrs, they are called to believe in the glorious name for which the martyrs are dying. Perhaps many people were in fact converted by the noble courage they observed. Thus, through the shedding of their blood, the martyrs served as "witnesses" to their eternal hope in Jesus Christ.

Apology 50

The Christians' Willingness to Suffer

You magistrates say to us, "Why do you complain that we persecute you, since you actually want to suffer? Shouldn't you appreciate the ones who bring about the suffering you desire?"

Certainly we are willing to suffer, but it's more like the way a soldier suffers in war. No one finds it enjoyable to suffer, since it always involves anxiety and risk. Even so, a man who complains about a battle ahead of time still fights the battle with all his strength, and he rejoices in the battle once he has gained the victory, because he receives glory and plunder. This is our "battle": that we are summoned to your law courts, where we fight for truth as we risk our necks. And this is our "victory": to hold fast to the truths for which we have fought. Such victory offers the "glory" of pleasing God, and the "plunder" of eternal life.

The Martyrs' Deaths Are as Noble as Pagan Examples

But we are struck down. Yes, that's true—but only after we have obtained what we want! Therefore we triumph at the very moment we are struck down. We find ultimate escape when we are led forth as captives. So feel free to mock us as "firewood" and "half axles" because we are bound to a half-axle stake and burned in a circle of firewood. This is the garment of our victory! This is our palm-embroidered toga! In such a chariot do we celebrate our triumph![16] Naturally we don't seem pleasing to the vanquished. Naturally we are viewed as hopeless and devastated. Yet you raise up exactly this sort of "hopelessness" and "devastation" like a heroic banner in your hands to celebrate glorious and famous deeds:[17]

Mucius willingly left his right hand on the altar. *"Oh,"* you cry, *"what a noble soul he had!"*

Empedocles offered his entire body to the flames of Mount Etna. *"Oh, what a strong mind he had!"*

That famous founder of Carthage escaped a second marriage by casting herself on a funeral pyre. *"Oh, what a prominent example of chastity and modesty!"*

Regulus, lest one man should live at the cost of many enemy hostages, endured crucifixion in every part of his body. *"Oh, what a steadfast man, victorious even in captivity!"*

While Anaxarchus was being pounded to death with a barley pestle, he exclaimed, "Pound, pound away at the bag that holds Anaxarchus—for you aren't pounding Anaxarchus himself!"[18] *"Oh, the lofty spirit of that philosopher, who could even joke about such a death as his!"*

I'll pass over those who earned praise for themselves by valiant deeds with their own swords, or by some milder form of death. For look! You even give prizes to those who win contests of torture. That Greek courtesan bit off her tongue after her torturer finally wore himself out. She spat it in the face of the enraged tyrant—thereby spitting out her own voice so she couldn't betray the conspirators, even if she wanted to after being overcome by pain. Or Zeno of Elea, when asked by Dionysius what philosophy has to offer, replied, "To become impervious

16. Tertullian pictures the martyr as a victorious Roman general who would wear a special purple robe decorated with palms as he rode in a chariot that paraded through the heart of the capital. For a Christian martyr, the moment of seeming defeat is actually a glorious triumph such as this.

17. See footnote 10 above for the background on several of these classical models of heroic endurance.

18. Anaxarchus was a Greek philosopher and friend of Alexander the Great in the fourth century BC. Though he was prone to utter witty sayings as a means of conveying wisdom, one of his quips infuriated the tyrant who ruled the island of Cyprus. When Anaxarchus later was forced to land there, the tyrant had him put in a large mortar to be pounded to death with pestles. But Anaxarchus's philosophy had taught him how to attain tranquility and indifference to the physical world, so he was able to disregard the death of his outer body because his true self was at peace.

to suffering."[19] Though he was subjected to the tyrant's lashes, he backed up his opinion even to the point of death. And surely the lashes of the Spartans, which are intensified while a boy's cheering relatives look on, bring honor to his house for his endurance in direct proportion to the amount of his blood that is spilled.

"Oh, what glory!" For you, this is legitimate glory because it goes to human beings. In such cases, when death and every kind of cruelty are scorned, you don't consider it an example of "devastation." You don't hold the view that it is "hopeless." It is permissible to suffer for one's country, one's empire, one's friends—yet martyrs are not allowed to suffer for God! And so for every one of these great men you mold a statue, you write their names on their images, you engrave epitaphs on their tombs for all time. So far as you can achieve it through monuments, you offer a sort of resurrection to the dead. But for the one who has the hope of a true resurrection from God, when he suffers for God, you call him insane!

A Final Challenge to the Magistrates

All right then, get on with it, good judges! The people will view you all the better if you sacrifice the Christians to them. Crucify us! Torture us! Condemn us! Eliminate us! Your unjust opposition only highlights our innocence—which is exactly why God allows us to suffer these things. In fact, when you recently condemned a Christian girl to *lust* rather than the *lion*, you admitted we consider a blemish on our chastity a far worse fate than any kind of punishment or death.[20] Yet nothing whatsoever is accomplished by your cruelties, even when each is more heinous than the last. Instead they serve as an enticement to our religion. Indeed, we supply a greater yield whenever you cut us down. The blood of Christians is seed![21]

Many among you offer exhortations to endure suffering and death. Cicero says this in his *Tusculan Disputations*, and Seneca in *Remedies for Accidents*, and Diogenes, Pyrrho, and Callinicus. Even so, their words don't manage to win nearly as

19. Zeno of Elea was a fifth-century BC Greek philosopher who lived in southern Italy and later came to Athens. Though Tertullian links Zeno with Dionysius here and in another of his works, he seems to be confusing Zeno's killer with a different tyrant, Dionysius of Syracuse, who actually lived at a later time. Zeno's primary biographer does claim the philosopher was slain by a tyrant—but one of a different name, and not in the manner Tertullian describes.

20. Tertullian makes a pun in Latin to describe a recent tragedy. He contrasts the *leno*, a pimp, with the *leo*, a lion. Apparently some unfortunate Christian woman known for her purity was condemned to the slow death of daily prostitution rather than being dispatched quickly by lions in the arena. Tertullian notes that the unjust judges who would order such a thing are implicitly recognizing the virtue of Christians in their cruel punishment.

21. An agricultural metaphor is applied to the Christians here. When wheat fields like those in North Africa were harvested, loose grains or cut stalks were often left behind. Gleaners would normally collect the remains, but if not, the seeds would eventually sprout. Tertullian likens the martyrs to stalks of grain being harvested. Ironically, the more you cut them down, the greater is the crop that springs up in their place!

many disciples as the Christians, who teach through their deeds. That very stubbornness you criticize in us is actually a teacher. For who, upon observing such stubbornness, is not so shaken by it that he must seek what lies behind it? And who, upon making this inquiry, does not give his assent? And when he assents, does he not eagerly long to suffer so he might acquire the whole grace of God, winning complete forgiveness from God by the payment of his own blood? For all sins are forgiven by this action.[22] This is why we give thanks at the very moment we are sentenced by you. Such is the fundamental contrast between divine things and human. As soon as you condemn us, God acquits us.

---

22. Tertullian is often noted for his theological understanding of salvation as a divine transaction in which an exchange with God must take place. God is pictured as a judge who must be recompensed in some way for the sins of humanity. This sort of thinking will become widespread in Western theology to explain the atoning work of Christ as a payment. Yet when Tertullian goes so far as to say the martyr's blood itself can pay for sins, we must criticize the excesses of his thought. In attempting to show how the martyr's willingness to die for the Lord demonstrates an absolute commitment to God that will certainly be honored, Tertullian overstates the case by attributing saving efficacy to the martyr's own blood. Even so, let us note Tertullian always intended to describe this forgiveness as a result of God's grace. Many early Christians viewed martyrdom as a "baptism of blood" (Luke 12:50) that so deeply identified the martyr with Jesus that his or her sins were washed away because of that union. Just as water baptism places a person "in Christ," so the act of suffering for the Savior creates a special oneness with him. A thematic linkage between the martyr's suffering and the cross of Christ can be found in biblical texts such as Revelation 12:11, "And they have conquered [Satan] by the blood of the Lamb and by the word of their testimony, for they loved not their lives even unto death." Note how this verse joins the "blood of the Lamb" and the martyrs' faithful testimony as the means of overcoming the Devil. Yet just as this Scripture obviously presupposes true faith as the basis for the martyrs' victory, so the church fathers never considered the dual baptisms of water or blood to have any efficacy apart from faithful adherence to the risen Lord. For further explanation of some of these martyrological themes, see footnote 7 in chap. 4 and footnote 17 in chap. 8.

10

Origen of Alexandria

A Theology of Martyrdom

Like Tertullian's treatise *To the Martyrs* in chapter 9, the present text serves as a letter of encouragement to fellow believers facing persecution. It is not an account of a martyr's arrest, trial, and execution but an exegetical and theological exploration of the underlying reasons for Christian martyrdom. The text is offered in this book because it comes from one of the most brilliant intellects the church has ever produced.

It is impossible to define a man of Origen's greatness in a few short words. When he was just sixteen his father Leonides was martyred, and only his mother's quick thinking prevented the zealous teenager from meeting the same fate: she confined him to the house by hiding all his clothes. Origen grew up to become a teacher of Christian converts in his hometown of Alexandria, Egypt. Throughout his ministry he remained bold in his affection for the imprisoned confessors. He often visited his former students in prison at great personal risk, and indeed, he eventually met a violent end himself. After a long and prolific career as the church's foremost scholar, the old saint was hauled into prison, where great effort was made to break him through torture. Although Origen held out until the persecution passed and he was released, the torture had taken its toll, and he died soon thereafter. Later generations began calling him Adamantius, a nickname that means "diamond." The title is appropriate, for Origen of Alexandria was both beautiful and unbreakable.

The *Encouragement to Martyrdom* was written nearly two decades earlier than all this, in AD 235. It is addressed to Origen's wealthy patron Ambrose and a presbyter named Protoctetus, both of whom were facing the possibility of martyrdom. The historical situation Origen addressed was the attempt by Emperor Maximinus Thrax to force the church's leaders to apostatize. The clergy were commanded to make a token sacrifice to the gods, swear an oath by them, and deny Christ. As we have consistently seen in this book for other ancient Christians, Origen considers this to be blasphemous idolatry—that is, demon worship—and just as much an abomination in Christian times as when God warned the Hebrews against it in the Old Testament.

Even a casual reader cannot help but notice how biblical Origen's treatise is. One glance will reveal the many scriptural quotations woven into every paragraph. The words of the sacred text, Old and New Testament alike, come pouring from Origen's mind. Yet perhaps we will be puzzled by the seemingly unbiblical theme of the martyr earning benefits from God and meriting rewards. Modern Protestants must try not to force every ancient expression into the category of "works salvation." Origen's remarks simply reflect the sort of thing Paul says in 1 Corinthians 9:24–27, that every athlete competes to receive a prize. Or read Luke 6:22–23—persecuted Christians should rejoice that their reward in heaven is great because of their persever-ance. Though salvation itself is not earned, there is a theological connection in the Bible between the quality of a Christian's sanctification and his or her final reward in eternity. That being said, Origen does go too far when he sug-gests the martyr's blood can have an atoning effect. (See footnote 22 in the previous chapter for a discussion of this theme.)

In any case, Origen's *Encouragement to Martyrdom* is an advanced text, one obviously produced by a brilliant mind. Due to his wide-ranging thought and scholarly tendency toward repetition, only about the first quarter of all he had to say in the treatise has been translated here. The purpose of its inclusion is to provide theological illumination for other texts in this book. Perhaps you've been struck by the martyrs' dogged refusal to acquiesce to the demands placed on them by the authorities. At times it may have seemed like willful stubbornness. Origen gives us another view. For the early Christians, to submit to the pagans' wishes was to deny the Lord Jesus Christ and elevate foul demons in his place. No ground can be ceded to the Devil—none at all. Origen is uncompromising on this. He is, no doubt, one of the most hard-core of the church fathers. Yet ask yourself: What would you do if someone ordered you to worship demons and curse the Savior who endured your punishment on the cross?

Encouragement to Martyrdom 1–12

Introduction: Encouragement for Martyrs from Isaiah 28

"All you who are weaned from milk and withdrawn from the breast: expect trials upon trials, as well as hope upon hope—for a little longer, just a little while longer—through contemptuous lips and a foreign tongue" [Isa. 28:9–11].[1]

You, my godly and devout friends Ambrose and Protoctetus, are no longer "carnal" or "infants in Christ" [1 Cor. 3:1] but have advanced in your spiritual age. You no longer need milk but now require solid food [1 Cor. 3:2; Heb. 5:12]. Therefore listen to what Isaiah says about those who are "weaned from milk and withdrawn from the breast." Not just one tribulation but "trials upon trials" are prophesied for you because you are "weaned" athletes. Yet notice also that whoever doesn't try to dodge these trials but welcomes them like a noble athlete immediately welcomes "hope upon hope" too. Such hope is enjoyed soon after the trials, which is why it says, "a little while longer."

So if any strangers to Holy Scripture's way of speaking should scorn and despise us, calling us impious or foolish, let's remember that this "hope upon hope" granted to us in "a little while" will be given "through contemptuous lips and a foreign tongue." Now, who wouldn't gladly accept numerous trials in order to receive numerous hopes afterward? Like the apostle Paul, we have considered "the sufferings of the present time as unworthy to be compared to the glory that God is about to reveal to us" [Rom. 8:18]. By these sufferings we are making a bid, so to speak, for blessedness.

Further Encouragement from 2 Corinthians

And all the more do we embrace trials, since they are "our temporary slight affliction" [2 Cor. 4:17]. The affliction isn't just being *characterized* here as slight; it's actually *experienced* as slight by those who aren't overwhelmed by their circumstances! The more such affliction abounds, the greater and more magnificent is the "eternal weight of glory it produces in us." Yet this is true only if, at the moment our persecutors seek to oppress our souls, we refuse to let our minds dwell on our sufferings. Instead of considering our present afflictions, we should focus on the rewards reserved by God's grace for those who through their patient endurance have competed like athletes in Christ "according to the rules" [2 Tim. 2:5]. Then God indeed multiplies his benefits. He grants favors far beyond what is deserved by the contestant's efforts. Such multiplication is proper, because God

---

1. Origen's quotation is based on the Greek Septuagint, a Jewish translation of the Old Testament that came to be widely embraced by the early Christians. The Hebrew text that serves as the basis of modern English Bibles reads somewhat differently.

doesn't give gifts like a miser—he gives generously! He knows exactly how to magnify his grace to those who with every ounce of their strength have proven by their disregard for their "jar of clay" [2 Cor. 4:7] that they "love God with all their soul" [Matt. 22:37].

Earnest Desire to Go and Be with God

Now, I think the people who "love God with all their soul" are those whose longing for union with him is so strong that they withdraw their souls and keep them away, not only from their earthly bodies, but also from all physical things. Such people aren't distracted or hesitant to put aside the lowly body when the time comes to strip away "the body of death" (in what only seems to be a death). Then they will hear the apostle's prayerful cry, "Wretched man that I am! Who will deliver me from this body of death?" [Rom. 7:24]. For what man among us, groaning in his earthly tabernacle because he's so burdened by a corruptible body [2 Cor. 5:4], would not give thanks to be free? First he would ask, "Who will deliver me from this body of death?" Then, seeing he has been delivered from the body of death by his relationship with God, he would utter the holy cry, "Thanks be to God through Christ Jesus our Lord!" [Rom. 7:25]. If anyone thinks this sounds difficult, he hasn't truly thirsted for the mighty and living God like "the deer pants for the springs of water," nor has he said to himself, "When can I come and behold the face of God?" [Ps. 42:1–2]. He isn't thinking the way the psalm writer was thinking when he was asked, "Where is your God?" [v. 3]. Every day he "poured out his soul" within himself [v. 4], constantly rebuking his soul's weakness at becoming sad and disturbed. "I will enter into the place of the wondrous tabernacle, to the very house of God," he said, "with cries of rejoicing and thankful shouts like people at a festival" [vv. 4–5].

Therefore, throughout your present struggle I beg you to remember the "great reward" laid up in heaven for those who are persecuted and reviled for the sake of righteousness, or for the Son of Man [Matt. 5:10–12; Luke 6:22–23]. Rejoice and be glad and leap about—just as the apostles rejoiced when they were "counted worthy to suffer dishonor for the Name" [Acts 5:41].

Look to God for Strength

And if you should ever find your soul shrinking back, let the "mind of Christ" in us [1 Cor. 2:16] say to your soul when it is trying its hardest to upset the mind, "Why are you downcast, O my soul, and why are you troubling me? Hope in God, for I will gave thanks to him." And this is repeated [Ps. 42:5, 11].

Come, then, don't let your soul be unsettled in the least! Even when you stand before the very tribunals, when unsheathed swords are laid against your neck, let your soul be guarded by "the peace of God, which surpasses all understanding" [Phil. 4:7]. Let it be calmed by considering that those who are absent from the body are at home with the Lord of the universe himself [2 Cor. 5:8]. And if we aren't strong enough always to maintain such inner peace, let's at least not allow our troubled souls to burst forth and be noticed by outward observers. That way we'll still have the opportunity to explain ourselves to God, saying, "O my God, my soul was troubled *inside of me*" [Ps. 42:6].

The Word[2] also encourages us to recall the passage in Isaiah that says, "Do not fear the reproach of men or be overcome by their contempt" [Isa. 51:7]. For God is in charge of all the movements of the heavenly bodies, and by his divine skill he supervises everything that is being accomplished among the plants and animals of the earth and sea [vv. 6, 13]. He oversees the beginning, the structure, the nourishment, and the growth of all things. So it would clearly be foolish to shut our eyes and not look to God, turning our terrified gaze instead upon mortal men who will soon die and be handed over to the punishment they deserve!

God once said to Abraham, "Go forth from your country" [Gen. 12:1]. Perhaps it won't be long before the words are spoken to us, "Go forth from the earth altogether." To obey him in this is a privilege, for he will quickly show us the heavens, in which we find the place called the kingdom of heaven.

The Difference between the Virtue of Believers and Unbelievers

Now, it is plain to see that life is filled with contests and contestants striving to attain different virtues. And in fact, many people who are completely alienated from God's community appear to have struggled for self-control. Indeed, some have even died courageously for their loyalty to an ordinary master. Those who are adept in the arguments of scientific inquiry seem to have paid attention to wisdom, while those who exhibit a righteous life appear to have devoted themselves to righteousness. Truly, unbelievers strive for each of the virtues with the "mind of the flesh" [Rom. 8:6] or any other human capacities they may possess.

However, the only people who contend on behalf of *religion* are the "chosen race, the royal priesthood, the holy nation, a people for God's own possession"

2. When Origen refers to the "Word," he normally means the second person of the Godhead, who became incarnate as Jesus Christ—not the written Bible (which is usually called "sacred Scripture" or something like that). The identification of Christ as the Word is based on John 1:1–14. The Greek term for "word" in that passage, *logos*, was a prominent concept in pagan philosophy to explain the mediating principle between the divine mind and the physical earth. Therefore many early Christian apologists employed this term to describe the one who mediates between God and man—the man Christ Jesus. Origen believed the eternal Word was active among human beings long before he became incarnate and was born of a virgin. And Jesus Christ, the living Word, continued to teach his people the hidden meanings of the Bible in the ancient church. Origen saw teaching and revelation as one of Christ's primary ministries to humankind.

[1 Pet. 2:9]. If a persecution arises against religious people, others don't even pretend to demonstrate a willingness to die for their beliefs. They don't prefer to remain faithful unto death rather than live an impious life. In contrast, everyone who wishes to be part of the "chosen race" is committed to listening at all times to God, who says, "You shall have no other gods besides me" [Exod. 20:3] and "You shall not recall the names of other gods in your hearts nor mention them on your lips" [Exod. 23:13]. And the true believer adheres to this even when those who falsely call themselves "polytheists"—but are actually atheists—plot against him.

The Importance of Verbal Confession

This is the reason why Christians "believe in God with the heart unto righteousness" and "confess him with the mouth unto salvation" [Rom. 10:9–10]. They understand they won't be justified unless they believe in God with hearts that are properly disposed toward him; nor will they be saved if their outward speech doesn't confirm their inner disposition. Those people are deceiving themselves who think it is possible to reach Christ as their final destiny simply by "believing with the heart unto righteousness," without accepting the rest of the verse, "and confessing with the mouth unto salvation."[3] Indeed, one might even say it is better to honor God with the lips while having a heart far from him [Matt. 15:8] than to honor him with the heart while refusing to "confess with the mouth unto salvation" [Rom. 10:10].[4]

What if, though, when God commanded, "You shall not make idols for yourselves nor any kind of image," and so forth [Exod. 20:4], he stated the command so as to make a distinction between "you shall not bow before them" and "you shall not worship them"? Then perhaps the person who really believes in idols might worship them. But as for the one who doesn't actually believe, yet out of cowardice goes through the motions so he can look religious like everyone else (which he describes as "being diplomatic")—this person might not technically

3. Origen's point here is reminiscent of twentieth-century debates over "lordship salvation." Is it enough to believe in Jesus in the privacy of your heart, or do your words and actions have to back up your stated beliefs? Origen here follows the majority position in the ancient church that if a person verbally denies his Lord—even out of fear of torture or death—he has become apostate from the Christian faith. The believer's public testimony must correspond to what he claims to believe. The early Christians took a strong stance against any capitulation to the Roman authorities when it came to denying Christ or sacrificing to idols. To do so was to honor demons above Jesus, and this was absolutely unthinkable. However, we should remember that when the persecutions eventually passed, the church offered mercy to those who had succumbed to pagan demands. Thus, the approach was to draw a stark line in the sand against all apostasy and denials *before* the contest—then grant forgiveness to the fallen Christians *afterward*. (Not everyone, though, wanted to grant such forgiveness, which led to the breakaway community known as the Donatists, who separated from the universal church and caused a schism.)

4. Origen seems to be saying that Christian hypocrisy (while never a good thing, of course) is less likely to result in eternal condemnation than an outright verbal denial of Jesus Christ.

"worship" the idols, but he certainly does "bow down to" them.[5] And I would argue that those who swear an oath in the courtroom denying they are Christians, or even before they are put on trial, are bowing down to idols even if they're not worshiping them *per se*. They take the name of "God" from the Lord God and apply it to lifeless, powerless substances.[6] In exactly the same way, the Israelites who defiled themselves with the daughters of Moab [Num. 25:1] "bowed down" to idols but did not "worship" them. The text clearly states, "They called them to the sacrifices of their idols, and the people ate of their sacrifices, and bowed down to their idols, and performed the rites of Baal of Peor" [Num. 25:2–3]. Notice the text doesn't come out and say here, "and they *worshiped* their idols." Indeed, it was impossible after such great signs and wonders[7] for the Israelites to be convinced in a single instant by the women they fornicated with that the idols were actual gods. And maybe something similar happened at the making of the golden calf in the exodus: they "bowed down" but didn't "worship" the calf they had watched being made [Exod. 32:8].

Therefore we ought to regard the present temptation to deny as a test and trial of our love for God. "For the Lord is testing you," as it says in Deuteronomy, "to

5. Some modern commentators suggest Origen was thinking of certain gnostic sects that avoided martyrdom because any deed done in the physical body doesn't matter, so the behavior of the Christian martyrs must be considered foolish, stubborn, and unnecessary. While this attitude is well documented among the heretical sects, it is not hard to imagine that many within the orthodox Christian church were also making rationalizations like the ones Origen addresses here. "I'll bow down to idols on the outside," they might say, "but inwardly I won't actually mean it." Probably many Christians today would say the same thing if faced with persecution. Origen, however, takes a hard line against such capitulation. Though he acknowledges a verbal distinction between those who "worship" with heartfelt belief and those who only outwardly "bow down," he insists Christians who go through the motions of pagan religion are just like the apostate Israelites who worshiped Baal in the Old Testament and received God's judgment. I will leave it to the reader to determine whether Origen's hard-line view has support from the words of Jesus (Matt. 10:33; Mark 8:38; Luke 9:26; 12:9) or Paul (2 Tim. 2:12).

6. The idols, or "cult images," of Greco-Roman worship were composed of various materials, including stone, bronze, ivory, gold, silver, and wood. Often they were painted to look lifelike. Idols were normally housed in the interior room of a temple called the *cella*. Most worshipers did not enter the temple but only watched the rituals from outside. Often they left an offering on the temple's steps to compel the god to grant a wish or to thank the deity for a prayer answered. But the early Christians—like the ancient Jews before them—considered this behavior foolish because idols were made by human hands.

7. By "signs and wonders" Origen has in mind all the events experienced by the Israelites during the exodus as described in the book of Numbers (the first Passover commemoration, the cloud and fire over the tabernacle, the provision of quail and manna, divine judgments, military victories, the bronze serpent, Balaam's talking donkey, etc.). Origen thinks the Israelites could not so quickly forget these events and believe the pagan idols were actual gods. Yet by bowing down to these images, the Israelites became blameworthy before God even though they didn't accept the false religion in their hearts. So too, Christians who go through the motions of pagan worship are guilty no matter what they say they believe.

know whether you love the Lord your God with all your heart and soul" [Deut. 13:3]. But when you're tempted, "you will walk after the Lord your God and fear him and keep his commandments"—especially the one that says, "You shall have no other gods besides me" [Exod. 20:3]—"and you will hear his voice and attach yourselves to him" [Deut. 13:4]. For God takes you away from the present regions and attaches you to himself to bring about what the apostle Paul calls "the growth of God" that occurs in him [Col. 2:19].

Honoring Idols Is an Abomination

But here is what I say:[8] if "every evil utterance is an abomination to the Lord your God" [Prov. 15:26], how great an abomination is the evil utterance of a denial? Or the evil word of publicly hailing another god? Or the evil act of swearing oaths to the spirit that brings good fortune to men—which is utterly pointless? When this oath is demanded of us, we should remember the words of him who said, "But I say to you, do not swear at all" [Matt. 5:34]. The person who swears by heaven violates the very throne of God. He who swears by the earth utters blasphemy in making what is called "God's footstool" into a god. Swearing by Jerusalem is sinful as well, for it is the city of a great king, and even making an oath by one's own head is offensive [vv. 34–36]. So then, how much more sinful must it be to swear by someone's empowering demonic spirit? At such times we would do well to recall the saying "You will give an account for every idle word in the day of judgment" [Matt. 12:36]. And what word is more idle than an oath of apostasy?

The Error of Worshiping Created Things

Of course, the Enemy will probably seek to outwit us. He'll try to use every trick at his disposal to get us to worship "the sun, moon, or starry hosts of heaven," but we will respond that the word of God "has commanded us not to do this" [Deut. 17:3]. By no means should we ever worship the creation in the presence of the God who created all things—the God who now sustains the world and awaits the prayers of us all!

Nor would the sun even want to be worshiped by those who belong to God. In fact, it probably wouldn't want to be worshiped by anyone at all. It would respond exactly like he who said, "Why do you call me good? No one is good except God the Father alone" [Mark 10:18; Luke 18:19]. The sun would, we might imagine, respond to anyone who wanted to worship it by saying:

8. Having acknowledged a technical verbal difference between "bowing down" and "worshiping," Origen now proceeds to argue either one is evil. Any worshipful recognition of demons is an abomination to God.

Why do you call me God? There is only one true God—so why do you bow down to me? For it is written, "You shall bow down to the Lord your God and serve him alone" [Matt. 4:10]. I am something created. Why do you want to worship a thing that offers worship itself? For I too bow down to God the Father and serve him. In obedience to what he has decreed, I am "subjected to futility by the will of the one who subjected" me. Yet I also have the hope to be "set free from bondage to decay." Though I am now entangled in a perishable body, I await "the glorious freedom of the children of God" [Rom. 8:20–21].

It is also to be expected that some false prophet might arise—maybe more than one—who speaks a word to us as if from the Lord, yet telling us to do something the Lord has not commanded [Deut. 18:20]. He might offer a message that seems to be wise but is actually foreign to wisdom, intending to slay us with the word of his mouth. But as for us, whenever such a sinner comes and stands before us, let us say, "I am like a deaf man who does not hear, like a mute man who does not open his mouth. I have become like a man who does not hear" [Ps. 38:13–14]. For it is right to be deaf to immoral words when we find ourselves unable to correct those who speak evil.

God's Jealousy

Whenever we are faced with a decisive confrontation, it is a good idea to consider what God wants to teach us when he declares, "I the Lord your God am jealous" [Exod. 20:5]. In my opinion it's like a husband who pays attention to his bride to help her live a chaste life, devoting herself entirely to her spouse and taking every precaution to avoid intimacy with any other man but him. So if the husband is wise he will display some jealousy, exhibiting this demeanor toward his bride as a sort of medicine. The Lawgiver does exactly the same thing—especially if he is recognized to be "the firstborn of all creation" [Col. 1:15].[9] He informs his bride, the soul, that God is jealous, thereby keeping his hearers away from any fornication with demons and so-called gods. And God is speaking as a jealous husband when he says to anyone who has ever gone chasing after other gods, "They have made me jealous with what is no god; they have provoked me to anger with their idols. So I will make them jealous with those who are not a people; I

9. It is not obvious why Origen suddenly leaps to this verse from Colossians, but I think the answer may be as follows. He recalls the passage in Ephesians 5 where Christ is described as the bridegroom of the church. Verse 27 says Christ intends to "present" his bride to himself as "holy and blameless." This makes Origen think of Colossians 1:22, where Christ again "presents" Christians as "holy and blameless." In that passage it is clear that the one who accomplishes the chaste presentation is the "firstborn of all creation" (1:15), thus creating a connection between the two texts in Origen's mind. He was obviously a man steeped in the language of Holy Scripture. Biblical word associations often burst into his consciousness.

will provoke them to anger with a foolish nation. For a fire has been kindled by my anger, and it will burn all the way to the depths of hell" [Deut. 32:21–22; Rom. 10:19].

It isn't for his own sake that the Bridegroom steers his betrothed away from all defilement—for since he is wise, he isn't motivated by passionate emotions. Rather, it is for *her* benefit that he does it. When he sees any defilement and filth in her, he will do everything he can to restore her and win her back. Treating her as a person endowed with freedom of choice, he offers arguments to dissuade her from fornication. For what worse corruption could you possibly imagine befalling a soul than for it to proclaim another god and fail to confess the one true Lord alone? To me, just as "he who unites himself with a prostitute becomes one body with her" [1 Cor. 6:16], so anyone who confesses some god—especially at the moment his faith is being tested by a trial—intermingles and unites himself with the god he is confessing.

Consequences of Apostasy

Now, a denial causes the denier to be severed as if by a sword stroke from the one he rejects. He suffers amputation by being cut off from the one he disowned. Be aware, then, that it's probably because of the logical necessity that confessors be confessed, and deniers be denied, that Jesus said, "Whoever confesses me before men, I will also confess him before my Father in heaven, but whoever denies me before men, I also will deny him before my Father in heaven" [Matt. 10:32–33]. Thus, to the confessor as well as the denier, he who is the very Word of Truth himself might say:

> "With the measure you use it will be measured back to you" [Luke 6:38]. Those of you who have measured out a confession of me, truly filling your measuring cup, will receive back the full measure of my confession—"pressed down, shaken together, running over, poured into your lap." But you who measured out a denial of me will receive my denial of you in exact proportion to your own denial.

Requirements for a Full Confession

Let me offer a few additional thoughts about how the "measuring cup of confession" is either filled to the brim or found to be lacking. Suppose through the whole course of our testing and trial we give no foothold to the Devil in our hearts [Eph. 4:27]—he who wants to infect us with evil thoughts of denial, or doubt, or some kind of rationalization urging us to act contrary to our martyrdom and final perfection. And further suppose we don't defile ourselves with any statement that would undercut our confession, but instead we endure all our enemies' insults, ridicule, laughter, slander, and even the pity they pretend to have for us when they take us for idiots who have been tricked, calling us "badly mistaken." And suppose beyond this we don't waver from our path even when our hearts are tugged by tender love for our children, or their mother, or the people we consider our dearest friends in the world, such that we might cling to them and this earthly life. Instead we turn away from all these things and devote ourselves to God and eternal life in his presence, knowing we will fellowship with his only-begotten Son and everyone who has a share in him. Only then would I affirm we have truly filled up "the measuring cup of confession." But if we lack even one of these things, we haven't filled the cup. Instead we've contaminated it and mixed in something foreign. Then there will be a shortcoming in us, like the shortcoming in those who built on the foundation with "wood, hay, and straw" [1 Cor. 3:12].[10]

The Christian's Requirement to Deny Himself

We also need to recognize that when we embarked on the Christian life we entered into what are called "covenants" with God, that is, certain agreements we made with him. And one of our agreements with God was to embrace the whole lifestyle of the gospel, which makes the claim, "If anyone wishes to come after me, let him deny himself and take up his cross and follow me. For whoever wishes to save his life will lose it, but whoever loses his life for my sake will save it" [Matt. 16:24–25]. On many occasions we've also been inspired by hearing the words, "For what will it profit a man if he gains the whole world and forfeits his soul? Or what will a man give in exchange for his soul? For the Son of Man is about to come with his angels in the glory of his Father, and then he will repay each person according to his works" [vv. 26–27].

---

10. Origen sets the bar very high, doesn't he? Perhaps you may be wondering whether he was willing to back up his words with actions. The church historian Eusebius of Caesarea records what happened to Origen at the end of his life. About a decade and a half after he wrote the present treatise, Origen was imprisoned during the persecution of Emperor Decius. By then he was an old man in his mid-sixties. Knowing their prisoner was a very famous Christian, the jailers were especially fierce in their attempt to break him. Eusebius states that through these demon-possessed torturers, the Devil fought against Origen "with every available machine and all his power, assaulting him far beyond anyone else being persecuted at the time" (*Church History* 6.39.5). Origen was chained in the innermost dungeon, where he endured untold tortures, such as burning with fiery implements or being left in the stocks for many days with his legs forced apart into a splits position. Yet he bore these things steadfastly and maintained his confession, even when the contentious judge did his best to prolong the suffering instead of ending it through execution. At last the emperor died, and the persecution ended. Origen appears to have been released at that time, surviving for perhaps a year or two, though no doubt in constant pain from his injuries. Eusebius says he left behind words "full of comfort for those who need aid" until he finally breathed his last. The modern reader might wish to fault Origen's treatise *Exhortation to Martyrdom* for being too strict, but the one thing it can't be called is hypocritical.

But it's not only Matthew, in the text I just quoted, who records that we must deny ourselves, take up our cross, and follow Jesus. Mark and Luke say it too. Listen to Luke's version: "And he was saying to them all, 'If anyone wishes to come after me, he must deny himself and take up his cross and follow me. For whoever wishes to save his life will lose it, but whoever loses his life for my sake will save it. What does it profit a man if he gains the whole world but loses or forfeits himself?'" [Luke 9:23–25]. Likewise Mark says, "And he summoned the crowd with his disciples and said to them, 'If anyone wishes to follow after me, he must deny himself and take up his cross and follow me. For whoever wishes to save his life will lose it, but whoever loses it for the sake of the gospel will save it. What will it profit a man to gain the whole world and forfeit his soul? For what will a man give in exchange for his soul?'" [Mark 8:34–37]. As you can see, we long ago accepted the obligation to deny ourselves and say, "It is no longer I who live" [Gal. 2:20]. Now is the time to reveal whether we've taken up our crosses and followed Jesus! And this is exactly what happens if "Christ lives in us."[11]

If we want to save our soul and receive it back as something better,[12] let us lose it in martyrdom. For if we lose our soul for Christ's sake, casting it at his feet by dying for him, we will attain its true salvation. But if we do the opposite, we'll be told it profits us nothing to gain everything the physical world has to offer at the price of losing or forfeiting our very selves. Once someone has forfeited his soul, there is nothing he can give in exchange for that loss even if he owns the whole universe. Why? Because the soul that was made in the image of God is more valuable than all physical things put together. Only one person is able to offer a substitution for our soul after it has been lost—the one who has redeemed us with his own precious blood!

---

11. Origen quotes only some brief excerpts of Galatians 2:20 here, but in the present context of martyrdom the verse is worth pondering in its entirety: "I have been crucified with Christ. It is no longer I who live, but Christ who lives in me. And the life I now live in the flesh I live by faith in the Son of God, who loved me and gave himself for me." The church fathers felt that any person who believes this—who *really, truly* believes it—will gladly die for his or her faith.

12. What is meant by the term "something better"? Origen held the rather strange view that souls were rational "intelligences" that had cooled and fallen away from the warmth of God. Upon returning to him they would be rewarmed—and then the term "soul" (which Origen connected with the Greek word for "cooling off") would no longer apply. The soul would now be improved to the status of a "mind" that is united with God's own mind. This intriguing but completely unscriptural idea did not gain much traction with the other fathers of the ancient church.

11

The Great Persecution

The Church's Hour of Fiery Testing

Emperor Diocletian is normally portrayed as a villain of church history because he sponsored the worst persecution of the ancient period, but in fact he was a good ruler in terms of civil administration. When he rose to power in AD 284, the Roman Empire had just endured what came to be called the Crisis of the Third Century. Gone were the days of supremely powerful emperors from aristocratic families ruling over an expanding and stable domain. Now civil wars, breakaway kingdoms, barbarian invasions, plague, economic woes, and a merry-go-round of soldier emperors had turned the middle decades of the third century into an age of chaos. At last, Diocletian managed to settle things down—and in this way he set the stage for the long and prosperous reign of Constantine the Great. Though Rome's fall was still inevitable, these effective emperors managed to push back its demise by another century or two.

Diocletian recognized the empire had grown too large to be managed by one person. He needed to initiate an "imperial college" in which he would remain the supreme ruler yet others could supervise some of the more turbulent portions of the empire on his behalf. At first he used a two-man system, then later expanded it to four in what modern scholars call the Tetrarchy. The two figures with the highest power were given the title "augustus," while two junior emperors, known as "caesars," reigned under the senior men and would replace them when the time was right.

Though this system worked for a while, its fatal flaw was its lack of a clear mechanism for succession. When Diocletian abdicated the throne along with his co-emperor in 305, the two junior rulers moved up to the supreme rank. However, too many people wanted to be part of the imperial college—and they all had loyal armies. Soon various rivals were vying to be named a caesar, then one by one the caesars started proclaiming themselves augusti. Other powerful men jumped directly to augustus, backed up by their legions. All these ambitions formed a tangled web of simmering feuds, secret alliances, and familial bonds. Only brute force would decide the matter.

One of the main political decisions within the Tetrarchy was whether to adopt a policy of persecution against the Christians. This did not arise from pure religious hatred or bigotry. As you will see below, Christians were suspected of plots against the emperor and, more basically, of being disloyal to the empire and its gods. For this reason, some figures, such as Galerius, were ardent supporters of persecution; while others, like Constantine's father, Constantius Chlorus, did not support a vigorous crackdown. Constantius seems to have considered himself a monotheist of sorts, worshiping the supreme deity as personified by the Victorious Sun. Such solar monotheism would likewise serve as Constantine's entrée into the Christian faith.

Sometime around 310, while marching on a military campaign, Constantine witnessed a solar phenomenon that refracted the sun's light into crossed lines. At first he connected the event with the sun god Apollo, but later he began to wonder about other interpretations. A second supernatural omen then caught the general by surprise. He dreamed a divine figure came to him by night with instructions to make a battle standard that employed an x-shaped emblem. After consulting some Christian leaders, Constantine learned the cross was a sign of great cosmic power. Now he could sense the one true God was elevating him to supreme authority. Yet an archenemy stood in his way: Maxentius, the powerful son of an original tetrarch. Firmly entrenched in Rome, Maxentius commanded the elite Praetorian Guard along with an impressive regiment of imperial horsemen. Since Maxentius was also empowered by occult magic, Constantine knew he would need extra help from heaven to defeat his foe.

After a brief campaign in northern Italy, the two rivals finally met at the famous Battle of the Milvian Bridge in AD 312. Maxentius foolishly crossed the Tiber River and left himself no option for retreat. Carrying banners and shields marked by the sign of the cross, Constantine's veteran troops pressed the enemy backward into the river's muddy waters. The defeated army fled, and Maxentius was drowned. His corpse was fished from the river so its severed head could be mounted on a spear as Constantine marched triumphantly into Rome. Though he did not abandon pagan religion right away, the jubilant conqueror had every intention of offering tolerance to the Christians and rewarding the people whose God had granted him victory. And so it was that Emperor Constantine's rise to power changed the course of church history forever.

———————— ▬ ————————

Two important texts have been selected in this chapter to illustrate the events of the Great Persecution. The first comes from an early Christian orator and scholar named Lactantius. Originally from Africa, Lactantius made his way to the imperial court in Nicomedia (modern-day Izmit, Turkey) to serve as a professor of rhetoric. The city of Nicomedia was one of the capitals of the Tetrarchy, which gave Lactantius the opportunity to rub shoulders not only with the empire's elite but also with the many Christians who lived there as well. After converting to Christ, he resigned (or lost) his professorship just as the Great Persecution got going. Many scholars think he moved to a safer part of the empire where hostility against Christians was less intense. During this exile, Lactantius occupied himself by writing apologetic works in defense of the true faith.

After the persecution passed, Constantine recognized Lactantius's great learning and raised him from poverty to a high station once more, even asking him to tutor his own son. This newfound respectability gave Lactantius the opportunity to write his treatise *On the Deaths of the Persecutors*, a description of the terrible fates that befell the pagans who persecuted the church. The book is permeated with the psychological attitude known as *Schadenfreude*, or delight in the misfortune of enemies. Even so, because Lactantius moved in upper-crust circles, he had a unique vantage point from which to describe what was happening behind the scenes in the halls of power. In this first selection we get a look at the Great Persecution's beginnings from someone who had every reason to watch it closely.

Lactantius, *On the Deaths of the Persecutors* 10–15

Diocletian Enraged at Christians

Because of Diocletian's nervous disposition, he was very devoted to investigating the future through divination.[1] One time while he was conducting business in

---

1. The practice of divination was common among the Romans, but the sources suggest Diocletian was an especially avid consultant of soothsayers. This type of forecasting, which the Romans learned from the Etruscans, typically consisted of watching the flight of birds or examining animal entrails to discover omens about the future. Major decisions often depended

the eastern regions, he was sacrificing cattle and examining their livers to predict what was about to happen. But during the sacrifice some of his attendants who knew the Lord were standing nearby, and they made the everlasting sign on their foreheads. At this the demons fled away, which disrupted the sacred rites. The soothsayers grew anxious at not seeing the usual signs in the entrails, so they tried several more sacrifices as if the first ones hadn't been favorable; yet the slaughter of further offerings revealed nothing. Finally the chief priest Tagis (either through a hunch or by what he had observed) declared the reason the sacrifices were not providing an answer was because sacrilegious men were present at the holy ceremonies.

At this Diocletian flew into a rage. He ordered not only those who were ministering at the sacrifice but everyone who lived in the palace to make an offering. Anyone who refused was to be severely flogged. He also sent letters to the military officers directing that every soldier be forced to make the impious sacrifice or be dismissed from the army. But this was as far as Diocletian's furious anger went. He didn't do anything further against the law and religion of God.

Galerius Urges Empire-Wide Persecution

Then after some time had passed, Diocletian came to Bithynia to spend the winter. The caesar Galerius arrived there too, inflamed with the wicked desire to convince the weak old man to persecute the Christians as he had already begun to do. And I have discovered the root of Galerius's madness to be as follows.

His mother was a highly superstitious woman and a worshiper of the mountain gods. When she was [*text missing*], she used to hold religious banquets almost every day and offer the sacrificial meat to the villagers of her district. But while she was feasting with the pagans, the Christians abstained and continued with their fasts and prayers.[2] Thus, she conceived hatred for them in her heart. And by

---

on whether the signs were auspicious. Portents of the future frequently occurred in the sky, so when Constantine encountered his cross-shaped "vision" in 310, it was entirely in keeping with Roman sensibilities to interpret it as a divine sign. The only unusual thing about it was the God who Constantine decided had spoken to him.

2. In 1 Corinthians 8 and 10, the apostle Paul says eating meat sacrificed to idols is not a sin *per se*, yet if a fellow believer's conscience warns against it, the mature Christian should abstain for the sake of his brother or sister. This advice would pertain to meat obtained in public markets or served to guests in a pagan's home. However, Paul makes a clear distinction (see especially 10:18–21) between purchasing meat in shops and participating in religious banquets in conjunction with temple sacrifice. Eating at such banquets is idolatrous fellowship with demons. The situation in Bithynia under Galerius's mother, Romula, fit the latter category. Enjoyment of the meat she distributed would have been not a mere purchase from a butcher shop but an act of religious devotion. In addition, eating the meat would have violated the voluntary fasts to which some of these Christians had committed themselves. They had no choice but to abstain, and Romula took offense at this.

constantly complaining the way women do, she provoked her son, who was no less superstitious than she, to get rid of these men.

So Diocletian and Galerius held exclusive meetings all through the winter. Everyone assumed they were discussing matters of the highest importance to the empire. For a long time the senior man resisted the younger's madness, pointing out how destructive it would be for the whole world to be destabilized by a lot of bloodshed. The Christians, Diocletian observed, were quite accustomed to dying for their principles. It would be enough to prohibit those in the imperial household and the army from that religion.

But since Diocletian couldn't restrain the insanity of that rash man, he decided to test the opinions of his friends. (For this was one of Diocletian's character flaws: that when he decided to do something good, he did it without counsel so he could take the credit for himself; but when he intended to do something evil that he knew would be criticized, he called together many advisers so the blame for whatever he did wrong could be pinned on others.) Thus, a few judges and military officers were summoned and questioned in the order of their social rank. Now, some of them, out of their personal hatred of Christians, recommended they be exterminated as enemies of the gods and opponents of the state religion. But even those who held a different view understood what Galerius's wishes were—and so, whether out of fear or flattery, they concurred with the opinions of the rest.

Despite all this, the emperor wasn't persuaded to give his assent. He intended above all to consult the gods, so he sent a priest to the oracle of Apollo at Didyma.[3] Apollo answered exactly as one would expect from an enemy of divine religion. Thus, Diocletian was drawn away from his original purpose; yet while he could no longer resist his friends, and the caesar, and Apollo, he still tried to preserve a policy of moderation.[4] He ordered the affair to be conducted without bloodshed, though Caesar Galerius wanted those who wouldn't sacrifice to be burned alive.

3. The sanctuary at Didyma was, along with Delphi, one of the most important centers of oracular prophecy in the Greek world. Founded so far back in the misty ages of prehistory that no one knew its true origins, the shrine had become, in Diocletian's day, a favorite place for Roman generals and politicians to determine the will of the gods. A great promenade adorned with statues connected the temple to the nearby city of Miletus. Those who came to Didyma brought lavish gifts, and if Apollo was pleased with them he gave a reply to the question being asked. Note that Lactantius does not doubt a real spiritual force was offering oracles here. Indeed, Apollo gave exactly the sort of answer one would expect from a demonic enemy of Christianity.

4. In contrast to this description, Emperor Constantine depicts his predecessor Diocletian in much more bloodthirsty terms. Looking back on the beginnings of the Great Persecution from the stance of a committed Christian, Constantine says the cowardly, insane, and anxious Diocletian was desperate to identify the "righteous on earth" who were disrupting the prophecies of Apollo. The god's priests had recently been lamenting the failure of their oracles. When Diocletian was told the Christians were to blame, he grew enraged and immediately issued the edicts of persecution. Judges were ordered to invent the cruelest forms of torture they could

The Persecution Begins

A suitable and lucky day was sought for carrying out this business, and the festival of Terminalia on February 23 was chosen as best. In this way a sort of "boundary" could be imposed on the Christian religion.[5]

"That day was the first cause of death; it was the first cause of evils"[6] — evils that befell not only the Christians but also the whole world! When this day dawned, the two augusti were in their eighth and seventh consulships.[7] Suddenly, as the sun was just coming up, the prefect arrived at the church in Nicomedia along with several generals, senior officers, and treasury agents. They tore away the doors and searched for an idol of God. They found the Scriptures and burned them. Everything was given away as plunder. The whole church was full of ransacking, terror, and people dashing back and forth.

Meanwhile Diocletian and Galerius watched it all from their high vantage point, for the church was built on a hill and could be seen from the palace. They argued for a long time whether the building should be set ablaze. At last Diocletian won the debate with the reminder that starting such a great fire might cause some other part of the city to go up in flames, since the church was ringed on all sides by many mansions. So instead the Praetorian Guard arrived in full battle formation, carrying axes and other iron tools. After being let loose against the building from every direction, they razed that very lofty temple to the ground in a matter of hours.

The next day an edict was posted warning that those who adhered to Christianity would lose all rank and social standing. They would be subject to judicial torture no matter what order or grade they came from.[8] Any lawsuit brought against them

---

devise. The barbarians at that time put the persecutors to shame by offering the kind of humane tolerance toward fleeing Christians that the supposedly civilized Romans had exchanged for brutish savagery. According to Constantine, Diocletian and his cronies are now being punished for these wicked crimes in the pit of Hades (Eusebius, *Life of Constantine* 2.49–54).

5. Terminus was the Roman god who watched over boundary markers. In a society where the entire countryside was composed of large estates, the division of property was vital and had to be marked with stone monuments. Landowners met at the stones to conduct religious rites that sealed the goodwill between neighbors. Since Terminus was a god of boundaries, his annual festival seemed like a good day to *terminate* Christianity.

6. Lactantius, a highly educated literary man, often uses quotations from the Latin writer Virgil to illustrate his points. Here Lactantius cites the epic poem *Aeneid* 4.169–70.

7. As noted in footnote 2 of chap. 7, the consulship was an elected office in ancient Rome that was used to keep track of dates. The year referred to here is what we call AD 303.

8. Roman society was divided into strict hierarchies, and not everyone enjoyed the same legal privileges. Our Jeffersonian notion that "all men are created equal" would have been inconceivable to an ancient mind. People of different classes were thought to have different intrinsic worth. At the bottom of the barrel were slaves, who had no rights whatsoever and were subject to the whims of their masters. Among the free classes, a sharp distinction had emerged in the late imperial period between the *honestiores* ("more honorable") and the *humiliores* ("more lowly"). The upper class consisted of aristocratic senators and wealthy knights, as well as

would be valid, while they themselves could not sue those who wronged them, or committed adultery with their wives, or stole property from them.[9] From this moment on, they would have no freedom or voice.

There was a certain man who—though admittedly not doing what was right, yet showing great courage nonetheless—yanked down the edict and tore it to pieces, crying in a mocking voice, "Behold your victories over Goths and Sarmatians!"[10] He was apprehended immediately. And he was not merely tortured, but to put it more precisely, he was cooked over a grill fire. After displaying admirable endurance, he finally died from the burning.

Christians Framed for a Palace Fire

But Caesar Galerius wasn't content with the conditions of the edict, so he made plans to come at Diocletian by another strategy. In order to force him into a policy of viciously cruel persecution, Galerius got secret conspirators to set the imperial palace on fire. When a certain part of it had been consumed by flames, the Christians were blamed as public enemies. Then, just like the palace, the Christian name blazed up with the fire of tremendous hatred. It was rumored the Christians had made a secret pact with the eunuchs to kill the emperors, both of whom had nearly been burned alive in their own homes.

Diocletian, who always wanted to appear astute and intelligent, suspected nothing of the trick. Instead he was inflamed with anger and immediately began to torture everyone in his household. He presided over the investigation himself and had innocent people roasted with fire. Meanwhile all the judges—in fact, all the civil servants in the imperial administration—were given the power to apply torture. They competed with one another to be the first to discover something.

---

soldiers and local city councilors. These *honestiores* possessed considerable legal protections that the masses of *humiliores* did not have, such as exemption from torture and degrading forms of capital punishment. Many Roman clans had worked hard over decades or even centuries to raise their family's social standing and achieve higher *dignitas* ("respectability"). By the third century AD, the class of *honestiores* would have included numerous Christians. For them to be suddenly stripped of their hard-won rights, exposing them to all the harshness that Roman law meted out against the lowly, was a very severe blow.

9. Christians were barred from legal redress for wrongs committed against them by a devious strategy: Diocletian required a token sacrifice to the gods before any court proceedings could begin. Since Christians would not do this, they essentially could not use the court system—and therefore anyone could harm them or steal from them without fear of retaliation.

10. The martyr's name is recorded in later tradition as Euethius. His story is also told by Eusebius (see the selection below translated from his *Church History*). In Lactantius's version, the author does not feel he can approve of Euethius's scornful tone and voluntary martyrdom, yet he has to admire the man's courage. The insult Euethius shouts as he shreds the edict refers to Emperor Diocletian's titles, *Gothicus* and *Sarmaticus*, which he gained after winning victories over those tribes. In this defiant act, the martyr symbolically rejects everything Diocletian stands for. Such disrespect for the emperor's majesty was bound to bring swift punishment.

Yet nothing was found anywhere, for no one in Galerius's entourage was put to the test.

And Galerius himself was right in the middle of all this, urging it on, never allowing the wrath of the gullible old man to ease up. After fifteen days he started yet another fire. This one was discovered more quickly, though the culprit was never found. Then the caesar, who had been making plans to depart since midwinter, rushed off that very day. He called everyone to witness that he was fleeing for his life lest he be burned alive.

The Terror Spreads

Now Emperor Diocletian began to rage, not just against his domestic servants, but against everyone in the imperial household.[11] First of all he forced his daughter, Valeria, and wife, Prisca, to be polluted by sacrificing. Eunuchs who had once been very powerful, upon whom Diocletian and the whole palace used to rely, were put to death. Presbyters and deacons were arrested and condemned without any evidence or confession, then led off to execution along with their families. People of every age, both male and female, were carted off to be burned—not individually, but encircled by flame in large groups because their number was so great. Many members of the imperial household had millstones tied to their necks and were plunged into the sea.

But the persecution bore down with no less violence on the broader population. Judges were dispatched to all the temples to compel everyone to sacrifice. The prisons were overflowing. Previously unheard-of forms of torture were invented. To prevent a just verdict from accidentally being granted to a Christian, altars were erected in law courts and in front of tribunals, so that every litigant would first have to offer sacrifice and only then be allowed to make his case. In this way the judges were being approached as if they were gods!

Furthermore, bulletins were sent to Maximian and Constantius ordering them to carry out the same policy (though no attempt had been made to consider their opinion on such important matters).[12] The senior ruler Maximian readily enforced

11. The emperor's household would have included much more than his family and the necessary domestic servants. The palace was the seat of the imperial government, and as such it included an array of judges, clerks, military men, and civil servants of various ranks. Historians today consider the era of Diocletian to mark a transition in which the relatively lean government of previous years became bloated with layers of bureaucracy. The emperor was isolated like a divine being, surrounded by a posse of sycophants who curried his favor. Many of the palace staff were eunuchs: castrated men who were viewed with disdain, yet who could be entrusted with power because they lacked aggressive tendencies and family allegiances. This climate of raw power and sneaky double-dealing was the perfect atmosphere to spawn a vicious pogrom against a religious minority like Christianity.

12. Maximian (the augustus) and Constantius (the caesar) were the other two men who made up the original Tetrarchy. Their territories lay in the western half of the empire. As Lactantius

the order throughout Italy, for he was by no means a merciful man. As for Constantius, to avoid seeming to disobey the instructions of his seniors he allowed the demolition of some churches—that is, the physical walls, which can be rebuilt. But the true temple of God, which is the people themselves [1 Cor. 3:16–17; 6:19; 2 Cor. 6:16; Eph. 2:21–22], he preserved unharmed. And so it was that the whole earth was afflicted. Three wild beasts raged with utmost ferocity everywhere from east to west, except in Gaul.

———————————— ▬ ————————————

Our second text on the Great Persecution comes from the famous *Church History* by Eusebius of Caesarea. This book is one of the most precious documents to have come down to us from the early church. Without it, our knowledge of ancient Christianity would be greatly diminished.

Eusebius was born in the 260s and educated in a city that was experiencing its heyday. The port of Caesarea on the coast of Palestine (now a few miles north of Tel Aviv, Israel) had risen to become an important political and cultural center by Eusebius's time. The biblical king Herod the Great had given it an impressive harbor, a grand theater, and an aqueduct, all of which can still be visited today. Caesarea was also an important intellectual center for the early Christians, since the brilliant scholar Origen spent two fruitful decades there, and Eusebius's mentor Pamphilus continued the tradition by building up a great library. Thus, Eusebius was in an excellent position to consult whatever source documents the church had to offer as he composed his ten-volume history of Christianity, covering the period from Jesus to Constantine.

The selection translated here overlaps with what Lactantius recorded about the beginnings of the Great Persecution. Although Eusebius was not as highly placed as Lactantius, he was directly acquainted with Constantine and knew the intricate politics of the age. Eusebius had lived through the age of persecution, so he decided to make martyr stories his special area of historical research. While we must recognize the *Church History* is always arguing a case for Christianity and is never a purely objective account, the facts it records are usually reliable and based on available sources. With a careful and critical reading of Eusebius, we can learn much about the events of the early church.

points out, these two men responded very differently to Diocletian's command to persecute: Maximian obliged in Italy and Africa, while Constantius resisted in Gaul, Spain, and Britain. Less than a decade later, all four tetrarchs were dead and the sons of the western pair were locked in a struggle for supremacy. Constantine defeated Maxentius at the Battle of the Milvian Bridge in AD 312 to assume sole rulership of the West.

Eusebius, *Church History* 8.2–3, 5–7

Emperor Diocletian's Edicts

It was the nineteenth year of Diocletian's reign, in the month the Romans call March, just as the celebration of the Savior's Passion was approaching, that an imperial edict was published everywhere.[13] It ordered that all church buildings be demolished and the Scriptures be consumed by fire. In addition it gave notice that anyone who had attained high social rank would be stripped of it, while servants working in the imperial household who continued to adhere to Christianity would be deprived of their right to freedom and become slaves. This was the content of the first edict against us. Two more edicts followed soon after, one ordering the imprisonment of all the church's leaders across the empire, the next commanding that every available means be used to force them to sacrifice.

The Martyrs' Terrible Ordeals

At that time many of the church's leaders chose to bear up courageously under terrible tortures, and in so doing provided inspirational stories of perseverance through great suffering. Yet countless others whose souls had already been dulled by cowardice quickly succumbed at the first sign of trouble.

Among those who persevered, each underwent a variety of torments. Some had their bodies shredded by the whip; others were punished with disjointing and unbearable slicing, so that their lives came to a truly horrific and grisly end. Yet others came through the conflict in a different way. One was forcefully dragged by several men to the impure, disgusting sacrifices, then released as if he had made the offering though he certainly had not. Another who had not even approached such an abomination, much less touched it, was declared by the authorities to have sacrificed. He silently bore the slander as he went away. There was one gravely sick person who was arrested and then tossed out on the assumption he was as good as dead, while another man was dragged along the ground by his feet for a long distance and was included among those who had sacrificed. Some publicly proclaimed at the top of their lungs their utter rejection of the sacrifices; some shouted that they were Christians, taking pride in confessing the name that brings salvation; some earnestly maintained they had not sacrificed and never would. Despite their courage, these men were silenced by many punches from a large squad of soldiers dispatched for that purpose. They were beaten on their faces and cheeks until they were driven away. All of this demonstrates how the opponents of

---

13. This is the same year as described by Lactantius, AD 303. The persecution in Diocletian's capital began on February 23, but it must have been late March by the time the decree arrived in Eusebius's city of Caesarea. Easter that year was April 18.

righteousness put great stock, above all else, in seeming to have gotten the best of us. Yet none of these strategies gave them success against the holy martyrs. What word of mine can ever suffice to capture their amazing story?

[Eusebius makes some remarks about Christian soldiers who endured persecution, then continues his account.]

Terror and Triumph at Nicomedia

No sooner had the edict against the churches been published in Nicomedia than a certain man of no small reputation in town—in fact, a man highly esteemed according to the world's value system—was so overcome with zeal for God and aroused by red-hot faith that he seized the decree from where it was posted in a public square and ripped it to shreds as something unholy and profane.[14] And he did this while the two emperors were present in the city—the most senior of them and the one who occupied the fourth position of command. Then this martyr, the first of many who distinguished themselves for such behavior in that day, immediately suffered the natural consequences of such a daring act. Yet he remained tranquil and undisturbed right up to his final breath.

Among all those who have ever been celebrated in song, or whose courage has ever been proclaimed among Greeks or barbarians, our present age has produced its own godly and magnificent martyrs: the imperial palace servants led by Dorotheus. They had been esteemed worthy of highest honors by their masters, being treated by them as nothing less than their very own sons. Even so, these martyrs considered insults and afflictions for the sake of the gospel—not to mention the many new methods of execution invented for them—to be a truly greater form of wealth than all the eminence and luxuries that life has to offer. Allow me to recall how one particular individual met his end. I will leave it to my readers to gather from that instance what happened to the rest.

In Nicomedia a certain man was brought into a public place by the rulers I have just mentioned and was commanded to sacrifice. When he refused, he was ordered to be raised on high completely naked to have his entire body shredded by barbed whips, until at last he would give in and do as he was told even though he didn't want to. But when he remained steadfast despite suffering these things, they next poured a mixture of vinegar and salt on the deteriorated parts of his body, into wounds so grievous his bones were already showing through. And when he likewise treated these agonies as nothing, their next move was to bring out a brazier of hot coals. What remained of his mangled body was set over the grill fire like a piece of meat being cooked as food—not his whole body at once lest

14. The man was Euethius, who was described above by Lactantius. His action angered the most senior emperor, Diocletian, and the fourth member of the Tetrarchy, Galerius.

he die quickly, but rather he was burned little by little. The torturers who put him on the fire were not allowed to let up until such terrible treatment would force the man to agree to do what he was commanded. Yet he clung to his principles with unwavering determination. At last, victorious in the midst of his tortures, he released his spirit. Such was the martyrdom of one of the imperial household servants, a man truly worthy of his name—for he was called "Peter."

As for the rest, though their deeds were no less great, I will omit them for the sake of keeping my word limit to a minimum. I will only mention that Dorotheus and Gorgonius, along with many others from the imperial household who endured various types of torment, were strangled to death and carried away the prizes of their God-given victory.

It was at this time that Anthimus, who then presided as bishop of the church in Nicomedia, was beheaded for his testimony to Christ. And a great crowd of martyrs was added with him in the same moment; for a devastating fire had broken out in the imperial palace at Nicomedia (I know not how), and due to a false rumor, word circulated that our people were to blame.[15] By imperial command, entire families of godly believers perished in great heaps—some struck down by the sword, others killed by fire. Record has it that husbands and wives flung themselves onto the pyre with a kind of divine readiness that is impossible to comprehend. A large number of others were tied up by the public executioner and put on boats to be cast into the depths of the sea. And as for the imperial servants whose dead bodies had been committed to the ground with proper burial rites, their supposed masters, wanting to wipe the slate clean, thought it necessary to dig them up afterward and toss them in the sea as well. For they feared some of us would actually regard them as gods (such, at least, was their imagination) and we might worship them where they lay in their tombs.[16] These, then, were the things that happened at the beginning of the persecution in Nicomedia.

15. Compare Eusebius's account here to that of Lactantius above. Eusebius does not blame Galerius for framing the Christians; apparently he does not know any of those details. Several years later, Emperor Constantine will say the fire was caused by lightning. In the end, of course, we cannot know for sure what started the fire. Yet we should not be too hasty in assuming there could not have been any Christian involvement in setting it. In that age of extremism and desperation, an assassination attempt on the emperors' lives to stop the persecution could well have been possible. Perhaps a modern analogy would be the purported involvement of Dietrich Bonhoeffer (whom everyone acknowledges to be a very devoted Christian) in the plot to kill Adolf Hitler to spare the lives of his many future victims. Some ancient Christians might have justified arson on similar grounds.

16. The Christians did not, of course, worship dead bodies as gods. Their religion was emphatically opposed to polytheism. Yet as we have seen, devotion to saints and martyrs had already made its appearance in the church by this era. Both the archaeological and the literary evidence reveal a significant funeral cult had developed by the early fourth century (see the introduction for a discussion of this). It is easy to imagine how the Romans would mistake such respect for

Pastors Everywhere Are Persecuted

But when an uprising a little while later in the area called Melitene, and another in the region around Syria, tried to overthrow the empire, an imperial decree went out that the bishops of the churches in every place were to be bound in chains and imprisoned.[17] The spectacle of what happened next defies all description. Everywhere you looked, countless numbers of Christians were being locked up. Dungeons that were originally constructed to hold murderers and grave robbers now overflowed with bishops, presbyters, deacons, readers, and exorcists, so that there was no longer any room for those who had actually committed crimes! This decree was soon followed by another, stating that if the prisoners offered sacrifice to the gods they would be allowed to go free, but if they persisted, they would be torn to shreds by numerous tortures.

How, indeed, could I begin to number the great host of martyrs in every province, especially from distant Africa and Mauretania, or Egypt and the Upper Nile? Egypt in particular sent out many who were noted for their martyrdoms in other cities and provinces. Yet at least I know something about those who were noteworthy in Palestine, or Tyre in Phoenicia. What witness of these events was not astonished by the steadfastness of these utterly amazing champions of godliness under countless lashes? Or their struggle against man-eating beasts that immediately followed the whipping, such as leopards and various types of bears and wild boars and bulls enraged by a hot iron—each attack of which these noble heroes faced with admirable endurance? I myself was present when those events were happening. In that hour I could see the ever-present divine power from the One to whom they testified—our Savior Jesus Christ himself—clearly manifested in the martyrs!

---

bones and relics as "worship." The emperors did not want the tombs of Nicomedia to become an inspirational rallying point for the Christians—a possible stimulus to further treason.

17. This is the second decree of Diocletian from the early summer of 303. Little is known about the uprisings or whether Christians were involved, but the upshot was that persecution now fell not only upon the imperial household and the army but also on church leaders across the empire. The action put incredible strain on the Roman prison system, which was designed to hold only a few accused criminals awaiting trial, not masses of long-term inmates. Such overcrowding explains why the authorities quickly reversed their policy in a third decree (November 303) and tried to empty the jails—though only after going to great lengths to ensure, or at least make it seem, that the Christians had first offered sacrifice. Diocletian's fourth and final decree, in early 304, was the most terrible of all: it ordered everyone in the empire to sacrifice to the gods or be executed. Yet this law was enforced unevenly, with most of the oppression happening in the East. Due to the complicated political situation, quite a bit less persecution occurred in the West, though it did take place for a few years in Italy, Africa, and perhaps some parts of Spain.

12

The Peace of Constantine

An Empire Conquered by the Cross

Constantine is widely known as the "first Christian emperor." It was he who, broadly speaking, ushered in the Peace of the Church, the time when Roman persecution finally ceased. Our first textual selection recounts how this successful general and politician came to view himself as an adherent of the Christian religion. The story comes from the *Life of Constantine*, a writing composed by Eusebius much later than his *Church History*. This biographical work is noted for its constant tone of flattery and adulation—which does not, of course, mean nothing in it is true. Eusebius typically does not resort to outright fabrications in his historical narratives. Rather, he presents a heavily theologized version of historical events as he understood them, often with the sort of exaggeration and credulity that was common among ancient historians. Yet if we set aside Eusebius's exaltation of the emperor as God's specially chosen instrument, we can still discern many important facts about the man Constantine himself.

On the other hand, to completely disregard the underlying theology would be to misunderstand the historical moment in which Eusebius was writing. The vital thing about Constantine is not simply *what happened* but what Christians *believed to have happened*. As a bare historical fact, the rise to power of Emperor Constantine brought a permanent end to the policies of previous rivals who had been prone to persecute the church. However, we would fall short as historians if we failed to notice how Christians of that age discerned God at work in the man who now ruled the Roman Empire.

Nothing convinced the early Christians of divine favor more than miracles. And when it came to Constantine, the miracle most often remembered as signifying God's hand of blessing was the vision of the cross that preceded the Battle of the Milvian Bridge. This became a stock scene in later histories of the period and in the many medieval biographies of Constantine. Indeed, twelve hundred years later, when the great Renaissance artist Raphael was ready to paint a series of Constantinian frescoes for a room in the pope's personal apartments, he intended to cover two of the four walls with depictions of these very events. Though it was Raphael's students who actually executed the paintings after their master's death, the Hall of Constantine in the Apostolic Palace of the Vatican still symbolizes the high esteem in which the "first Christian emperor" is often held. For this reason, we must begin our present chapter with one of the most famous conversion stories ever to echo down through the halls of church history.

Eusebius, *Life of Constantine* 1.26–30, 32–39

Constantine Seeks a Divine Protector

Constantine perceived the whole structure of the earth was like a great body whose head, the imperial capital of Rome, had fallen under the domination of a tyrannical slave master. At first he gave the more senior men who ruled other parts of the empire a chance to defend it.[1] But when none of these men was able to provide any relief, and those who did try ended up meeting a disastrous outcome, Constantine declared his life was not worth living while he could see the imperial city afflicted like this. Then he began to make plans to overthrow the tyrant.

However, because the tyrant Maxentius made ample use of wicked occult magic, Constantine was firmly convinced he would need more powerful assistance than just what his soldiers could provide. Therefore he sought some kind of divine aid, assigning the abilities of foot soldiers or large numbers of troops

1. The tyrant mentioned here is Maxentius, against whom two unsuccessful campaigns were mounted in AD 307: first by Severus, a henchman of Galerius, and later the same year by Galerius himself. In both cases, Maxentius managed to turn back the armies that had invaded Italy to snatch Rome from him. But by 312, Constantine had allied himself with a man named Licinius, and both men agreed Maxentius had to be taken down. Realizing that whoever acted first would claim Italy as his prize, Constantine began to mobilize his army for an Italian expedition as soon as the mountain passes could be crossed. This was against everyone's expectation—but Constantine believed he had favor from on high.

to a secondary level of importance—for he believed without the help of a god, these things counted for nothing. Only what came from a god's cooperation, he declared, is irresistible and invincible.

So he was considering what kind of god he should adopt to help him, and as he was reflecting on this matter, a very clear insight crystallized in his mind. He realized that out of the many men before him who had earnestly desired to rule, those who linked their personal ambitions to multiple gods by honoring them with drink offerings, sacrifices, and gifts often found themselves deceived by flattering prophecies. Despite oracles that pronounced an auspicious outcome, these rulers frequently met an unfortunate end. Furthermore, none of these gods faithfully stood by the side of these men to shield them from natural disasters. Only one person—Constantine's own father—had turned in the opposite direction by condemning their error. Throughout his life he honored the God who is supreme over all, finding him to be a savior and guardian of his empire, the provider of every good thing.[2]

These thoughts tumbled over and over in Constantine's mind. He reflected long and hard on the fact that those who relied on many gods had run into many forms of ruin, so that no family, descendants, or offspring were left to them, nor any fond remembrance among mankind, whereas his father's God had bestowed

---

2. Eusebius represents Constantine's father, Constantius Chlorus, as a worshiper of the highest God, presumably meaning the Christian God. At an earlier point in his historical narrative (*Life of Constantine* 1.17), Eusebius suggested this even more clearly when he claimed Constantius filled his household with "holy men" and caused his family and servants to worship the Supreme God, so that his palace was not much different from a church. Yet there is little solid evidence that Constantius explicitly worshiped the God of the Bible. While recent historical scholarship has entertained the possibility that his first wife (or perhaps concubine), Helena, the mother of Constantine, was a Christian from an early stage, it is far more likely Constantius himself worshiped Sol Invictus, the Unconquered Sun. As has already been noted, solar worship was viewed in antiquity as a type of monotheism, for the sun symbolized the highest principle of the cosmos (cf. Ps. 84:11). Jesus was often depicted in early Christian art—and even in Scripture (Luke 1:78; Eph. 5:14; cf. Mal. 4:2)—through solar imagery. Therefore it seems Eusebius has combined Constantius's solar monotheism and the fact that he surrounded himself with Christian servants and advisers to prove that the emperor must have been on the road to authentic faith. Whatever the actual case may have been, there is little doubt that sun worship served as the religious entry point by which Constantine likewise began to consider the reality of a single supreme being. Eventually this spiritual exploration led to his adherence to full-blown Christianity. At a more mature stage of his life, Constantine even summoned the great Council of Nicaea in AD 325, where the doctrine of the Trinity was formally established. After this event, he left sun worship behind. Though Sunday continued to be a legal day of rest in the empire, it was now dedicated to Christ instead of Sol. (Some scholars, however, believe Constantine's sun worship continued throughout his life. They point to a marble column erected in 330 that was topped, so they claim, by a statue of the emperor arrayed like a sun god. But I follow the opinion of scholars who argue the statue did not convey solar themes, only the normal appearance of a glorious Roman emperor. The statue is long gone today, though its column still stands in the heart of Istanbul, Turkey.)

on him many obvious signs of divine empowerment. Constantine also considered the men who had already attacked Maxentius the tyrant. The polytheists had assembled all their forces but endured embarrassing defeats: Galerius was forced to retreat in disgrace without giving battle, while Severus was executed in the midst of his own army, becoming yet another example of death. So then, collecting all these thoughts in his mind, Constantine concluded that in light of such convincing proofs, it was an act of sheer lunacy to grasp after gods that did not exist and keep straying from the truth. He decided to worship his father's God alone.

The Vision in the Sky

Therefore Constantine began to call upon this God in prayer, earnestly begging him to reveal who he was and extend his right hand of assistance for what lay ahead. And as he was making these fervent and heartfelt prayers, an astonishing heavenly sign appeared to the emperor. (Now, this probably wouldn't be easy to believe coming from any other person. But since the victorious emperor himself recounted it to me many years later when I was privileged to be acquainted with him and have opportunities for conversation, and he confirmed it by swearing oaths, who could hesitate to accept the account—especially since the subsequent events offered indisputable evidence for what he claimed to have seen?)

He related that sometime during the middle part of the day when the sun had already begun to move toward evening, he witnessed with his own eyes a cross-shaped trophy formed of light suspended in the sky across the sun. A text was attached to it that said, "Conquer by this."[3] Amazement seized Constantine at this spectacle, along with his whole army that was accompanying him on a mission somewhere, and the soldiers likewise were gazing up at this wonder.

3. The image of a heavenly cross with an attached victory message immediately found its way into popular Christian imagination, where it has remained firmly lodged ever since. What actually happened? Many scholars believe Constantine witnessed a meteorological phenomenon called a "solar halo," in which arcs of light encircle the sun. Sometimes the light is refracted into radiating lines as well, resulting in "sun dogs" (parhelia). Wispy clouds often enhance this cross-shaped appearance. One ancient source refers to Constantine seeing "wreaths" of light, which he initially interpreted as victory laurels from Apollo. Later he came to understand the omen as a Christian cross. As far as the heavenly words "Conquer by this," I consider it a case of mistaken meaning. Constantine recounted this story to Eusebius fifteen years after the event. Though it is possible the emperor invented the miracle for effect, this isn't likely, because he swore oaths that would have cursed him if he were lying. It is more plausible that (a) Constantine's years of adulation as God's representative on earth enhanced his memory until he convinced himself he saw actual writing, or (b), most probable of all, the emperor said something to the effect that the cross was a clear and indubitable message declaring which sign would win the day, and the over-awed Eusebius took his words literally. Whatever theory is put forward, Constantine definitely encountered something in the sky that moved him in the direction of Christianity.

The Revelation of the Battle Standard

Constantine also told how he was musing to himself later about what the sign might mean. While he was considering it with much deliberation, nightfall came on, and then in his sleep the Christ of God came to him with the sign that had appeared in the sky. He exhorted Constantine to make a copy of the heavenly sign he had seen and use it as a defense against the attacks of all his enemies. When day came he arose and told his friends about the mysterious visit. After this he summoned goldsmiths and jewelers and sat down in their midst so he could describe the shape of the sign. He instructed them to copy it precisely in gold and precious stones.

[At this point Eusebius stops to give a detailed description of the banner's construction. The version he has seen is probably a more ornate one used in later battles. Then, realizing he has gotten ahead of himself chronologically, Eusebius returns to the campaign against Maxentius.]

That was, however, a little bit later. At the time I was just talking about, the emperor was astounded by the incredible vision [in the sky]. He decided not to worship any other god except the one who had visited him [by night]. So he summoned those who were experts in the god's words, asking them who this god was and how to interpret the vision he had seen about the sacred sign. They explained the god was the only-begotten Son of the one true God, and the sign that appeared in the sky was the symbol of eternal life. It stands as a trophy of the victory over death that Jesus achieved when he formerly sojourned on earth. Then they began to teach the reason for his coming, laying out the exact rationale for his incarnation among humans.

Constantine became their disciple in all these matters. He marveled at the divine wonder he had been allowed to see with his own eyes. After comparing the vision in the sky to the interpretation he was hearing, he made up his mind it was true, confident that the knowledge of these things had been granted to him through divine teaching. Now he resolved to devote himself to reading the sacred Scriptures. Furthermore, taking the priests of God as his assistants, he considered it right to honor the God who had appeared to him with all proper church services. So being shielded now by good hope in God, Constantine was ready to embark on his mission to extinguish the fiery threat of the tyrant.[4]

4. Eusebius's primary fault in his description of the vision and dream is his apparent compression of the time frame. Either the stories he received were vague and he didn't understand the chronology, or he was just plain sloppy in his narration. Yet upon closer inspection, we catch hints of an extended sequence. The actual events appear to be separated by about two years. In the spring of 310 Constantine witnessed a solar halo as noted above. For about a year he considered it a sign from the sun god Apollo, but gradually he began to wonder if it pertained to the Christian God instead. By the early months of 312 Constantine was preparing to embark on an expedition against Maxentius as soon as the spring thaw arrived (for he would have to cross the Alps). In this restless state of mind—obsessed, perhaps, with war plans against a great rival—he dreamed a powerful deity appeared to him with instructions about a battle standard. Could

Figure 12.1. The Vision of the Cross. Raphael Rooms, Hall of Constantine, Apostolic Palace of the Vatican. (Wikimedia Commons)

Maxentius's Tyranny in Rome

Meanwhile, he who had seized control of the capital city was busily engaged in abominations and wickedness. Among his depraved and filthy activities, no sort of

---

this have been Jesus? Since many Christian leaders were in Constantine's retinue or immediate vicinity, it was no difficult matter to summon a few churchmen and inquire about the meaning of all this. Based on their words, the emperor became convinced the "Christ of God" had finally given him the help for which he had prayed. Constantine now ordered the fabrication of a battle standard displaying the Christian cross in the form of the Chi-Rho (☧), which are the first two Greek letters in the name of Christ. We need not assume the heavily jeweled version Eusebius later saw was the one initially used. Even so, some kind of cross-emblazoned banner, along with markings on the troops' shields, probably did go ahead of Constantine's army at the Battle of the Milvian Bridge in October 312. Let us note once again that these events occurred over an extended time period. Eusebius is guilty of compressing the narrative so everything seems to occur on the eve of the momentous battle. That makes for good drama, and certainly it is the impression later generations have wanted to take away (as is vividly portrayed in the Raphael Rooms at the Vatican; see figure 12.1). Unfortunately, although this wasn't exactly what Eusebius recorded, his unclear presentation confused the matter for centuries to come.

atrocity was left undone.[5] He took lawfully wedded wives from their husbands, used them for his foul purposes, then sent them back to their men. And he did this not just to obscure commoners. He even rampaged among those who held the highest offices in the Roman Senate! Yet though he shamefully violated countless freeborn women, he still couldn't figure out how to satisfy his unrestrained and exorbitant appetite.[6]

But when he tried to lay his hands on Christian women, he could no longer use such tactics to carry out his adulterous plans. For the women would more readily yield their lives to execution than hand over their bodies to him for defilement. There was one lady—a Christian woman—whose husband was a senator and also served as the city's mayor. She learned that the tyrant's thugs who organized these crimes had arrived at her house, and her fearful husband had agreed to let them seize her and take her away.[7] So after asking for a little time to adorn her body in her usual way, she entered her private chamber. Once she was alone, she plunged a dagger into her breast and fell down dead. All she left to the pimps was her corpse. And so through her actions that spoke louder than words ever could, she proclaimed to all mankind—both in her generation and in future ones—that the only invincible and indestructible thing is the famous chastity produced among Christians. And this woman was seen to be just such a person.

5. Though it helped Eusebius's purposes to display Maxentius in the worst possible light, his scornful depiction might actually have been exaggerating the situation for the sake of Constantinian propaganda. Maxentius appears to have been quite popular during the early part of his reign. Yet several historical sources (and not just Christian ones) portray the end of Maxentius's rule as abusive and depraved. Considering the terrible behavior of other emperors—Caligula, Nero, and Commodus come to mind—it is not hard to believe Maxentius could have behaved likewise. However, while Maxentius may have tyrannized the aristocracy and commoners, he did not pursue a policy of active religious persecution. In fact, he granted tolerance to the Christians early on, though he then undercut this decision by dragging his feet in returning confiscated church properties. He also exiled some troublesome Roman bishops and formed a political alliance with a fierce persecutor in the East. Even so, none of this seems to have stopped construction from proceeding undisturbed on one of Rome's most ancient church buildings, the remains of which now lie beneath the church of San Crisogono. Furthermore, the site of San Sebastiano originally housed a Christian funeral banquet facility right across the street from the emperor's suburban villa. Under Maxentius, everyday Roman Christians were not penalized for their religion. Therefore when Eusebius reports travesties such as the Christian lady who committed suicide rather than be ravished by the lusty emperor, we must consider it an instance of "tyranny" rather than "persecution." The woman's predicament did not stem from her faith *per se*. Eusebius casts Maxentius as the church's great enemy, but in truth he was willing to leave the Christians alone. Constantine, however, was primed for active favoritism, and the believers in Rome could sense it. No Christian mourned the passing of Maxentius, so Eusebius took the liberty of vilifying him in church history.

6. Enslaved people in Roman society had no rights and could be used sexually at the whim of their masters. Here Eusebius is shocked that even freeborn women, who should have been protected by law from such mistreatment, are subject to Maxentius's advances.

7. The husband's name was Junius Flavianus. After his wife's death, he resigned his political office earlier than normal, letting another man finish out his term. He never again served as city mayor.

So the whole city cowered before the man who committed such atrocities. Commoners and rulers, the prestigious and the lowly—all were oppressed by the fearsome tyrant. Not even by keeping their heads down and enduring the cruel slavery could they find relief from Maxentius's bloodthirsty cruelty. One time, for some trivial supposed offense, he handed the populace over to slaughter by his Praetorian bodyguards. Thousands of Roman citizens were slain right in the middle of the city, not by the spears and weapons of Gothic barbarians, but by their very own countrymen! And I couldn't even begin to calculate how many senators were murdered as part of a plot to acquire their property. Untold numbers were executed on one trumped-up charge or another.

But the high point of the tyrant's crimes even reached to sorcery. In order to discover magical knowledge he sometimes ripped open the stomachs of pregnant women or examined the entrails of newborn babies.[8] He also slaughtered lions for this. And he employed certain dark arts to conjure up demons or turn away attacks. By all these methods he hoped to attain victory. I can't even begin to describe the ways this tyrant reduced his Roman subjects to slavery. In the end, he caused the kind of famine and lack of necessities in Rome that no one in our day can ever recall happening before.[9]

The Battle of the Milvian Bridge

But Constantine, meanwhile, was so stirred against all this by compassion that he began to arm himself with every kind of military preparation to defeat the tyranny.

8. It is hard to know whether these rumors are true, though such behavior certainly wasn't out of the question at the time. Ancient people are sometimes reported to have practiced human extispicy, that is, divination from the marks discerned on entrails. Historians believe that in the late Roman Empire, human sacrifice no longer played a large part of that society's religious devotion (despite some claims to the contrary from the church fathers). Nevertheless, the powerful in ancient Rome often treated the lives of the weak as utterly expendable. The ritualized torture and slaughter in the Colosseum is only one example of the many that could be produced. If Maxentius thought he could gain knowledge from soothsayers who examined the guts of some helpless pregnant woman, nothing would have prevented him from doing so. Likewise, unwanted babies were often thrown on trash heaps as garbage; so cutting one open would not have violated the sensibilities of the age. Since Maxentius's consultation of magic oracles is confirmed by Lactantius, and a speech by a pagan orator similarly condemns his "superstitious wickedness," it appears the emperor did indeed dabble in occult practices. Though his sacrifice of human beings cannot be verified for certain, the accusation is not outside the realm of possibility.

9. When the governor of North Africa, Domitius Alexander, rebelled against Maxentius in 308, he cut off the African corn supply on which Rome depended. Severe famine was the immediate result, and the Roman people rioted in protest. Maxentius dispatched his Praetorians to put down the disturbance, killing around six thousand people. Though the rebel Alexander was quickly defeated and the shipments of grain restored, the Romans now held a simmering grudge against their emperor.

He took as his patron the God who is over all and called upon Christ to be his Savior and defender. Having set the victorious trophy, the sign of true salvation, at the front of his bodyguard and troops, he led forth his entire army to reclaim for the Romans the freedoms their ancestors had won for them.[10]

Maxentius, on the other hand, put his trust more in magic arts than in the loyalty of his subjects. Though he himself did not dare venture beyond the gates of Rome, he deployed countless legions of soldiers and very many units to guard every region and city under his control. But the emperor who clung to the help of God advanced against the first, second, and third of the tyrant's stations, easily defeating each one on his initial attack. Thus he made his way straight into the heart of Italy.[11]

He was now very close to Rome itself.[12] Suddenly, to spare Constantine from having to fight against the Roman people because of the tyrant ruling them, God drew Maxentius a long way out of the gates as if by a kind of divine chain. And then, through his mighty deeds God openly confirmed to the eyes of all who beheld these wonders—believers and unbelievers alike—the things written long ago against the ungodly. (These words are widely considered legendary, but in truth they were recorded in the holy books for full acceptance by the faithful.) Just as in the former days of Moses and the godly Hebrew people, [God]

cast Pharaoh's chariots and strength into the sea, and his chosen chariot captains he drowned in the Red Sea [Exod. 15:4],

10. The establishment of the Roman Republic in 509 BC was considered to have thrown off the tyrannical power of kings. With Maxentius playing the role of a more recent tyrant, Constantine is hailed as the liberator of the Roman people, who have become oppressed once again.

11. Constantine moved his troops—veterans of numerous battles with the barbarians, and many of them Germanic mercenaries themselves—down from the Rhine frontier to the Cottian Alps of France. After vaulting the mountains through a low pass, he captured the towns of Susa, Turin, and Verona with relative ease. Resistance collapsed as most of the besieged cities of northern Italy welcomed the invader as a savior. Now nothing stood between Constantine and his showdown with Maxentius at Rome.

12. In antiquity, the Milvian Bridge spanned the Tiber River in the suburban countryside about two miles north of the city walls. Today it stands in an urban area near the athletic complex built for the 1960 Olympics in Rome. Maxentius had already withstood several sieges and probably should have stayed behind the walls. However, because he doubted the people's loyalty, and because certain omens suggested he should go out and give battle, he left the safety of the city to meet Constantine head-on. Good strategy would have forced Constantine to fight his way across the river, but instead Maxentius crossed the Tiber and thereby cut off any chance for a large-scale retreat. Eusebius suggests he did this because he had destroyed the stone bridge and fashioned a booby-trapped version made from wooden pontoons. Evidently some latching mechanism could be released to make the bridge collapse with Constantine on it. Unfortunately for Maxentius, he "fell into the hole he had made" (Ps. 7:15; see below). The latch separated while he was luring Constantine across, and he was drowned. Eusebius interprets the event in biblical fashion, casting the victorious emperor as a new Moses. Just as Pharaoh's chariots

so too Maxentius and all his guards and troops, as they fled from God's power
that accompanied Constantine, tried to cross the river that was in their way and

sank to the bottom like a stone [v. 5].

Maxentius had connected the riverbanks quite well by building a bridge of
pontoons—but actually he had constructed a machine of his own destruction in
his desire to capture God's ally. For Constantine's God was at his side even as
the cowardly Maxentius was creating the secret contrivance that would be his
downfall. Of him it was said:

He dug a pit and hollowed it out and will fall into the hole he has made. His toil will
return on his head, and on his own skull shall his wickedness descend [Ps. 7:15–16].

Therefore by God's sovereign decree, the secret mechanism in the bridge's
linkage failed at an unintended time. The bridge sank, and the pontoons immediately plunged to the bottom with all the men on them. And the wretch himself
went down first, then the guardsmen and infantry around him, just as the divine
prophecies had predicted:

They sank like lead into the turbulent waters [Exod. 15:10].

So while it wasn't with actual words, certainly by their deeds those who claimed
this victory from God sang the same hymn as the followers of his great servant
Moses, who cried out against the impious tyrant of old, saying:

Let us sing to the Lord, for he has been gloriously honored! The horse and its rider
he has thrown into the sea. He has become a helper and protector for my salvation.
[Exod. 15:1–2]

and

Who is like you among the gods, O Lord, who is like you? Glorified in holy works,
honored in awesome deeds, accomplishing wonders! [Exod. 15:11]

Then, after Constantine in his own time—just like Moses, the great servant of
God—proclaimed through his deeds these praises and many similar ones to the

---

were swamped in the Red Sea, so the tyrant of Rome was engulfed by the waters of judgment.
Constantine is depicted as a deliverer who releases captives from slavery and humbly brings the
law of God to his society.

Ruler of all (the true reason for his victory), he marched triumphantly into the imperial capital.

Rome Receives Its Liberator

Immediately, all the senators and other notable or distinguished persons in the city—freed, as it were, from a cage—joined with the rest of the Roman populace to receive Constantine with acclamations of unbridled joy. Their radiant faces beamed with the happiness bursting from their souls. Men with their wives and children, and huge throngs of slaves, couldn't stop cheering as they hailed Constantine as their deliverer, savior, and friend.

The emperor, however, possessed true reverence for God in his heart. He didn't get puffed up at all the shouting, nor did the praises go to his head. Conscious as he was of the help he had received from God, he immediately offered prayers of thanksgiving to the One who had given him the victory.[13]

Almost every ancient history textbook makes the claim that Emperor Constantine issued the Edict of Milan in 313 to end the age of Christian persecution. At last the church received official freedom from the harsh laws of oppression. Yet the truth is, the document was not an "edict," it did not make any difference in Milan, and it did nothing to change Constantine's existing policy. What, then, is the big deal about the Edict of Milan?

Let us recall the historical background here. We have already seen in chapter 11 how Emperor Diocletian set up a Tetrarchy, or rule by four, to govern the

---

13. The reader might be interested to know what happened next. Constantine spent very little time in Rome, departing for Milan after a two-month stay. Even so, he left his mark on the city. Within three years the Senate had honored him with a triumphal arch that ascribed the emperor's military victories to "the Divinity," a term that could be referring to the Christian God. Constantine also sponsored a building campaign of his own. For example, he took over and completed a vast civic hall that had been started by his rival. In place of the intended statue of Maxentius, the Basilica Nova featured a colossal sculpture of an enthroned Constantine gazing into the heavens. The famous statue's head, with its faraway stare, now resides in Rome's Capitoline Museums. Interestingly, the ancient sources also report the statue's right hand held a cross-shaped banner that resembled a military standard but could also be interpreted by Christians as a cross. To make sure the emperor's support for Christianity was clear to everyone—and to trumpet his defeat of Maxentius—Constantine razed the camp of his enemy's horse troops and donated the property to the bishop of Rome. A church was erected on the spot, now known as the Papal Archbasilica of St. John Lateran. Although the architecture has changed over the centuries, the church continues to be the official cathedral of the pope of the Roman Catholic Church. Yet Constantine's support for the true faith wasn't seen only through construction. His reign also brought a permanent end to the Roman Empire's policies of Christian persecution. The document that best symbolizes this historical development is the so-called Edict of Milan, which is our next selection.

western and eastern halves of the empire. Beginning in 303, various figures within that complex political arrangement—including Diocletian himself—found it expedient to persecute Christians. This became known as the Great Persecution. However, others were favorable toward the church, such as Constantine's father, Constantius. Eventually the tumultuous politics of the day resulted in Constantine bringing an army down from the German frontier to confront his enemy Maxentius in Rome. As we have just seen, Constantine defeated Maxentius handily, then entered the city as a triumphant liberator and took control of the western half of the Roman Empire.

The empire's eastern half, however, was not yet his to command. One of the key eastern rulers was Licinius, who at that time was Constantine's ally. The two men had decided to cement their alliance by having Licinius marry Constantine's half sister. The wedding took place at Milan, which had become the western capital instead of Rome because it was better situated to give quick access to the alpine passes by which invading armies might enter Italy. While gathered at the impressive imperial palace (a few remains of which can still be seen today on Milan's Via Brisa), the two allies, now related by marriage, agreed that in their respective territories, tolerance would be granted to the Christians. This decision meant little in the West, where persecution had long since ceased and church properties were restored. But the death toll had been horrendous in the East, continuing right up to 313 in some areas, so Constantine's agreement with Licinius signaled the end of a much more recent and bloody period of martyrdom in the eastern provinces. Licinius at first supported Constantine's pro-Christian policy by overthrowing the final tetrarch who was still persecuting the church. Eventually, however, Constantine had a falling out with his brother-in-law and went to war against him. After defeating Licinius soundly, Constantine had him executed. Now sole rulership of the empire was in the hands of a man who considered himself a devout follower of Jesus Christ—and he intended to prove it.

The significance of the Edict of Milan, then, is not that it changed an existing program of empire-wide persecution. Instead, its enduring value is symbolic: it marks the threshold between one governmental stance and another. After the Battle of the Milvian Bridge, and even more so after defeating Licinius, Constantine began to implement a policy of imperial favor toward the Christians. As his power kept growing, so did his patronage of the church. Anyone who might have been inclined to renew a persecution had now been removed from the scene, while Constantine, the last man standing after the Tetrarchy fizzled, pursued a steadfastly pro-Christian religious strategy throughout his life. Therefore, in hindsight the year 313 appears to mark the vital tipping point when the demons of paganism lost and Jesus won. A new era of peace had dawned in the history of the church. For the Christians who lived through the Great Persecution, this could only be the mighty work of God.

The Edict of Milan comes down to us as a joint letter that circulated in Licinius's territory and perhaps also in Constantine's as a reiteration of the standing imperial religious policy. Addressed to the provincial governors (in this case, the one at Nicomedia), it instructs them to give freedom of religion to everyone and to restore confiscated properties to the Christians so that "the Divinity" might be favorable to the co-emperors. The Latin text is preserved by Lactantius in *On the Deaths of the Persecutors*.

The Edict of Milan (Lactantius, *On the Deaths of the Persecutors* 48.2–12)

The Right of Universal Religious Freedom

When I, Constantine Augustus, as well as I, Licinius Augustus, met on a happy occasion at Milan, we took the opportunity to consider everything that related to the public's best interest and security. We thought that, among the many things we perceived would be profitable for the majority of the people, the first order of business was to secure proper reverence for the Divinity.[14] Thus, we granted to Christians and everyone else the freedom to follow the religion each one preferred, so that whatever Divinity is seated in heaven might be favorable and well disposed toward us and to all who have been placed under our rule. In light of this beneficial strategy and completely logical way of thinking, we judged it appropriate that absolutely no one should be denied the right to devote himself to the observance of the Christian faith or to whatever religion he might deem most fitting. Thus, the supreme Divinity, whose religion we follow with free minds, may be inclined to show to us his usual favor and benevolence in every way.

14. The word "Divinity" appears to be a vague reference to the Christian God, yet without being too explicit about it in the complicated politics of the age. Constantine was just beginning to explore his relationship to the church, and his empire was still overwhelmingly pagan. When it came to his interaction with the imperial bureaucracy, he had to use traditional religious language and could not introduce obvious Christian piety into public affairs. Yet the singular word "Divinity" certainly is noteworthy. One would normally expect references to "the gods" in the plural. Apparently the Roman Senate understood the delicate balance Constantine was trying to achieve, for the senators quickly dedicated a triumphal arch in Rome that claimed Constantine had defeated his rival at the Milvian Bridge "by the prompting of the Divinity." The Arch of Constantine still stands today next to the Colosseum, and the word "DIVINITATIS" is clearly legible in its lofty inscription (see fig. 12.2 on p. 164; see also the previous footnote for more about the imperial building campaign initiated in Rome after Constantine's victory).

Figure 12.2. Arch of Constantine, AD 315. Rome, Italy. (Wikimedia Commons)

Therefore we wish your eminence to know it has pleased us to cancel every one of the regulations about the Christian faith formerly sent to your office in various letters. Now anyone who has the desire to observe the religion of the Christians should hasten to do so freely and openly without any disturbance or molestation. We thought this should be commended to your care with utmost clarity, so you might know we have granted to those Christians an unhindered and unconditional right to practice their religion. And when you see we have awarded them this freedom, your eminence will understand that others too have been given the same open and unrestricted right of religious observance, as is fitting in our peaceful times. Thus, every person shall have free opportunity to engage in whatever religion he has chosen. We have decreed this so it won't seem like we have discriminated against any form of worship or religion.

Confiscated Church Property to Be Restored

Concerning the matter of the Christians, we have also decided to command this: that if in the immediately preceding period someone appears to have purchased (whether out of the imperial treasury or from another person) any properties at which the Christians were previously accustomed to gather—the properties about which a definite rule was expressed in recent letters sent to your office—the owners must now restore them to the Christians without taking payment or requesting any compensation whatsoever, setting aside all attempts at obstruction or deception.[15] And anyone, moreover, who received such properties as a gift must likewise hand them back to the Christians right away. If those who bought properties or received them as a gift are inclined to seek compensation from our imperial benevolence, they should make a request of the Regional Deputy to be considered for our leniency. Through your mediation, all these places must be restored immediately to the corporation of the Christians without any delay.

And since these same Christians are known to have possessed not just the properties where they normally assembled but additional properties[16] that legally belonged to their corporation—that is, to the churches as a whole, not the individual members—you will order, in accordance with our above-stated law, that all these properties be restored to the corporate assembly of these Christians without any hesitation or dispute whatsoever. And as you do this, you will of course maintain the principle stated above that those who restore the property without receiving any payment may, as we have said, expect to receive compensation from our benevolence. In everything, you ought to give the aforesaid corporation of Christians your most earnest efforts at mediation so our command may be all the more

15. We saw in chap. 11 how Diocletian's Great Persecution began on February 23, 303, with an edict that ordered the destruction of all church buildings. The hilltop church in the eastern capital of Nicomedia was then leveled to the ground by soldiers with axes and iron tools. However, during the ensuing decade the original law was unevenly enforced. Church buildings were sometimes confiscated without being destroyed. What exactly were these structures snatched up by the authorities? Though the earliest Christians had met in the private homes of their wealthier members, by the third century AD the church in each city (or perhaps the bishop as its legal representative) would typically own a house or meeting hall as its regular place of worship. In a sizable urban area like Rome, several such buildings might be dotted around the city (see footnote 4 in chap. 5 for more on this background). The right of Christians to own property had been granted by Emperor Gallienus in 260, but Diocletian and his allies revoked that privilege in 303. After the Peace of the Church, Constantine not only restored lost ecclesiastical properties, he actually paid for the construction of additional churches. In so doing he introduced a new building option: the *basilica*, a spacious hall that originally served a civic or judicial function but now became the quintessential architectural style of an ancient Christian church.

16. These church properties beyond the regular meeting places might have included donations of land whose income could fund charitable endeavors. A letter from Constantine to an African governor commands restoration of the church's "orchards" or "plantations" along with its "houses" (Eusebius, *Church History* 10.5.17). Furthermore, the restored properties almost certainly would have included cemetery lands in which to bury the Christian departed. In Rome, for example, the church owned several suburban burial complexes in addition to its meeting places within the city walls. Large funeral halls over important grave sites were not yet being constructed, but this practice was about to begin now that Constantine's patronage made it possible. The cult of the martyrs was about to take off.

swiftly carried out. This will likewise be conducive to public order through our generosity in this matter.

All of this shall be done to the fullest extent so that, as we have noted above, the divine favor toward us, which we have experienced in such important matters,[17] will continue for all time to enhance our successes and bring about public blessing. Moreover, in order that the nature of our benevolence as expressed in this decree might be brought to everyone's attention, it shall be suitable for you to publish this letter everywhere and announce it as common knowledge, having displayed it alongside an edict of your own. In this way no one can fail to notice this declaration of our bounteous goodwill.

---

17. Given the setting of this document's composition only a few months after the Battle of the Milvian Bridge, the "important matters" mentioned here probably refer to Constantine's victories in the Italian campaign that he won through heavenly help. And by the time this document was publicly posted in the summer of 313, Licinius had experienced his own divinely assisted victory after an angel gave him a prayer his troops could use to seek God's aid against a rival. The Edict of Milan reflects its coauthors' firm belief that they had been empowered for war by the Christian God, which explains their joint policy of offering imperial favor to the church.

13

Augustine of Hippo

Honoring the Martyrs' Memory

In this final chapter we are well into the age known as the Peace of the Church. When the sermon translated below was originally preached, the Edict of Milan was already a hundred years old. By now, Roman law had not only granted equal rights to the church, it had actually made Christianity the official religion of the empire. Paganism was on the run; Jesus had vanquished the gods of the Roman state. The great Christian preachers of that day looked back on the age of the martyrs with fondness and affection—and not a little exaggeration as well.

Our selection here is the second of three sermons honoring Perpetua and Felicity on the anniversary of their martyrdom. The sermon comes straight from the lips of Saint Augustine, the renowned bishop of Hippo Regius in North Africa. Augustine is often cited as one of the ancient church's greatest orators. Though he is most widely known for his spiritual autobiography, the *Confessions*, or his vast theology of history, *City of God*, a large part of Augustine's surviving corpus is made up of everyday sermons. Well over five hundred of his "Sermons to the People" have lasted into modern times, plus many more on the Psalms and the Gospel of John. In all, Augustine probably preached something like eight thousand sermons over the course of his forty-year ministry. Scholars have numbered them, and the ones about Perpetua and Felicity are designated 280–82 (the last of which was recently recovered in full text from a newly discovered manuscript). It is hard to tell exactly what years these three sermons were delivered, though it was probably sometime in the early 400s. Yet we know the month and day for sure: March 7, the annual feast day when the early church commemorated the African martyrs' deaths.

As you read the text of Sermon 281, you should picture Augustine seated in an elevated chair in the curved apse of his church. Out in the nave, women stand in one aisle and men in the other. At the rear is a throng of unbaptized believers who are allowed to hear the sermon but must leave before Holy Communion is celebrated. From high above, light filters into the spacious hall through windows lined with translucent crystal panes. A row of columns defines each aisle; mosaics and gravestones adorn the floor; the roof is made of timber and terra-cotta tiles. The bishop, who would normally sit with a portion of Scripture in his lap, would instead on this special day have open before him the Latin text of *The Passion of Saints Perpetua and Felicity* (translated in chap. 8). The story has just been read aloud to the congregation. Now a stenographer is poised to record whatever wise observations the great bishop might offer to his flock. Though these scribes didn't always capture the preacher's every word, their presence in the church ensures that the text below is a faithful synopsis of what Augustine had to say about Perpetua and Felicity.

The primary theme that emerges in this meditation can be discerned in Sermons 280 and 282 as well. Augustine was fascinated by the courage of the female martyrs, whose bravery rivaled the strength of the masculine sex. It is easier, Augustine says, for most men to admire these martyrs than actually follow their example. Endurance of pain to the point of death was viewed in Roman times as a uniquely masculine virtue. Indeed, the word *virtus*, meaning "bravery" or "excellence," comes from the word *vir*, or "man." But Augustine proclaims to his congregation that in the glorious martyrdom of Perpetua and Felicity, the women have, like the very noblest of men, demonstrated their utter devotion to Christ and renunciation of the earthly world. Other prominent themes that unify all three sermons are the women's parallelism with Eve, their victory over the Devil, the martyrs' special intimacy with Jesus, and the eternal heavenly rewards that await those who maintain their confession unto death. Augustine's Sermon 281 serves as a fitting conclusion to this book because it illustrates, in rich and beautiful language, how later Christians honored their courageous forerunners and passed their legacy to future generations. This is exactly what I have hoped to accomplish as well.

Sermon 281, "On the Anniversary of the Martyrs Perpetua and Felicity"

The Women Exhibit Manly Courage through Christ

The honors that are due, and even the very names of Perpetua and Felicity, the holy maidservants of God, shine forth with supreme brightness among their fellow martyrs. Indeed, the crown is more glorious where the sex is weaker. Why? Because a manly spirit has obviously accomplished something much greater in women when they, despite their natural feminine frailty, refuse to give in under incredible pressure.[1]

Perpetua and Felicity did so well because they cleaved to one Man—he to whom the one church is presented as a chaste virgin [2 Cor. 11:2]. They did well, I say, because they clung to that one Man from whom they drew strength to resist the Devil. And what happened? The women struck down the enemy who had previously struck down the human race through a woman![2] Jesus, who was made weak for these martyrs, was shown to be invincible in them. The very one who "poured himself out" [Phil. 2:7] to plant his seed in them has filled them with strength to reap them as a harvest.[3] The one who had to hear taunting accusations for the

1. On the basis of statements like these about women's weakness, many feminist historians suggest the church fathers were hopelessly sexist. While it is true the fathers had traditional notions of female roles like everyone else in Greco-Roman society, the reality is that ancient Christianity was liberating to women. The church taught men to be gentle, faithful husbands. It condemned the abusive treatment so often heaped on women in ancient times. Though modern people may complain about sexism according to contemporary standards, the fact remains that numerous ancient women found great promise in Christianity. This new religion gave them dignity and worth before God, as well as better treatment from men than pagan society would typically provide. The church also respected women enough to offer them the opportunity of a life of full-time service instead of traditional familial roles. Even so, most women in ancient society were physically and socioeconomically weaker than their male counterparts. Christian teaching about how to deal with this reality is encapsulated in 1 Peter 3:7: "Husbands, live with your wives in an understanding way, showing honor to the woman as the weaker vessel, since they are heirs with you of the grace of life." Such ideas are probably what Augustine has in mind here.

2. Augustine is referring to Genesis 3, where the Devil was victorious over humankind because of Eve's sin. But now in a great reversal of that earlier defeat, the two female martyrs have metaphorically canceled the moral weakness of the original woman. Perpetua's conquest of the Devil was predicted when she tread upon the head of the dragon in her vision of the ladder, and again when she crushed the head of the Egyptian gladiator underfoot. When the female martyrs maintained their confession all the way to death, they denied Satan any triumph over them. In this way, Perpetua and Felicity demonstrate that although the Devil used a woman to introduce sin into the world, Christ has caused women to be instruments of his victory. (See footnote 5 below for further reflection on God's victory through women in the parallelism between Eve and Mary.)

3. In this meditation on the roles of women and men, Augustine gives symbolic significance to the central act of marriage, sexual intercourse. Ancient people understood sex to consist of the man planting his vigorous and life-giving seed into the woman, who nurtured and brought

women's sake has now escorted them into these words of honor and praise. He who mercifully lowered himself to be born of a woman on behalf of Perpetua and Felicity enabled them to die in firm faith like men.

Now then, anyone with a godly mind will delight to consider something as amazing as what the blessed Perpetua recorded as being revealed about herself. She described how she turned into a man and fought against the Devil. As you can see, in that struggle she was already hurrying on "to mature manhood, to the full measure of Christ's adulthood" [Eph. 4:13]. But that crafty old enemy of ours, who had once tricked the man Adam through the woman Eve, rightly perceived how Perpetua was interacting with him as a man. So, not wanting to miss any opportunity for treachery, he tried to conquer her in the form of a man. Yet he didn't try to bring her *husband* into the struggle. He knew the lofty-minded Perpetua was already living in heaven. Any hint of sexual temptation would just make her blush and resist even more. So instead the Devil taught beguiling words to Perpetua's *father*. He hoped her devout mind, which couldn't be softened by any urge for physical pleasure, could instead be broken by her strong impulse toward family devotion.[4]

A Daughter's Faithfulness to Christ

However, Saint Perpetua answered her father with remarkable moderation. She avoided violating the commandment that calls us to honor our parents, yet she didn't yield to the trickery that the true enemy was practicing against her. Seeing how he was defeated at every turn, the Devil caused Perpetua's father to be beaten with a rod. That way, she would at least have to suffer with his lashes despite successfully resisting his words. And she really did grieve the abuse of her aged father! Though she never gave in to what he wanted, her affection for him remained strong. She obviously hated her father's foolishness, yet not the man himself. She repudiated his unbelief, not her relationship to him as a daughter. Thus, Perpetua

forth the life supplied to her by the man. Augustine employs the analogy of sex to show how Jesus has consummated a holy relationship with the female martyrs. By "pouring himself out" on their behalf, Christ infused the women with the seed of his strength so they might become his abundant spiritual harvest. In this way, Augustine uses sexuality within marriage as a profound indicator of spiritual realities.

4. Father/daughter relations in the ancient world were not like they are today in Western society. Girls in the Roman Empire were under immense cultural pressure to obey the patriarchs of their homes. The feisty daughters of "Disney princess" movies who defy their father's wishes and then bring him around to their point of view were not part of the ancient cultural landscape. Therefore Perpetua's renunciation of her father required incredible inner strength. Only her absolute loyalty to Christ could enable her to resist her father's pleas. Yet Augustine goes to great lengths to show that Perpetua honored her father just as the Bible demands. She loved the man himself, the preacher declares, but she could never obey her father's order to deny her true Lord.

earned even greater honor because—while it pained her to witness her father's beating—she steadfastly rejected the bad advice of a father she loved so much. To the extent that her sorrow was incapable of shaking her firm resolve, it added to the praiseworthiness of her martyrdom. Indeed, "all things work together for good to those who love God" [Rom. 8:28].

A Pregnant Mother's Faithfulness to Christ

As for Felicity, she was pregnant while in prison. By giving birth there, her feminine voice testified to her female condition. Eve's punishment wasn't missing; yet the grace of Mary was present too.[5] Though the curse owed by women had to be fulfilled, he who was born of a virgin brought relief.[6]

At last Felicity delivered her baby—ready to be born, though still undeveloped by a month. This is indeed an act of God: that a woman's womb should lay down its burden at the wrong time so the honor of martyrdom might not be delayed to the wrong time. This event, I repeat, is a divine miracle: that a fetus should be brought forth before its due date; yet in that very moment, Felicity was restored to her proper "due date" with such great comrades! For if it hadn't happened like that, the martyrs would not only appear to be lacking one of their companions—they would actually be lacking *felicity* itself, which is the martyr's reward.

Exhortation to the Congregation

So then, what these two women were named, that is the gift granted to all martyrs.[7] For why do martyrs endure what they do, if not to delight in the glory of

---

5. Genesis 3:16 institutes pain in childbirth as the punishment for Eve's sin of eating the forbidden fruit at Satan's bidding. Felicity had to endure this pain, just as all women do. Yet verse 15 had promised the "seed" of the woman would crush the Devil. By Augustine's day, a parallelism between Eve and Mary had emerged from this text, similar to the correspondence between Adam and Christ. Following the interpretive lead of several other church fathers, such as Justin Martyr and Irenaeus, Augustine compares two archetypal women in the Bible—one by whom sin entered the world, the other by whom a Savior was born. The parallel here should be understood as an expression of rhetorical balance, not Marian doctrine by which the Blessed Virgin supplies saving grace. Augustine declares that although the Devil overcame one woman (Eve), Christ used another woman (Mary) to defeat humanity's greatest enemy. Felicity's experience of birth pangs (the curse of Eve) and final victory (through the son of Mary) testifies to this truth.

6. Recall that when Felicity cried out in the agony of childbirth, a prison guard overheard it and mocked her. "Ha!" he exclaimed. "So you're suffering now? What are you going to do when they toss you to the beasts? Little did you think of them when you refused to sacrifice!" But with steadfast faith, Felicity replied, "Right now I must endure what I'm suffering. But on that day there will be someone inside me to bear the pain on my behalf, since I'll be suffering for him." This is what Augustine means when he says that Christ brought Felicity relief. Even in her labor pains, Felicity's eternal hope gave her comfort and strength.

7. The name Perpetua means "continuous," and Felicity means "happiness." Augustine uses these two names to symbolize the perfect and unbroken blessedness that all Christians can

"perpetual felicity"? And the truth of the matter is, those women were called to the same destiny we all are! This is why, though a great host of martyrs was present at the contest, it is by the two names of "Perpetua" and "Felicity" that we describe the whole group's eternal destiny—and also designate the church's annual commemoration of them.

---

anticipate in the eternal city of God. The church celebrates Perpetua and Felicity by name because all believers can look forward to perpetual felicity in the presence of the Lord.

Epilogue

The Meaning of the Martyrs

In this book we have encountered a lot of difficult things. At times, it's hard to believe the martyrs were actually victors. Yet it is often in the midst of disturbing circumstances that we begin to see things with new eyes. Since you have allowed me to be your guide this far, perhaps I can now offer some final thoughts about the meaning of the martyrs. What did they do for the ancient church? And what do they offer to contemporary Christians as well?

1. The martyrs refused to make Jesus into just another god. Ancient Rome was full of borrowed religions. New gods constantly flowed into the empire and pooled in the capital. Jesus could have easily taken his place among the other heroes and saviors and lords—except the early Christians insisted on worshiping him to the exclusion of all rivals. This was, as we have seen, a cultural offense. The Romans were prepared to kill for it. Yet they offered an easy way out. "Just worship our gods too," they said. "You can have Jesus if you'll just set him alongside Jupiter." But there's one problem here: that isn't who Jesus really is. The martyrs understood this. They felt it so deeply that they enthroned Jesus right where he should be, as King of kings and Lord of lords. In so doing, they passed on the enduring Christian faith that is still practiced today instead of just another gnostic cult we can read about in history books.

2. The martyrs counted the cost and gave up everything. It's tempting to think the martyrs "weren't like us"—that they didn't have the same love for friends and families, the same enjoyment of life's little pleasures, the same hopes for a long Christian life. If nothing else, Perpetua's prison diary puts that notion to rest. We hear in this woman's own words how she feared for her baby, how she suffered in prison, how she grieved the loss of a life that once was. Yet she declared to her father, and likewise to the judge, "I am a Christian, and I can't be called anything else." Perpetua had counted the cost, and it was a cost she was willing to pay. The martyrs knew the pain in store for them—they knew it all too well. No one was ignorant of what Roman torture meant. And still they chose Jesus. That was the nature of their radical devotion. What attachments to this world are we being asked to repudiate today? What sufferings are we being asked to endure for the sake of God? Since we have so great a cloud of martyrs surrounding us, let us run our own race with equal endurance. Eyes on the finish line!

3. The martyrs were utterly confident in their eternal hope. People like to say Christianity is about "getting into heaven." That's too simplistic—yet sometimes, simple sayings hide core truths. It would be hard to identify an experience all human beings share in common, but one would certainly be *death*. It is our great enemy. Its icy hand claims the mighty and lowly alike. World religions have been spawned to grapple with it. The aged fear it. And Jesus has overcome it. "O death, where is your victory?" asks the apostle Paul. "O death, where is your sting? . . . Thanks be to God, who gives us the victory through our Lord Jesus Christ" (1 Cor. 15:55, 57). It is no coincidence that the martyr's final cry became *Deo gratias!*—"thanks be to God"! They knew what lay on the other side of the veil. Christians rightly grieve the finality of death. But they do not grieve like others do, who have no hope. The martyrs rejoiced at their sunset from this world, confident in the knowledge the bright Morning Star would greet them soon.

4. The martyrs call us into unity with the ancient church. It is easy for modern people to feel distant from the early Christians. They wore different garments, ate different foods, thought in different ways. Even so, they insisted that the church is "universal" across the span of time. A common confession unites all Christians, regardless of whether we are ever called to die for it. In other words, the martyrs remind us that the church is *catholic*. This is a good word, not one to be feared. Lots of issues may divide us today, but the historical life, death, burial, resurrection, ascension, and return of Jesus Christ—these truths form a story that unites every Christian into a "catholic" whole. The early church martyrs, despite their chronological distance from us, understood what really mattered. We can't claim their lifestyles and beliefs were just like ours. Yet they did know our same Jesus. He is the Alpha and Omega, the explosive beginning and final destiny of cosmic history. "Jesus Christ is the same yesterday and today and forever," exclaimed the writer to the Hebrews (13:8). Since the martyrs died for the same Lord whom we worship, they call us into fuller union with the whole body of Christ. This unity crosses all the ages. The martyrs belong to Protestants, Catholics, and Orthodox alike. The ancient church is the wellspring for all who truly follow the risen Lord. Even those who are not "capital-C" Catholics—in other words, not in communion with the bishop of Rome—can still embrace "little-c" catholicity. Many have done so already. I hope you will too. For the church needs its *martyres*, or witnesses, in every generation.

Index

Abraham, 98n8, 129

Africa, 87–88, 91–92, 139, 144–45n12, 149n17, 158n9, 167–68

afterlife, 23, 69

  in heaven

    as dwelling place of God and Christ, 33, 41, 59, 62, 95–96, 101–2, 115

    martyrs' desire to attain, 50, 90, 104, 174

    as reward awaiting the martyrs, 56n7, 69, 116, 119, 126, 128–29, 170–72

    See also salvation

  in hell or Hades, 23n6, 56, 60, 77, 98n8, 142

angels, 56–57n8, 101–2, 116, 166n17

Antioch, 19, 46. *See also* Ignatius of Antioch

Antiochus IV, 19–20, 26n13. *See also* Maccabean martyrs

Apocrypha, 20

athletes, 76, 116–17, 126, 127

Augustine of Hippo, 15–16, 32n5, 83n14, 98n8, 167–68

baptism

  of blood, 104–5n17, 108, 124n22

  and renunciation of Satan, 9n9, 42n25

  as rite of entrance into the church, 94n3, 95, 115–16n5

beasts, condemnation to

  Christians' confident acceptance of, 48–49, 57, 106

  and hunting games, 80–81, 105n19, 119

  as Roman punishment, 5, 60, 104

Bible, 20, 90n5, 127, 129n2, 142, 146, 168

Blandina. *See* Lyons and Vienne, martyrs of

blood

  of Christ, 50, 136

  as leading to conversions, 108, 121, 123

  saving value of, 28n16, 56n7, 124, 126. *See also* salvation

  shed by martyrs, 42, 62, 102, 104–5, 108

bones. *See* relics

Carthage. *See* Africa; Perpetua: and Carthage; Tertullian: and Carthage

catacombs. *See* relics

Cecilia. *See* cult of the saints

Chi-Rho, 156n4

Christ. *See also* salvation

  imitation of, 14, 50, 55–56, 58n10, 63–64, 80–81

  lordship of

    over all Christians, 33, 86n17, 88–89, 101, 130n3, 170n4, 173–74

    over demons, 9, 59n12, 88–89, 126

  as one who suffers with the martyr, 56n6, 61n16, 76–77, 85n15, 103, 107, 171n6

church, ancient

  burial practices of. *See* relics

  called "catholic," 55n3, 58, 63–64, 174–75

  and house churches, 68n4, 114n2, 165n15

  as a "mother," 82n11, 112, 113n1

  and property ownership, 6, 12, 68n4, 142, 157n5, 161n13, 164–66

  Roman Catholic Church

    beliefs of, 15n15, 20, 36n13, 43n28, 98n8, 174

    and bishop of Rome or "pope," 43n28, 48n2, 55n3, 68n4, 98n8, 152, 161n13

    history of, 11